CW00330060

The Macroeconomic Environment of Business

Core Concepts and Curious Connections

The Macroeconomic Environment of Business

Core Concepts and Curious Connections

Maurice D Levi
University of British Columbia, Canada

World Scientific

NEW JERSEY · LONDON · SINGAPORE · BEIJING · SHANGHAI · HONG KONG · TAIPEI · CHENNAI

Published by

World Scientific Publishing Co. Pte. Ltd.

5 Toh Tuck Link, Singapore 596224

USA office: 27 Warren Street, Suite 401-402, Hackensack, NJ 07601

UK office: 57 Shelton Street, Covent Garden, London WC2H 9HE

Library of Congress Cataloging-in-Publication Data
Levi, Maurice D., 1945–
    The macroeconomic environment of business : core concepts and curious connections / by
Maurice D Levi (University of British Columbia, Canada).
        pages cm
    ISBN 978-9814304344
    1. Macroeconomics. I. Title.
    HB172.5.L48 2014
    339--dc23
                                                        2013030052

British Library Cataloguing-in-Publication Data
A catalogue record for this book is available from the British Library.

In-house Editors: Chye Shu Wen/Sutha Surenddar

Typeset by Stallion Press
Email: enquiries@stallionpress.com

Printed in Singapore by World Scientific Printers.

To the Levi gene pool

When Albert Einstein is lost on a desert island he meets three men. He asks each about their IQ. The first replies 190. 'Wonderful,' exclaims Einstein. 'We can discuss quantum mechanics. The second answers 150. 'Good,' says Einstein. 'I look forward to discussing the prospects for world peace'. The third mumbles 50. Einstein pauses. 'So what's your forecast for the economy next year?'

Anon.

CONTENTS

A WORD TO THE INSTRUCTOR

In writing this short one-semester book on the macroeconomic environment of business an important objective has been kept in mind throughout, namely, to preserve as much as possible the macroeconomics content of the best full-year economics texts. Of course, maintaining content in substantially fewer pages than is found in typical full-year texts means confronting the essence of the economic problem itself, requiring difficult choices over what to include. Fortunately, so much material has been assimilated into many full-year texts that while the task of meeting the stated objective seemed formidable at first, the author feels comfortable that the completed book has if anything gained from making the choices over content. The gain arises from the clearer flow between economic principles when nonessential matter is avoided, and from the quicker pace of learning that brevity allows.

As the book proceeds with presenting economic principles, Connections sections are included at the end of each chapter to show the interconnectedness of economics to a wide range of subject areas that students may have studied or be currently studying. The connections that are drawn link economics to a most eclectic array of subjects from theology to physics, history, law, psychology, sociology, business, and even English literature. The purpose of showing the connections between economics and other areas of inquiry is to demonstrate that economics does not exist in a vacuum, having influenced other disciplines, having been greatly influenced itself, and having interests in common with other areas of inquiry. With many students in one-semester introductory economics courses being majors in the humanities, natural sciences, business, law, medicine, and other social sciences, no presumption can be made that they come with a strong motivation to master the subject. Indeed, many one-semester students take economics as a program requirement, often with great reluctance. The quick demonstration of the payoffs from learning economics and the steady stream of connections explained in the Connections sections are aimed at such otherwise disinterested, sceptical students.

Economics instructors, whose passion by choice of discipline is economics, can easily forget that students' interests lie elsewhere. Therefore, even though some instructors may consider bridges between economics and psychology, biology, marketing, theology, physics or literature a distraction from the task at hand, the student majoring in one of these fields may view the matter very differently. Indeed, identification of just one or two close connections might be the spark that lights the fire of interest in economics, showing it is not detached from the student's other subjects. The variety of connections considered is purposely large to provide lots of sparks. Of course, because the range of disciplines to which economics is linked is very wide, all but the rare polymath may find a few connections somewhat obtuse. Therefore, instructors should explain that the Connections sections are not for studying or learning in the same way as the main body of the text. Rather, these sections are for reading to gain a sense of how economics connects to the body of human knowledge. The connections go beyond the busy two-way flow of traffic of ideas between economics and other areas of scholarly inquiry. Some of the connections involve no intellectual arbitrage between economics and other fields, but represent, e.g., a common interest in a matter, even if the matter is viewed from a very different perspective. Every effort has been made to make the material accessible and include something of interest to everyone.

As well as relating economics to an eclectic array of disciplines, this book has a few other idiosyncratic features. One difference is that rather than describe concepts and methods at the beginning in an abstract way, we define terms and explain concepts as they are used. They therefore appear, not in a vacuum, but in the context of the initial application. This is a more natural way of learning, and corresponds to what has been learned in language education. (Extensive research has shown the rote method of learning lists of vocabulary, verb conjugation and so on, is an ineffective way of learning a foreign language. We can most effectively learn languages by using them in context.)

Instructors quickly glancing through this book might think it looks unusually difficult for a one-semester text. Indeed, it is at a relatively high level. The reason the slightly more challenging material is included is to allow one-semester students who are so turned on by economics that they want to take further courses, to be able to get up-to-speed with students having a two-semester introductory experience.

A WORD TO THE STUDENT

While most of the steps in economic arguments are not difficult to follow, the cumulative effect of the many steps it can often take to reach conclusions sometimes leaves the student dizzy. This problem can be overcome by taking a number of precautions.

In order to ensure that you recall conclusions when they are used later as a part of an argument, it helps to periodically close the textbook and to retrace the argument you have just read. This can be done by jotting it down on a writing pad, making sure to include all graphical figures, complete with labelling of axes. This procedure of retracing arguments with the book closed is useful both for committing the material to memory, and for checking whether you are ready to move ahead. You should be meticulous about re-reading the parts you are unable to retrace. Even if it takes several re-readings it is well worth doing. If you try to push ahead when you have been unable to retrace the preceding few pages you are almost certain to eventually become stuck. Moreover, once stuck, it may not be obvious where you need to turn to find the step needed to clear up your confusion. It is difficult to overstate this need to ensure you understand everything before moving ahead because otherwise at some point, after a long chain of reasoning, "if A then B, if B then C," and so on, you may face the statement, "if A then D," and you won't know where it came from or even where to look in order to find out.

After you have opened and closed the book and reached the end of a chapter, you should look over the summary that is provided to ensure that every point is completely clear. Only after you feel comfortable with the statements in the summary should you move on to the next chapter.

The preceding warning should make it clear that economics is not the sort of subject you can casually read during the semester, and expect to learn during the last couple of weeks to take the final exam. Economics is a subject you must work at. In this sense it is like mathematics. However, it does not take any mathematics beyond that from high school to read this book. What it takes is your own patient testing that you properly understand what you are reading before you move ahead. If you do this, you will not only move ahead with little difficulty, you will also know what you need to know when the final exam rolls around.

On the subject of exams, it might comfort you to know that the author has included the Connections sections at the end of each chapter, not to be studied and learned like the main body of the text, but to be read for a sense of how economics relates to other areas of enquiry. Students majoring in the sciences, business, law, history, political science, literature and so on are likely to be surprised at the connections between their principal interest and economics. Because of their different purpose, you can read the Connections sections more quickly than other parts of the book. However, you are advised to read them all. They give the broadest possible perspective on economics.

ACKNOWLEDGMENTS

The approaches taken in this book to explain macroeconomics principles have evolved from preparing class notes for numerous courses over many years, making it difficult to apportion credit to the many universities in which I have taught or done research. Therefore, I would like to thank all of them in the chronological order in which they have played a role: the Hebrew University of Jerusalem, the University of California at Berkeley, MIT, the London Business School, the University of Exeter, the University of New South Wales, and of course, the Sauder School of Business of the University of British Columbia. As the university which has been my home between my various visits to other universities and which has treated me so well, my debt could not be repaid. I am also thankful to Ms. Sutha Surenddar, Editor, Academic Consulting and Editorial Services and Ms. Chye Shu Wen, Editor, World Scientific Publishing Company for their complete involvement and dedication in realizing this book.

CHAPTER 1

NATIONAL INCOME AND NATIONAL PRODUCT

"Every short statement about economics is misleading (with the possible exception of my present one)."

Alfred Marshall

Key Concepts: Domain of macroeconomics versus microeconomics; different measures of national income and national product; difficulties in calculating national income and product; real versus nominal gross domestic product; economic growth; comparing economic performance over time and between countries; consumption, investment and other components of GDP.

INTRODUCING MACROECONOMICS

The two major divisions of economics are microeconomics and macroeconomics. Microeconomics is concerned with the prices and outputs of individual products and the prices of the inputs, often called **factors of production**, used to make these products. On the other hand, macroeconomics is concerned with the condition of the economy taken as a whole. In particular, macroeconomics is concerned with the price level and output of the entire economy, and with the total income of all the factors of production in the economy. Of course, the entire economy consists of the aggregate of all the individual outputs and inputs which are dealt with in microeconomics, and therefore there are close connections between macroeconomics and microeconomics. However, somewhat different perspectives and methods are required to view matters at the level of the entire economy than when considering individual products and inputs that make up the economy.

Microeconomics is concerned with prices and outputs of individual products and factors of production. Macroeconomics is concerned with the price level and output of the entire economy.

In what follows we take a phenomenological approach, discussing matters around the main macroeconomic phenomena that are subject to study and debate, specifically national income and product, national debt, money supply, inflation, unemployment, interest rates and exchange rates. In the first three chapters, we introduce the necessary background for dealing with these important macroeconomic matters. This involves explaining the nature and measurement of output and income at the level of the economy, the meaning and importance of the national debt, fiscal deficit, and the economically important characteristics of money, including the role commercial and central banks play in the creation and management of the nation's supply of money and credit.

Each chapter is devoted to one of the principal macroeconomic phenomena — inflation, unemployment, economic growth, interest rates, and so on. We first describe how the phenomenon is measured, then we explain what causes it to vary over time and to differ between countries, and finally we consider what effect it has on people and companies. For example, when discussing inflation we start by describing how to measure inflation facing consumers, companies (producers) and the overall economy: yes, consumers, companies and the overall economy can face different relevant rates of inflation. Then we explain what makes inflation increase or decrease and why some countries have had run-away inflation of thousands of percent per year while other countries have enjoyed generally stable price levels. Finally, we discuss who gains and who loses from inflation. We find that when inflation is higher than had been anticipated at the time interest rates were determined — interest rates reflect expected inflation — there are gains by people who owe money, corporations and governments which have issued bonds, and so on. Also, businesses which have contracted the wages offered to employees gain from unanticipated inflation. There are also losers from unanticipated inflation, such as people who have lent money, workers whose wages buy less than they had anticipated, and purchasers of bonds. More generally, what we find is that a critical matter determining gains and losses from inflation is the extent to which inflation turns out to be higher or lower than had generally been expected.

On some matters in macroeconomics there is a general agreement among economists, but this is not always so. Where there are differences of opinion between economists, we present the main schools of thought, not with the purpose of arguing which school is correct, but rather to indicate that different opinions exist and may not be mutually exclusive. Indeed, it is the author's opinion that depending on the circumstances and issue at hand, each of the major schools of macroeconomic thought may have something to offer.

This chapter begins our exploration of macroeconomics by explaining the way the output of the economy is measured, namely, via the **gross domestic product (GDP)**. We show how the GDP can be used for evaluating the economic performance of a nation over time, and for comparing the economic well-being of people in different nations. We explain that the GDP is only one of a number of important statistics given in the **national income and product accounts**. Among the other important statistics are those on the main components of a nation's output, specifically, consumption, investment, government spending, and exports.

This chapter is followed by an appendix on the measurement of the distribution of income and the associated issue of poverty. These matters are important because when comparing incomes over time or between countries it is important to consider how the national income is divided among citizens: are there a small number with fabulously high incomes while the majority of people are desperately poor, or is income more evenly distributed? There have been times when national incomes have advanced quite rapidly with a small percentage sharing the gains while others experience static or even declining incomes. Also, there are countries where a tiny minority enjoys a vast proportion of the national income and where the majority of citizens scrape out a meager existence.

MEASURES OF INCOME AND PRODUCTION

Defining Gross Domestic Product

The GDP is an estimate of the combined value of all the final goods and services produced within a country during an interval of time, such as a calendar quarter or year. The GDP includes the total value of loaves of bread, shoes, airplane journeys, haircuts, new homes, and everything else produced in the economy. For example, if domestic production involves $25 billion of bread, $50 billion of shoes, $75 billion of airplane travel, $10 billion of haircuts, and so on, we say the GDP is $(25 + 50 + 75 + 10 + \cdots)$ billions. More generally we can write the GDP for a given year, say 2012, as:

$$\text{GDP}^{2012} = \sum_{i=1}^{N} p_i^{2012} q_i^{2012} \qquad (1.1)$$

where p_i^{2012} is the price of product i in 2012, and q_i^{2012} is the quantity of product i produced in 2012. Therefore, the multiplication of the price and quantity of each item, $p_i^{2012} q_i^{2012}$, is the dollar *value* of i produced during 2012. We add the value of all products, where in the Eq. (1.1) we assume there are N different items.

Only **final goods and services** are included in the GDP. These are the end result of the production process. We exclude items used in the course of production which are considered as inputs. For example, we include the value of bread, but not the value of flour and labor used in baking bread. We measure the amount spent on air travel and not the fuel, wages paid to crews and payments made for use of airports. To include the final goods and services as well as the inputs would be to include the value of the inputs twice. We would be **double counting**.

The GDP is an estimate of the total value of all final goods and services produced within a country during a given interval of time.

As stated in the definition, the GDP is an ***estimate*** of the value of goods and services produced within a country, and as an estimate, is subject to possible errors. Fortunately, the estimation of the GDP is in some ways made easier by the close connection that exists between the value of goods and services produced — the GDP — and the value of incomes received, or earned — the **national income**. The national income, as you might expect, is the total value of all the incomes earned in a country during an interval of time. The national income is roughly equivalent to the nation's GDP. Let us examine the reason for the rough equivalence of national income and GDP before turning to problems of measuring and interpreting these important macroeconomic magnitudes.

National income is roughly equivalent to the GDP.

Equivalence of National Income and GDP

We can illustrate the approximate equivalence of national income and GDP, along with some other aspects of national income and product accounting, by referring to this economics book you are currently reading. The copy of the book in front of you is a part of the GDP of the year or calendar quarter in which it was manufactured. It enters the GDP statistics at a value equal to what you paid to purchase it — assuming you bought it new. (If you bought the book in a used bookstore, it was part of the GDP of the year when it was originally produced and sold, and only the value added by the used bookstore is part of the current year's GDP.) But why is this value of the book also equal to the income derived in producing it? This can be explained by looking at what goes into producing a book.

In producing this book, it was first necessary for loggers to chop down trees to be used for paper production. The trees were sold to a paper manufacturer whose output was sold to the printer who, for simplicity, we assume is also the publisher. The publisher printed and bound the book and sold it to the bookstore. From there it was sold to you.

The various stages of producing a book with a selling price of $40 are shown in Table 1.1. We show logging as the first stage, with no payments being made to any previous stage of production. The amount of wood required to make the paper for the book is $4, with this wood being sold to the paper producer. This $4 appears as the value of sales on the bottom line of the logging operation, and as the payment to the previous stage on the top line of paper production.

In the table, we assume the logging company pays $2 of wages and salaries, and $1 of rent and interest, so that the $4 it receives from the paper producer leaves $1 of profit. The $3 that the logging company pays as wages, salaries, rent and interest is income for the people who receive it, while the $1 that remains as profit is income for those owning the logging company. Therefore, the total income generated by the first stage of production is $4.

The paper producer pays the logging company $4. It then hires workers for $3, this amount being income for those receiving it in their wages or salaries. The paper producer also pays $2 of rent and interest which is income for those who receive it. After meeting all these costs which add up to $9, the paper producer sells the paper for $12. Therefore, it has

Table 1.1.   National income and gross domestic product are equivalent.

	Logging operation	Paper production	Printing/ publishing	Bookstore sales
Payment to previous stage	0.00	4.00	12.00	28.00
Wages/salaries	2.00	3.00	8.00	5.00
Rent/interest	1.00	2.00	4.00	3.00
Profits	1.00	3.00	4.00	4.00
Income generated at each stage of production	4.00	8.00	16.00	12.00
Values of sales	4.00	12.00	28.00	40.00

The total amount of income generated by all stages of book production is given by adding the $4 earned in logging, the $8 in paper production, the $16 in printing/publishing, and the $12 in retailing by the bookstore. The total of these is $40, which is the total income earned by people involved in producing the book. This is equal to the selling price of the book. The sum of incomes generated equals the amount paid for the book because somebody earns every dollar received. The income earned therefore equals the value of production.

$3(= \$12 - \$9)$ of profit which is income for the paper producer. We find that the total income resulting from paper production is $8 consisting of the sum of $3 paid as wages and salaries, $2 paid as rent and interest, and $3 remaining as the paper producer's profit.

We do not include the $4 paid for wood as part of income generated by the paper producer since this is not income due to paper production. Rather, this $4 is paid out by or earned as profit by the logging company, and if we were to include the cost of wood in the paper producer's added value we would be double counting; we would be counting the wood twice, as part of the income generated in paper production and also as income from logging.

If the cost of inputs were included along with the value of outputs of goods and services produced, there would be double-counting.

We see from Table 1.1 that the printer/publisher pays $12 for paper and sells the book to the bookstore for $28. The printer/publisher is therefore responsible for $16 of income, part of which is profit. This $16 consists of $8 paid as wages and salaries, $4 paid as rent or interest and $4 remaining as profit. The bookstore buys the book for $28 and sells it for $40, and therefore generates $12 of income. The composition of income generated at these last two stages of production into wages, interest, rent, and profit, is shown in Table 1.1.

The sum of all of the incomes generated by all stages of production combined is the sum of the amounts in the second-from-bottom row, namely $40 = \$(4 + 8 + 16 + 12)$. This is equal to the amount paid for the book. The sum of all incomes earned in producing and selling the book equals the price of the book because somebody gets paid for every activity going into producing and selling it. The price paid for the book is the value of final production.[1] We discover that the total value of incomes earned equals the value of final production. Note that this means that the value of incomes earned in producing the book is equal to the perceived value of the book to the final buyer. The value the buyer attaches to the book must be at least as high as the price paid for the book or it would not have been purchased.

The income generated at each stage of production is called the **value added** by that stage of production. It follows that if we add up the values added by all stages of production we have a total that is the same as the value of final production. This is also equal to the total of incomes earned, and is a conservative estimate of the presumed pleasure/benefit people derive from consuming the products.

The GDP and national income consist of the values added at all stages of production of all the goods and services produced within a country during an interval of time.

Because the value added at each stage of production equals the amount earned as wages and salaries, rent, interest and profits, we can calculate national income from summing these different types of income. Specifically, by adding across the rows in Table 1.1 for wages/salaries, rent/interest, and profits, we find:

Wages/salaries $= \$(2 + 3 + 8 + 5) = \$18.$

Rent/interest $= \$(1 + 2 + 4 + 3) = \$10.$

Profits $= \$(1 + 3 + 4 + 4) = \$12.$

---

[1] The book is a final product, while the wood, paper and so on are **intermediate products**.

The sum of these amounts earned, $40 = \$(18 + 10 + 12)$, is the national income, and also the GDP.

In the example of the book, we have ignored the possibility that some foreign-owned factors of production could be used in producing the book. Indeed, the author of this book lives in Canada, and some (very small) part of the income derived from producing the book — the author's royalty — is not part of U.S. national income. Of course, at the same time that non-residents of the U.S. earn income in the U.S., residents of the U.S. are earning incomes in other countries. The presence of **factor incomes** paid to foreigners or received from foreigners is one of the reasons we said there is only a *rough* equivalence between GDP and national income. Let us consider the effect of such factor income payments abroad and receipts from abroad before turning to the other reasons why GDP and national income are not exactly equal.

GDP versus Gross National Product

As we have said, the GDP measures the value of goods and services produced *within* a country during an interval of time. For example, the GDP of the United States is the value of goods and services produced at locations in the United States during a calendar year or calendar quarter.

Some of the goods and services produced within the United States are not made using factors of production provided by residents of the United States. For example, as mentioned, the author's labor in writing the book was provided by a non-resident. More importantly in terms of magnitudes, some of the automobiles produced in the U.S. are made in factories owned by Japanese companies such as Honda and Toyota, some financial services within the United States are provided by foreign-owned companies such as HSBC from London/Hong Kong, Nomura securities of Japan and so on. Furthermore, to the extent that non-residents own property in the United States, have made loans to U.S. businesses or to the federal government or government agencies, and have invested in shares of U.S. businesses, then some of the rent, interest and dividends earned in connection with goods and services produced in the United States are earned by non-residents.

Just as non-residents provide some of the labor and capital, and own land used in producing goods and services within a country, so do residents provide labor and capital and own land used in producing goods and services outside the country. For example, Americans have built factories and acquired property abroad, work in other countries, and have made investments and provided loans to foreign-based businesses and to foreign governments.

With foreign-provided factors of production contributing to the output within a country, and some of a country's factors of production contributing to output in other countries, there is a difference between the value of goods and services *produced within a country*, and the value of goods and services produced with *factors of production provided by the residents of a country*. The former, as we have seen, is called the GDP. The latter, i.e., the value of goods and services produced with factors of production provided by the residents of a country, is called the **gross national product (GNP)**.

GNP is the value of goods and services produced with factors of production provided by a country's residents. On the other hand, GDP is the value of goods and services produced within a country.

Until 1992, the United States emphasized the GNP as its principal measure in the **national income and product accounts**, but in that year it switched to emphasizing the GDP. This switch brought the United States in line with most other countries which shifted from GNP to GDP somewhat earlier.

The different bases of measurement of GDP and GNP concern incomes earned by foreign factors of production in a country, and incomes earned by resident-owned factors at work in other countries. Table 1.2 shows the connection between GDP and GNP in the United States. The table shows that in order to calculate the U.S. GNP from the U.S. GDP, it is necessary to add to GDP the amount Americans earned from supplying factors of production to other countries, and to subtract the amount earned by factors of production supplied by foreigners to the United States. This means adding the **net foreign factor income**. In terms of an equation:

$$\text{GNP} = \text{GDP} + \text{Net foreign factor income,} \qquad (1.2)$$

where

Net foreign factor income = Factor income receipts from foreigners

−Factor income payments to foreigners.

Table 1.2.   The GNP equals GDP plus net factor income from abroad.

	Billions $
GDP	14,265
+ Factor income receipts from foreigners	798
− Factor income payments to foreigners	665
= GNP	14,398

Source: *National Income and Product Accounts, U.S. Survey of Current Business*, 2009.

The GDP is the value of goods and services produced **within** a nation, whereas the GNP is the value of goods and services produced by factors of production **provided by a nation**. Therefore, to obtain the GNP from the GDP we need to add factor incomes received by residents from foreigners, and subtract factor incomes paid by residents to foreigners.

> *Net foreign factor income is factor receipts from foreigners minus factor payments to foreigners. The GNP is the GDP plus net foreign factor income.*

The difference between aggregate production in the United States, the U.S. GDP, and aggregate income earned by Americans, the U.S. GNP, is relatively small. However, for a country such as Ireland where a large number of businesses are owned by foreigners, and for countries such as India and Pakistan where many citizens are employed as guest workers abroad, the differences between GDP and GNP can be quite significant. Furthermore, the **rates of change** of GNP and of the GDP can differ substantially even in countries for which the **levels** of the two magnitudes are similar.

GNP versus National Income

Factor incomes received from foreigners and paid to foreigners are only one cause of a difference between the value of production in a country, and the income earned by people in that country. Another cause of a difference between the value of production and income is **depreciation**, also referred to as **consumption of fixed assets**, involving the need to spend as machines wear out in order to maintain production potential.

In our example involving the production of this book, we defined profit as the difference between the value of sales at a stage of production on the one hand, and the amount paid as wages, salaries, interest, rent, or to the previous stage of production on the other hand. For example, the profit from printing/publishing is $28 received for the book from the bookstore, less $8 for wages/salaries, $4 for rent/interest, and $12 for paper. This leaves a profit of $4 = $(28 − 8 − 4 − 12).

In reality, some of what we call profit in the example is not available for the owners of the publishing company to take as their income because printing machines and other capital wear out and need to be replaced. The extent to which capital wears out is called **capital consumption**, or more briefly, depreciation, and this part of what is received is not really part of somebody's income. On a national scale too, it is necessary to subtract capital consumption from the value of goods and services produced by factors supplied by a country in the course of calculating national income. Subtraction of depreciation from GNP gives the **Net National Product (NNP)**.

Depreciation, which is also called capital consumption, is the value of capital that wears out during an interval of time. GNP minus Depreciation is NNP.

The connection between GNP and national income is also affected by **indirect taxes**, specifically, sales taxes and tariffs (taxes) on imports. These taxes are called "indirect" because rather than being paid directly to the government by the purchaser of a product, they are collected by the seller of the product, and then remitted by the seller to the government. Indirect taxes are part of the value of goods and services entering into the GNP, but are not part of national income; they are included in the value of what people produce and pay for, but are not part of people's incomes.[2] In the context of our example in Table 1.1, if $2 of the $40 received for the book is sales tax, then the net income of the bookstore is not $4 as shown and labeled "profit", but is only $2. That is, in calculating national income it is necessary to deduct sales tax, as well as depreciation, from the GNP.

Indirect taxes consist of sales taxes plus import duties. These are indirectly paid by consumers who pay taxes to product providers who then remit to the government.

---

[2]Indirect taxes are part of GNP and GDP because the value purchasers attach to products is at least what they pay or they would not buy them, whether or not what they pay includes tax.

The fact that national income excludes depreciation and indirect taxes, both of which are contained in the GNP, is summarized by

$$\text{National income} = \text{GNP} - \text{Depreciation} - \text{Indirect taxes}. \quad (1.3)$$

Both depreciation and indirect taxes are small relative to GNP, nevertheless they are the reason why national income and GNP are only ***roughly*** equivalent.

National income is GNP minus depreciation and indirect taxes.

If we wish to compare national income to GDP rather than to GNP, we can use Eq. (1.2) in Eq. (1.3). This gives

$$\text{National income} = \text{GDP} + \text{Net foreign factor income}$$
$$- \text{Depreciation} - \text{Indirect taxes}. \quad (1.4)$$

Alternatively, since NNP is GNP minus Depreciation, we can shorten the link between national income and national product to

$$\text{National income} = \text{NNP} - \text{Indirect taxes}. \quad (1.5)$$

That is, if we add wages, salaries, rent and profits to find the national income, this should correspond with the value of goods and services produced, provided we use NNP and subtract indirect taxes as in Eq. (1.5).

PROBLEMS IN CALCULATING GDP AND NATIONAL INCOME

Measurement Difficulties

The national income accountant must consider a number of potential measurement problems when calculating GDP, GNP, and national income. Among the more important sources of measurement errors are:

Double-counting: As noted in our example, we have identified the value of the book as $40, the amount paid at the bookstore for the final product. We would not want to add to this $40, the $28 that the bookstore paid the publisher, since this $28 is already included in the $40: if we added the $28 paid to the publisher we would be double-counting that amount.

In the same way, we would not want to include the $12 the publisher paid the paper producer, or the $4 the paper producer paid to the logging company for trees. These other payments are for **intermediate transactions**, and we must be careful to include only the value of final products when calculating the GDP.

When we avoid double-counting by including the value of final production only, our measure of national income or product is not influenced by the level of **vertical integration**. The degree of vertical integration concerns the extent to which the various stages of production are combined within individual firms. For example, if the logging and paper production for this book were done by the same integrated firm, we would have to combine the first two stages as in Table 1.3. We find in Table 1.3 that since we do not include the payments to previous stages of production within national income or GDP, vertical integration does not affect these magnitudes.

The level of vertical integration concerns the extent to which different stages of production are handled by separate firms or by a single firm. The degree of vertical integration does not affect the GDP or national income.

Table 1.3. The amount of vertical integration does not affect the GDP or national income because we avoid double-counting.

	Logging/paper production	Printing/ publishing	Bookstore sales
Payment to previous stage	0.00	12.00	28.00
Wages/salaries	5.00	8.00	5.00
Rent/interest	3.00	4.00	3.00
Profits	4.00	4.00	4.00
Value added	12.00	16.00	12.00
Value of sales	12.00	28.00	40.00

This table is obtained from Table 1.1 by adding the wages/salaries, rent/interest, and profits of the first two stages of production. We find by comparing the top row of this table with that of Table 1.1 that when logging and paper production are done by the same firm, we have fewer intermediate transactions. However the sum of values added — the GDP or national income — is still $40, the same as the amount paid for the final product. The GDP is not affected since intermediate transactions are not included in the GDP.

Used goods: As mentioned earlier, if you purchased this book used, your purchase is not part of current GDP. Only newly manufactured goods enter the GDP, and this is true for items like houses and cars as well as books. We include only new goods because we want to measure production during the specified period of time, and used goods have already been measured. They were included for the time interval during which they were originally produced.

While the amount paid for used goods is not included in the GDP, the profit and other income earned on the purchase and sale of used goods *is* included. If a bookstore that sells used books buys a text for $20 and sells it for $30, they have presumably provided a service worth $10. This amount would be contained in the income generated by the bookstore in wages and salaries, rent, interest, and profits. Similarly, the services of real estate agents and used car sales people in selling older homes or used cars are included in GDP, even though the used homes and cars are themselves not a part of the current GDP.

> *Used goods are not included in the GDP. However, incomes earned and values added from buying and reselling used goods are included.*

Exports and imports: In practice, the GDP is obtained by measuring the value of ***expenditures*** on final goods and services rather than by measuring the value of ***production***. The value of expenditures on final goods and services, excluding all intermediate sales, is called **final sales**. The value of final sales includes the amount spent on goods produced abroad, that is **imports**, as well as the amount spent on goods produced at home. Imports include items such as automobiles from Japan, wines from France, teas from India, coffees from Brazil, and financial services from Britain. However, GDP measures the value of only those goods and services produced ***within*** the nation. We must therefore be careful to deduct the value of imports from final sales to obtain the GDP and national income. However, value added in the marketing and retailing of imports *is* a part of GDP. For example, if this economics book had been produced and published abroad and purchased by the local bookstore for $28, the value added by the bookstore is part of the U.S. GDP or national income. If the book sells for $40, the $12 markup or value added is included in the U.S. national income and GDP.

The remaining $28 belongs to the GDP and national income of the country in which the book was produced.

A similar problem arises with **exports**. Exports are items produced domestically but sold abroad, and therefore do not appear in a nation's statistics on final sales. However, since exports are produced within the country, they generate income and are part of the country's GDP and national income. For example, if this economics book had been produced in the U.S. and sold to a foreign bookstore for $28, the U.S. GDP and national income would include this amount. Since this $28 is not a part of the final sales statistics of the United States, the value of exports must be added to final sales to obtain the U.S. GDP and national income.

> *Imports are part of final sales in a country but are not included in the country's GDP or national income. On the other hand, exports, which are not part of final sales, are included.*

Change in inventory stocks: Another problem that derives from the way GDP is measured concerns changes in stocks of **inventories**, which are items that have been produced but not yet sold. As we have said, for practical reasons the national income accountant measures the value of the nation's final ***sales*** rather than the value of ***production***. As with imports and exports, the existence of inventories means that adjustments have to be made to final sales to calculate the value of production, i.e., the GDP. For example, if the GDP is being measured over a calendar year and some books produced and sold to a bookstore in that year remain unsold on the shelves of the bookstore on the 31st of December, the value of these books does not show up in final sales during that year even though they were part of GDP and national income for that period. In order to rectify this problem, the national income accountant adds the increase in inventories to the final sales to obtain the GDP.[3]

The inventory problem can work in either direction. Some goods sold in a given interval might not have been produced during that interval,

---

[3]The books would be valued at what the bookstore paid for them, $28 in our example, not at the price at which they could eventually be sold, $40 in our example. The difference of $12 of retailing service generated by the bookstore belongs to the year in which the service is performed, that is, when the book is sold.

but instead have been carried forward as inventory from an earlier period. For example, if 6,000 books had been sold but 1,000 came from inventory stocks, only 5,000 were produced in that year. In this case, the change in inventory stocks is negative. In such a case, we deduct the decline in inventories from final sales to determine the value of production.

> *Inventories are goods produced but not yet sold. An increase in inventories during the measurement period is added to final sales in determining GDP and national income. A decrease in inventories during the measurement period is deducted from final sales in determining GDP and national income.*

Government spending: Even in basically free enterprise economies like those of the United States, Canada, Western Europe and Japan, a large proportion of economic activity measured, e.g., by the number of people employed or other resources used, involves "production" by some level of government. Government production includes, e.g., national defense, law and order, public education, public health, and so on.

Little of what the government produces is sold in the market, and when it is the price may be subsidized. Therefore, most of what is produced by government does not appear in final sales. This forces us to calculate the value of the government's ***production*** from the amount the government ***spends***. This involves the summation of payments of incomes to bureaucrats, soldiers, teachers, healthcare and social workers. That is, government production is valued at cost rather than as the value of sales.

> *Government spending is included in GDP and national income, valued at cost.*

Goods versus "bads": All items produced during the measurement interval are valued at market prices and included in GDP and national income whether they are pornographic videos or new economics textbooks.[4] This is done so as to avoid making subjective judgments, but does cause problems in interpreting GDP as a measure of well-being. For example, the GDP will be increased if a massive oil spill sweeps onto our beaches.

---

[4]This assumes the pornographic videos are not sold in the **underground** or **informal economy** which is not observable to the law or the national income accountant. Of course, this points to yet another problem, that of illicit or tax-evasive activity, that may well represent an important component of overall economic activity but which is not recorded.

The payments made to emergency workers who toil around the clock to contain and remove the oil, and the payments for vessels moving floating booms, will all be included in the GDP. Provided these people and the equipment would not be called into service without the spill there is no offset from income or production lost elsewhere. As a result, a higher GDP will occur because of an oil spill. Similarly, if a major earthquake were to cause damage in California, the lost property would lower the GDP only to the extent that it lowers some peoples' incomes and disrupts output. However, all the extra building activity in replacing housing, roads, schools, and hospitals that were destroyed would be included in the GDP. Therefore, the GDP might be increased from a natural disaster like a hurricane or an earthquake.[5]

It is not possible for the national income accountant to select only some incomes or some products and value them as "goods", and to exclude or even subtract others that she or he considers "bads." Workers who are paid to produce wheat or to clean up after oil spills have all earned incomes and been involved in "production." Therefore, their incomes and the value of what they produce are included in the national income and product accounts. However, this does mean the GDP is at best only a general guide to the quality of life, and that increases in the measure do not necessarily mean improvements. But there is another factor that must be taken into account, and this is the rate of inflation.

The value of all production is included in the GDP and national income whether or not some of what is produced may be generally considered harmful.

Correcting GDP for Inflation

Inflation, which means a general increase in prices, will raise the GDP and national income; we will be adding higher values of goods or incomes because the prices of the goods and levels of incomes are higher. However, we do not wish to say a country is better off just because dollar values of production and incomes are higher. People are better off only if there is a

---

[5]Those natural disasters which affect the *flow* of production rather than the *stock* of capital do have a negative effect on GDP. For example, the U.S. GDP after adjusting for prices is reduced by severe drought because of its effect on farm income and output.

larger quantity of goods and services for them to enjoy. Similarly, people are better off only if their incomes will purchase a larger quantity of products.

In order to obtain a measure of real economic performance that does not show an improvement merely because prices have risen we need to measure the change in the GDP that would have occurred if all prices had remained unchanged. In order to do this the national income accountant:

(1) Measures physical outputs of everything each year, and
(2) values all outputs each year at the prices in a common, **base year**.

The physical outputs of all items each year are valued at the common base year prices before they are added up to obtain the GDP. By valuing the output of each year at the same base year prices the national income accountant derives the value of output at unchanged prices. The relevance of this measure, and the way it is calculated, can be seen by an example.

Adjusting GDP for Inflation: An Example: Imagine a very small and simple economy that produces only six items. Table 1.4 summarizes the amounts produced and the prices during two years that are a decade apart.

Table 1.4. Real GDP can be compared between years without the distortion of inflation.

	2002		2012	
	Output	Price	Output	Price
Bread	10,000 loaves	$0.80 each	15,000 loaves	$1.50 each
Rent	50 homes	$4,800/year	60 homes	$8,400/year
Utilities	1,000 units	$8/unit	2,000 units	$10/unit
Suits	50 suits	$100 each	60 suits	$120 each
Investment	20 machines	$5,000 each	22 machines	$5,600 each
Social Services	8 workers	$16,000/year	8 workers	$26,000/year
Nominal GDP (current prices)	$489,000		$884,900	
Real GDP	$489,000		$560,000	

Nominal or current-price GDP is the value of output each year at current prices. Real or constant-price GDP is the value of output during each year at base-year prices. Changes in real GDP occur only from changes in the volumes of outputs, and not from changes in prices. During periods of inflation real GDP increases less than nominal GDP.

The dollar value of GDP, where the value is assessed at prices prevailing at the time the goods and services are produced, is called the **nominal GDP** or **current-price GDP**. Sometimes the label **current-dollar GDP** is used. The nominal GDP's for 2002 and 2012 in our example are calculated as:

$$\text{Nominal GDP (2002)} = \$(10{,}000 \times 0.80) + (50 \times 4{,}800)$$
$$+ (1{,}000 \times 8) + (50 \times 100)$$
$$+ (20 \times 5{,}000) + (8 \times 16{,}000),$$
$$= \$489{,}000.$$

$$\text{Nominal GDP (2012)} = \$(15{,}000 \times 1.50) + (60 \times 8{,}400)$$
$$+ (2{,}000 \times 10) + (60 \times 120)$$
$$+ (22 \times 5{,}600) + (8 \times 26{,}000),$$
$$= \$884{,}900.$$

We find an increase in the nominal GDP of $395,900 = (\$884,900 - \$489,000)$, which is an increase of 80% from the 2002 level over the 10 years, 2002–2012. But how much better off are people in this economy?

Nominal GDP is the value of goods and services produced within a country assessed at prices prevailing at the time the goods and services are produced.

Table 1.4 shows that as well as there being more production of everything other than social work in 2012 than in 2002, there is also an increase in the price of everything. In order to discover how much of a real improvement has occurred in the economy when price increases are not included as part of the measured "improvement", we value the 2012 outputs, not at the prices in 2012, but instead at the prices prevailing in 2002. When this is done, GDP can increase only if more goods and services are available, not just because of higher prices. Computing this from Table 1.4 we have:

$$\text{GDP (for 2012 at 2002 prices)} = \$(15{,}000 \times 0.80) + (60 \times 4{,}800)$$
$$+ (2{,}000 \times 8) + (60 \times 100)$$
$$+ (22 \times 5{,}000) + (8 \times 16{,}000)$$
$$= \$560{,}000.$$

This is less than 15% larger than the 2002 GDP, also measured in 2002 prices ($560,000 versus $489,000).

Our example shows that during times of inflation, the growth in the GDP calculated in each year at base period prices is smaller than the growth in the GDP measured in current prices. When there is **deflation** — which means prices in general are falling — the nominal or current-price GDP could conceivably fall even if the GDP measured with base-period prices is rising. This occurs if prices are falling faster than output is increasing.

The name given to the GDP that is measured in the prices of a base year is **real GDP**. The titles of **constant-price GDP** and **constant-dollar GDP** are also sometimes used. The label "real" indicates that this measure of GDP is affected only by what *really* determines our standard of living, namely the physical quantity of goods and services produced, rather than the dollar value of goods and services. We define real GDP as:

> *Real GDP is the value of final goods and services produced within a nation during an interval of time measured in base-period prices. Real GDP is also called the constant-price GDP, or constant-dollar GDP.*

Symbolically:

$$\text{Real GDP}^{2012}\text{on 2002 base} = \sum_{i=1}^{N} p_i^{2002} q_i^{2012}. \qquad (1.6)$$

This is the real GDP for 2012, based on prices in 2002. The difference from the nominal GDP in Eq. (1.1) is that whereas nominal GDP is based on current prices, real GDP is based on prices prevailing in the base year. The real GDP is therefore increased only by increases in production.

An increase in real GDP is roughly equivalent to the extent national income increases faster than prices. The equivalence is because higher output of goods and services means more output is available to be bought, and for people to be able to buy more output their incomes must increase more than prices. Example 1.1 illustrates how some people just can't grasp this important fact — at least in Mark Twain's world.

Example 1.1. An Argument of Real Significance

Mark Twain understood very well how the real value of a given nominal income depends on the price level. What the following shows however, is that he, or at least his literary embodiment as the Connecticut Yankee, overestimated the comprehension of others about this matter.

"Dowley warmed to his work, snuffed an advantage in the air, and began to put questions which he considered pretty awkward ones for me, and they did have something of that look:

'In your country, brother, what is the wage of a master bailiff, master hind, carter, shepherd, swineherd?'

'Twenty-five milrays a day; that is to say, a quarter of a cent.'

The smith's face beamed with joy. He said:

'With us they are allowed the double of it! And what may a mechanic get — carpenter, dauber, mason, painter, blacksmith, wheelwright, and the like?'

'On the average, fifty milrays; half a cent a day.' 'Ho-Ho! With us they are allowed a hundred! ... 'Rah for protection — to Sheol with free-trade!' And his face shone upon the company like a sunburst. But I did not scare at all. I rigged up my pile-driver, and allowed myself fifteen min. to drive him into the earth — drive him *all* in — drive him in till not even the curve of his skull should show above ground. Here is the way I started in on him. I asked:

'What do you pay a pound for salt?'

'A hundred milrays.'

'We pay forty. What do you pay for beef and mutton — when you buy it?' That was a neat hit; it made the color come.

'It varies somewhat, but not much; one may say 75 milrays the pound.'

'*We* pay 33. What do you pay for eggs?'

'Fifty milrays the dozen.'

'We pay 20.'

. . .

I prepared now to sock it to him. I said: 'Look here, dear friend, *what's become of your high wages you were bragging so about a few minutes ago?'* — and I looked around on the company with placid satisfaction, for I had slipped up on him gradually and tied him hand and foot, you see, without his ever noticing that he was being tied at all . . . .

But if you will believe me, he merely looked surprised, that is all! He didn't grasp the situation at all . . . . I could have shot him, from sheer vexation. With cloudy eye and a struggling intellect he fetched this out:

'Marry, I seem not to understand. It is *proved* that our wages be double thine . . . .'

Well, I was stunned; partly from this unlooked-for stupidity on his part, and partly because his fellows so manifestly sided with him and were on his mind — if you might call it mind."

Source: Mark Twain, *A Connecticut Yankee in King Arthur's Court*, (Harper & Row, New York, 1889) pp. 295–297. (Emphasis in original.)

The Measurement of Economic Growth

Economic growth, which involves an expansion in the real national income and product, provides the basis of improvements in the standard of living. However, we must be careful when measuring living standards from the national income and product accounts to employ the correct statistics.

First, in measuring the rate at which the standard of living is advancing we would not want to use the rate of improvement in a nominal magnitude such as the nominal GDP, since this would show improvements even when the increases stem from inflation. Instead, we must use a measure based on a real magnitude which shows gains only from higher output of the overall economy which is the basis of gains in the standard of living.

Second, the standard of living in a country is more closely related to the GNP than to the GDP. This is because incomes accruing to factors of production provided by residents of a country include net factor earnings from abroad, and these are part of GNP but not GDP.

Third, as we have seen, the GNP includes the production of capital goods that are to replace those that are wearing out. We called this "depreciation". That is, part of what is produced is to enable the firm to keep on producing at the same rate and this requires replacing machines and other forms of capital that are wearing out. When depreciation is deducted from GNP the result is the NNP. Of course, the NNP must be put in real or constant-price form so as to exclude the effect of inflation. This is achieved by computing the real GNP, and then subtracting the real or constant-price depreciation. The calculation of real depreciation requires the valuation of the physical amount of wear and tear at the base period prices of capital equipment.

A further adjustment is necessary before obtaining a useful measure of the standard of living of an average individual. The NNP, like the GNP or any other measure of national income or product, will grow merely because there are more people engaged in production. However, what determines the amount of product available for an average citizen to enjoy is the amount of product per person, or **per capita**. Consequently, the real NNP must be divided by the number of people in the country.

DIFFICULTIES WHEN COMPARING LIVING STANDARDS

Comparing Living Standards between Years

We have already indicated that measures of national income and product such as the NNP count bombs and hospitals equivalently, and can perversely show an improvement after man-made or natural disasters. The NNP can be increased by many other factors which we would consider undesirable. For example, if spending is more each year on healthcare and on cleaning bills because of higher levels of air pollution, the real per capita NNP will increase even though we would not consider people to be better-off. In a similar way, higher crime rates which require that we incur higher expenditures each year to protect ourselves, to enforce the law, and to replace stolen or damaged property, also increase the real NNP.[6]

---

[6]Expenditures on crime protection made by individuals or by government *are* part of the GNP and NNP, but expenditures on crime protection by businesses, are *not* included in the NNP and GDP. Crime protection by business is considered to be an intermediate product that is included in the value of final products and is therefore left out in calculating the NNP and GDP.

Just as some undesirable developments are not included in the NNP, some desirable developments involving improvements in the quality of life are also left out. For example, restrictions on the cutting of trees in the wilderness reduce real NNP by lowering the number of trees available for building houses and furniture. Similarly, shorter work-weeks that are not offset by higher productivity reduce national output and hence the real NNP. Changes in the quality of the environment and amount of leisure are not likely to be dramatic enough to make comparisons completely meaningless when the years being compared are close together, but they make for questionable comparisons over longer spans of time.

> *Real per capita NNP, while being as good a measure of economic performance as we have, is nevertheless an imperfect measure of changes in the quality of life of an average citizen. It can be increased by pollution and crime, and reduced by environmental improvements and increased leisure.*

It is not only changes in the quality of the environment that may be missed when comparing real per capita NNPs over time. Changes in the quality of goods and services that constitute the national income and product may also not be captured. For example, newer motor vehicles provide a smoother ride and safer handling than earlier models. Electrical sound and viewing systems have greatly improved. On the other hand, construction standards in some furniture and homes and the quality of service in the gas station and at some stores have declined. Despite the development of statistical methods for handling changes in quality for measuring real NNP, they are a source of "noise" in the measurement of economic progress.

Comparing NNPs between Countries

If anything, a comparison of standards of living based on real per capita NNPs is more difficult between countries than between years within a country. For one thing, when we compare per capita NNPs between, e.g., Britain, Canada, Germany and the United States, we cannot compare pounds sterling in Britain with Canadian dollars, with euros, with United States dollars. In order to make comparisons we must express all NNPs in a common currency by, e.g., multiplying NNPs in the foreign countries by the number of United States dollars trading in the foreign exchange markets for each other currency. Then, e.g., a £25,000 income in Britain when there are

2 dollars per pound will be $50,000. We can then compare the per capita dollar-equivalent NNP or income in Britain with the dollar values of these magnitudes in the United States.

A potential problem arises when exchange rates do not reflect costs of living in different countries. Exchange rates reflect a variety of factors, and not just the prices of goods and services in one country versus another. As a result, after putting all NNPs in terms of the same currency it is necessary to make further adjustments for the cost of a typical consumer's "basket" of goods in different countries. (A typical consumer's basket is what an average or representative consumer purchases. The determination of a typical basket is discussed in more detail in Chapter 4.) However, "typical baskets" differ between countries. This is partly because people in different countries have different needs, tastes and customs.

Nature is kinder in some geographical locations than others. Those enjoying a temperate climate do not need to spend great sums heating their houses, and therefore home-heating expenditures are not a large part of a typical consumer's basket. Less lucky people who experience severe cold — as in northern parts of the U.S., and Canada — need more income just to pay the bills for keeping their homes warm. Similarly, in countries where communities are highly dispersed — as in Australia and Canada — large amounts are needed for travel. In more compact places, people can make visits and do business at lower cost. Generally, equal incomes do not mean equal standards of living when there are diverse needs.

Comparisons of real NNPs per capita between countries are distorted by different costs of living and different needs in different countries.

Another problem in comparing average per capita real NNPs concerns the distribution of incomes around the average. For example, in some of the richer countries measured solely by average real per capita NNP or national income there are a handful of fabulously rich families, and the majority of families live barely above the poverty level. Average incomes in such countries may be quite high because of the massive incomes of the very few, but we would not view such countries as providing a high standard of living for the typical citizen. In comparing countries, the equality or inequality of the distribution of income should somehow be taken into account. This problem can also arise in comparisons over time when there are significant changes in the distribution from year to year. For example, it has been claimed that in the 1990s and the first decade of the 21st century most of the economic progress of the United States was enjoyed by a small minority of people who already earned high incomes. The appendix to this chapter considers issues related to the measurement of the distribution.

Quality of the environment and conditions in the workplace are at least as much a problem when comparing living standards between countries as they are when comparing them over time. High per capita incomes that are earned at the expense of polluted air, dirty streams and lakes, the risk of technologically-induced nightmares, and toxic working conditions hardly qualify a country to head the league of the quality of life.

There are further problems related to the "value" of what is produced. For example, just as it causes problems comparing standards of living over time, international NNP comparisons do not distinguish between countries producing vast mountains of armaments, and other countries in which a similar fraction of NNP is spent on medical research for the benefit of humankind.[7]

A related problem concerns the composition of different countries' national outputs between goods and services for immediate or current enjoyment, versus goods and services to enhance future potential output. Countries putting aside for the future by devoting resources to improving capital equipment and to education may have similar current NNPs to those indulging in prolific consumption even though the potential for future economic growth is different.[8]

Since outputs and not inputs are measured in the accounts — except in the case of the contribution of the government — problems in comparison occur when the same outputs take very different inputs. For example, as in the case of comparing real NNPs between years, a country where the public enjoys a lot of leisure appears no wealthier than another where the same per capita real NNP is achieved by people typically working 50 or 60 hours a week. Countries with a long workweek and very little leisure

---

[7]To the extent that government expenditures can be broken into defense versus non-defense categories some allowances can be made. However, some budget items like research and development are difficult to disentangle.

[8]This problem is mitigated by the categorization of the national product as we explain later.

may even appear to have a higher NNP, some of which goes to doctors or for medications aimed at helping workers cope with work-related stress. Similarly, a country where a parent remains at home to raise the children will show a lower domestic product than an otherwise similar country in which both parents must work; work in the home is not counted in the GDP as Example 1.2 explains. Even the procedure for providing goods and services has an impact on real per capita NNP, and is a potential source of error when comparing NNPs between countries. For example, commercial television, which is supported by payments from the advertisers, is considered an intermediate product, or input — it is a component of marketing — and is *not* part of final output. This is despite the fact that the programming supported by the advertising provides viewers with pleasure. On the other hand, publically-funded TV *is* part of NNP — based on cost of providing it. This means that the NNP is influenced by the way television programming is provided.

Example 1.2. Should GNP Include Housewives and Resources?

Many of the points we have made concerning the inadequacies of the national income and product accounts are dealt with in the following article by David Francis in the *Christian Science Monitor*.

"Housewives don't count!

At least not in the national-income accounts. Because they are not paid in money, all the cooking, cleaning, and child-care hours of housewives (or, for that matter, house husbands) do not add one dime to the nation's GNP.

If a working couple hires a maid service to help in the home or pays for childcare, the charges are added to the national output of goods and services. But the same activities, done unpaid at home, are ignored by the statisticians in Washington.

The value of these activities is not questioned from a social standpoint. But they are considered too hard to measure accurately in dollars and cents. For example, could you determine by how much the multiplication of two-job families has reduced the time spent on household chores and childcare? Should you subtract that amount from GNP?

Robert Repetto has a different complaint about national income accounts. He says they fail to encompass the concept of sustainability. "A country could exhaust its mineral resources, cut down its forests, erode its soils, pollute its aquifers, and hunt its wildlife and fisheries to extinction, but measured income would not be affected as these assets disappeared," he states in a study for the World Resources Institute in Washington.

In keeping the national books, the statisticians subtract depreciation of manmade assets, including plant and equipment, from the value of national production. They do not subtract the depletion of natural resources.

"It should be considered," says an official in the United Nations Statistical Office. "We are all advocating that."

The UN system of national accounts provides a statistical standard and model that in its basic elements is closely followed by most countries. A UN Statistical Commission is expected to recommend by 1991 that nations turn out a 'satellite' account, separate from the current GNP standard account, that takes into consideration depletion (or restoration) of natural resources.

That commission is also reviewing, among other statistical controversies, the question of what to do about the unpaid production of goods and services by households.

In the U.S., the Bureau of Economic Analysis in the Department of Commerce plans to reevaluate its count of national output in light of what the UN Commission recommends. "We are watching closely what the UN experts are doing," says Carol Carson, a Bureau deputy director. She is actually one of the six 'core' experts consulted by the UN commission.

Because such a huge proportion of the U.S. GNP derives from services or industrial production, a full accounting of developments in natural resources might not make much difference in the GNP accounts. Though Americans think of their nation as being resource-rich, natural resources are not so important to total output as in some other countries.

Further, there are offsets in the book-keeping. Depletion of some mineral resources (say, crude oil) might be offset by new discoveries of other minerals or natural gas. Or forests being cut down in the West might be replaced by new forest growth in New England.

But in some developing countries, the failure to extend the concept of depreciation to natural resources can be important. Mr. Repetto says this lack can give "misleading signals about the status of the economy."

With a group of graduate students, he did a calculation for Indonesia of 'net' domestic product (NDP) — taking account of resource depletion. The annual growth rate of NDP from 1971 to 1984 on average came to 4%, way down from the 7.1% average annual growth calculated by the usual method of national accounting.

Moreover, their study only looked at the depletion of petroleum, timber, and soil resources. It ignored many other resources.

This study implies that Indonesia's natural resources are being depleted to finance current consumption.

"Such an evaluation should flash an unmistakable warning signal to economic policy makers that they were on an unsustainable course," holds Repetto. "An economic accounting system that does not generate and highlight such evaluations is deficient as a tool for analysis and policy in resource-based economies and should be amended."

Source: David R. Francis, *The Christian Science Monitor*, May 31, 1989, p. 9.

Real per capita NNP comparisons between countries may not reflect relative standards of living because they do not reflect the quality of the environment, working conditions, the types of goods and services produced, how goods and services are provided, and the distribution of income.

There have been efforts to form inter-temporal and inter-country comparisons from criteria other than real per capita NNP. Measures used include the number of automobiles and TVs per capita, the amount of open park space, the proportion of families in self-owned homes, the percentage of homes with refrigerators, telephones or inside plumbing, and the number of different newspapers from which to choose. Other measures have included the incidence of mental illness and crime. These different measures are, however, difficult to combine.

CATEGORIES OF THE GDP

Lumping all the different goods and services together in the GDP is useful for judging overall output of an economy, but hides some important categories of that output. Therefore, as well as reporting the total GDP, the national income and product accounts also show the GDP in terms of its major components as in Table 1.5.

The component of national output that is for current or "immediate" use is given under the heading of **personal consumption**. This includes such items as food and beverages, clothing, household appliances, entertainment and so on. The amount of consumption is determined primarily by the incomes consumers have available to spend. Consumption itself, which is over 70% of GDP, is divided into durable goods, nondurable goods, and services. The largest part of U.S. consumption is services, constituting 60% of consumption and over 40% of GDP. Sales and production of durable goods are affected not only by consumers' incomes, but also by the interest rate on consumer debt.

Consumption goods and services are for immediate use. Consumption depends primarily on consumers' incomes, but also on interest rates.

The value of output produced to assist future production and sales rather than for current enjoyment, such as new plant and equipment, is listed under

Table 1.5. The gross domestic product can be usefully divided into a number of components.

U.S. Gross Domestic Product (billions $), 2008		
Personal Consumption (C)		10,058
durable goods	1023	
nondurable goods	2965	
services	6070	
Investment (I)		1,994
Government (G)		2,882
Exports (Ex)		1,860
Imports (Im)		−2,529
Gross Domestic Product (Y)		14,265

Source: National Income and Product Accounts, U.S. Survey of Current Business, 2009.

the heading of "investment". The investment category also includes changes in inventory stocks, which as we have explained, are goods that have been produced but have not been sold. Business investment in new buildings and equipment and in inventories is frequently financed through debt or via the issue of new shares, and is therefore influenced by the interest rate on borrowing and the expected return offered to shareholders to induce them to invest. The interest rates businesses must pay on debt and the expected return they must offer to attract new equity investors — those buying the companies' stock — is referred to as the **cost of capital**.

Investment is current production designed to enhance future consumption and output, and includes plant and equipment and additions to inventories. Investment depends on the cost of capital.

After showing consumption and investment, the GDP account gives the "output" of the government. However, as we have observed, instead of measuring government *production*, the account measures the amount the government *spends* on labor and other inputs. That is, government contribution to GDP is cost-based rather than revenue-based. Government spending is normally assumed to be a matter of economic policy that is determined in the political arena. However, there is also pressure to vary spending according to the health of the overall economy, with **fiscal stimulus** being applied during recessions and **fiscal restraint** being exercised when inflation is of concern. Wars, political pressure to battle the national debt, benefit programs for the needy and interest rates paid to government bond holders who finance the national debt also affect the size of government spending.

The GDP account includes the value of goods and services produced for export. A country's exports depend on its prices compared to prices of similar goods and services elsewhere, with lower relative export prices increasing the quantity sold. Exports also depend on the foreign exchange value of a country's currency, and on incomes in foreign countries. Other factors affecting exports include import tariffs and quotas in potential markets.

While exports must be added to final sales, imports must be subtracted to obtain the GDP. The recorded values of consumption, investment and government spending include imports. This is done for practical reasons as it can be extremely difficult to isolate the domestic production from foreign production. For example, how much of a Honda assembled in the United States is part of U.S. GDP and how much is foreign? It is easier to treat the value of the car as U.S. consumption and then to deduct imports from that value, than to try and disentangle the domestic and foreign elements. Even exports contain imports — called **re-exports** — that must be deducted to obtain the GDP. Like exports, imports depend on a country's own prices versus foreign prices — with relatively lower prices at home increasing the incentives for import substitution — and also on exchange rates, incomes in the importing country, tariffs and quotas.

Table 1.5 summarizes our discussion of the components of GDP. We have written a symbol next to the various categories of the GDP using the following notation:

$$\text{Consumption} = C$$

$$\text{Investment} = I$$

$$\text{Government} = G$$

$$\text{Exports} = Ex$$

$$\text{Imports} = Im$$

$$\text{GDP} = Y.$$

We observe from the table that the GDP consists of the sum of the various categories of production, specifically:

$$Y \equiv C + I + G + (Ex - Im). \tag{1.7}$$

We have used an identity sign in Eq. (1.7) because it is a **tautology**, that is, it is always true. We see that the GDP is the sum of the outputs of consumption goods and services, C, investment goods plus inventory, I, government goods and services, G, and exports minus imports, (Ex − Im). The relationship (1.7) is known as the **national income accounting identity**.

The national income accounting identity shows the GDP as the sum of consumption, investment, government spending, and exports minus imports.

The relative importance of the components of GDP differs substantially between countries. Poorer countries tend to consume a large proportion of their GDPs; these countries need to spend a lot of what they earn on essentials such as food. In richer countries such as the United States,

Japan, and most members of the European Union, consumption is still the largest category of GDP, especially consumption of services, but represents a smaller proportion than in poor nations. There is also substantial variation between countries in the amount of GDP going into investment. In general, those countries which consume a small part of GDP invest a relatively large amount. For example, Singapore and Japan have high rates of investment and low rates of consumption.[9] China also has very high investment and low consumption, and a large **trade surplus** of exports versus imports (Ex − Im). Government spending and net exports also vary between countries. The importance of government depends on the amounts spent on defence, public health, education and welfare.[10] Net exports are a positive contribution to GDP in China and Japan, but a negative part in the U.S.; the U.S. has a **trade deficit**, with imports exceeding exports by about 5% of GDP as can be inferred from Table 1.5.

The composition of GDP between consumption, investment, government spending and net exports varies substantially between countries.

SUMMARY

(1) Gross domestic product, GDP, is the total value of goods and services produced within a nation during an interval of time such as a calendar year or quarter.

(2) Gross national product, GNP, is the value of production by factors of production provided by residents of a country. GNP is GDP plus net foreign factor income.

(3) National income and GNP are roughly equivalent. This is because values added in production are received by somebody as income, and the GNP is the sum of values added by all stages of production.

(4) The precise connection between national income and GNP is that national income is GNP minus depreciation and minus indirect taxes. Indirect taxes are primarily sales taxes, where rather than the buyer of

---

[9]As we shall explain in Chapter 6, countries which invest relatively more of their GDPs also have relatively rapid economic growth.

[10]Welfare is considered a **transfer** from taxpayers to welfare recipients and is not included in GDP, national income, or G, Government. However, the wages paid to bureaucrats and the other costs of administering the transfers are included.

a product directly paying tax to the government, the tax is collected by the seller of the product who remits the tax to the government.

(5) The national income accountant must avoid double-counting and must also not include the sales of used goods. The accountant must include exports, exclude imports, add in government spending and any change in inventories.

(6) Real GDP and real GNP value the national output at a constant set of base year prices. Real GDP and real GNP are not, therefore, distorted by inflation and deflation.

(7) Net national product, NNP, is the GNP minus depreciation.

(8) Economic progress can be measured from the growth rate in the real per capita NNP.

(9) National income comparisons between years can be misleading because of changes in outputs of undesirable products, and changes in the quality of goods and services.

(10) Income comparisons between countries can be misleading because exchange rates may not reflect differences in costs of living, because there are different requirements for a comfortable life, different degrees of equality of income distributions, different allocations between consumption and investment, different levels of inputs for the same national outputs, and different volumes of production of undesirables.

(11) GNP is frequently categorized into the type of output — consumption, investment, government expenditures, and exports. Because each of these components contains an imported component, imports must be subtracted in order to obtain a nation's output.

(12) The composition of GDP between its various components differs substantially between nations. The GDP accounts distinguish between consumption, investment, government spending and exports minus imports.

QUESTIONS

(1) Do accidents increase the GDP?

(2) What effect might the establishment of new national parks have on GDP?

(3) How might you go about developing a Gross National Happiness Index?
(4) Why do we calculate worker productivity as well as real GDP?
(5) Will advances in the real per capita NNP inevitably eventually come to an end, and either flatten out or even decline?

APPENDIX TO CHAPTER 1

"And the moral of that is — 'The more there is of mine, the less there is of yours.'"

Lewis Carol, *Alice's Adventures in Wonderland*

POVERTY AND THE DISTRIBUTION OF NATIONAL INCOME

Measuring the Inequality of Income

Aggregate measures such as national income and national product, even after we adjust for inflation, depreciation, and the number of people who share the income or product, do not tell the entire story. It is possible for these measures to suggest general improvements in well being over time when in fact the majority of people are not better off, and indeed could be worse off. It is also possible for these aggregate income and product measures to suggest a country's average citizens are better off than citizens of other countries when they are not. This is because the distribution of income — how the income is shared among individuals — can change significantly over time and can also differ substantially between countries. This appendix considers some of the issues that arise because of these distributional matters. We begin by showing how the equality or inequality of income in a particular country during an interval of time can be measured by a single number, the **Gini Ratio**.[1]

---

[1] What we say about the Gini ratio concerning the measurement of and character of the distribution of income can also be said about the distribution of wealth. Generally, the distribution of family wealth within a country or between countries is even more unequal than the distribution of income: it is not uncommon for 90% of wealth to be owned by fewer than 5% of families.

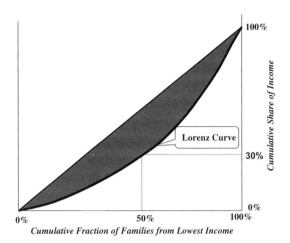

Fig. 1A.1.   The Gini ratio and the Lorenz curve.

The Lorenz curve indicates cumulatively how much of the total income of a country is earned by part of the population, grouped by family, starting with families with the lowest incomes. The Gini ratio is the shaded area between the Lorenz curve and the sloping straight line to the total area below the sloping straight line. If every family earns the same income the Gini ratio is zero: the Lorenz curve will be the sloping straight line. If all income is earned by one family and other families earn nothing at all the Gini ratio is one: the Lorenz curve will be the same as the labeled axes.

Calculating and interpreting the Gini ratio: The Gini ratio, named after the Italian statistician Corrado Gini, is a measure of dispersion that is based on the **Lorenz curve** developed by economist Max Lorenz. Fig. 1A.1 shows how the Lorenz curve is constructed, and how this can be used to calculate the Gini ratio.

The horizontal axis in Fig. 1A.1 shows the cumulative proportion of families, starting with those with the lowest incomes.[2] For example, if we go to the mid point on the horizontal axis, the point marked with 50%, this represents the bottom half of families in terms of incomes. The proportion of the country's income earned by this bottom half of the population is shown on the vertical axis. For example, if the combined income of the poorest half of families in the country is 30% of the total income of the country, the height

---

[2]Income distribution can be described in terms of individuals, but family income gives a better gauge of well-being than individual's incomes. For example, young children are likely to have no income at all and yet could be well-fed, housed and clothed.

of the Lorenz curve on the vertical axis is 30%. Inspection of the figure reveals that the more unequal is the distribution of incomes in the country, the more curved is the Lorenz curve. For example, if the poorest 50% of families share only 10% of the country's total income, the height of the Lorenz curve above 50% on the horizontal axis would not be 30% but would be only 10%. At the extreme where one family earns all the income and the others nothing, the Lorenz curve is the horizontal axis until the right vertical axis, and then is the vertical axis. On the other hand, if every family were to earn the same — not that this is the objective, as it would have adverse effects on incentives — the Lorenz curve would coincide with the slanting straight line: in such a situation the first 10% of families would earn 10% of the country's income, 20% would earn 20% of the total income and so on.

The Gini ratio is the ratio of the area between the Lorenz curve and the sloping straight line, divided by the area under the straight line. In the event that all the income is earned by one family with the others earning nothing at all, this ratio is 1.0, the maximum value that the Gini ratio can take. (Of course, it could never be that value or all would die of starvation except the one family with all the income.) On the other hand, if every family in the country earns the same income so the Lorenz curve is the slanted straight line, then the Gini ratio is 0, the lowest value it can take. More generally, the Gini ratio lies between 0 and 1.0, with the inequality of income being higher the closer the value is to 1.0.

Table 1A.1 shows the Gini ratio for family income in the United States over the 60-year period beginning just after the end of World War II. The ratio reveals an overall upward trend in the degree of inequality of Americans' incomes. This means that more of the economic progress that occurred during this time was enjoyed by wealthier families than by poorer families. Table 1A.2 shows that the United States has one of the more unequal family income distributions among a group of comparison countries, but it is by no means the most unequal. Japan and Sweden are among the countries with the most even family income distributions.

Problems in interpreting the Gini ratio: The simplicity of the Gini ratio, which summarizes the entire income distribution with a single number, comes at a price. We can see this if we consider the two parts of Fig. 1A.2.

Table 1A.1.   Gini ratio for income
of the United States over time.

Year	Gini Ratio
1947	.376
1952	.368
1957	.351
1962	.362
1967	.358
1972	.359
1977	.363
1982	.380
1987	.393
1992	.404
1997	.429
2002	.434
2007	.432
2012	.490

Source: United States Census Bureau
http://www.census.gov/hhes/www/
income/histinc/f04.html

Table 1A.2.   Gini ratio for sample of countries.

Country	Gini Ratio
Japan	.249
Sweden	.250
Germany	.283
France	.327
Pakistan	.330
Canada	.331
Switzerland	.331
United Kingdom	.360
Iran	.430
United States*	.466
Argentina	.522
Mexico	.546
South Africa	.578
Namibia	.707

Source: United Nations and CIA Factbook, 2009.
Copied from: http://blog.sustainablemiddleclass.
com/?page_id=162
*Based on more recent data than Table 1A.1.

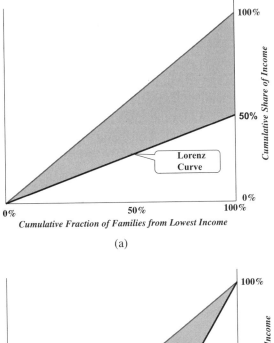

(a)

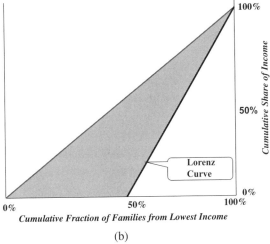

(b)

Fig. 1A.2.   Two Gini ratios equal to 0.5.

In Figs. 1A.2*a* and 1A.2*b* the Gini ratio, given by the shaded area divided by the area under the sloping straight line, is in both cases 0.5. However, the figures describe two very different realities. In Fig. 1A.2*a* the richest family has half the country's income while the remainder of the population — all other families in the country — equally share the other half of the income. In Fig. 1A.2*b* the poorer half of families earn nothing at all while the other half equally share all the country's income. Most people would probably agree that the situation in Fig. 1A.2*a* is less harsh than that in Fig. 1A.2*b*. In the case of the reality in Fig. 1A.2*b* the half of families with no income whatsoever will presumably die of starvation. In the case of the country with income distribution described by Fig. 1A.1*a*, if this is a rich country all the families other than the one enjoying half the income could be enjoying a high standard of living, albeit well below that of the one super rich family.

The problem with the Gini ratio that is illustrated in Fig. 1A.2*a* versus Fig. 1A.2*b* is that a single number comparison requires that the Lorenz curve has a rather smooth and symmetrical form, as is the case of the curve in Fig. 1A.1. This results in a shaded area that has its widest part in the center. The Lorenz curves in Fig. 1A.2*a* and Fig. 1A.2*b* have their widest part at the ends. The more the curves depart from the smooth symmetrical form the more the single number description gives a distorted picture.

One of the purposes of measuring income distributions is to provide a sense of the scale of the poverty problem in a country: are there many with very low incomes or do most families have a decent income? But what do we mean by poverty? Are there potential answers to solving the poverty problem?

Poverty Definitions

Relative deprivation: If poverty is viewed in terms of having a distinctly lower standard of living than is enjoyed by the average person, then the poor might be considered to be those who, e.g., are at the bottom 10% or 20% of the income distribution. This definition could be applied across the globe, just as it can to any individual country, but the definition has the distinct disadvantage of offering no measure of progress in the alleviation of poverty. Indeed, a relative deprivation measure suggests that poverty cannot be eliminated as long as any inequality remains. This does not mean that measures of relative deprivation have no value. In part, this is because it may well be the case that people are dissatisfied by seeing others enjoying substantially more affluence. For example, a very low income American may indeed feel poor because she or he sees so much affluence around them, even though on an international scale they may be relatively well-off. In addition, defining poverty as the "tail" of the income distribution can be useful if we are interested in the types of people who are poor, or in how much "turnover" occurs from year to year in the families turning up in the tail of the income distribution.

Absolute deprivation: It is possible to define the poor as those who lack the basic necessities such as adequate food, shelter, healthcare, and education. Of course, this does raise the question of what constitute the basic necessities, and what level of each is considered adequate? However, once these standards have been set, the proportion falling below the agreed poverty line can be used to judge, e.g., if progress has been made in fighting poverty and how many families need welfare assistance.

Unfortunately, while absolute standards of poverty are of some use in a domestic context, it is difficult or even impossible to define useful standards when making comparisons on an international scale. This is because the basic necessities of life differ markedly between nations. For example, housing, clothing and nutritional needs vary greatly with climate, energy needs differ greatly with norms of travel and home comforts, and so on. What might leave an American barely able to subsist might provide a princely life style on a South Sea island where heating is unnecessary and some food, such as fish and coconuts, may be available just for the taking.

The Causes of Poverty

While it is difficult for reasons we have cited, such as the great variations in needs for a comfortable life, to categorically decide on which countries are poor, there is little doubt that the richer countries include those in Europe, North America, Japan and Australia, while the poor countries are in Africa, the Asian sub-continent, and Central and South America. But what is it that has given rise to this global distribution, that to an extent, constitutes a "north-south" division, with the north generally being richer?[3]

An obvious candidate for an explanation of poverty versus affluence is **factor endowments**, by which we mean the good or bad fortune that

---

[3]More specifically, the richer countries tend to be in the temperate regions while the poorer ones are closer to the Equator.

countries have enjoyed or suffered in the global distribution of natural resources, including good soil and water. However, while this might explain the high living standards in North America and perhaps parts of Europe, it cannot explain why, e.g., Japan which lacks energy and other natural resources has a high standard of living, and why such city-states as Hong Kong and Singapore have done so well. The attribution of living standards to factor endowments also does not explain why parts of Africa which have large resource endowments remain desperately poor. Clearly, as a reflection about Africa reveals, political stability, education, motivation, the willingness to save and invest and to embrace the market mechanism all play a role. Development economists who specialize in the study of the sources of economic progress have indeed identified such characteristics as influencing the level and pace of development, although there is no consensus on *relative* importance of different factors.

The importance of investment, including investment in human capital that comes from allocating resources to education, helps point to the viciousness of the cycle of poverty in which so many desperately poor nations seem to be trapped. The very poor need all the income they can earn in order to subsist, and can afford little or nothing to save and invest for the future by building infrastructure, capital equipment, institutions of higher and vocational learning, and spreading literacy. Even childhood and elementary education may be lacking. Because these countries cannot invest they remain poor. It is little surprise that those countries that have managed to break themselves out of the vicious poverty cycle, such as, Brazil, India, China, South Korea, and Thailand have progressed rapidly after they have broken out of the poverty trap.

The Poor in America

Whether poverty in America is defined in relative or absolute terms, the same characteristics show up in who is likely to be poor. According to the U.S. Bureau of the Census, in the United States families headed by a female without a husband present constitute more than half the families facing poverty. Partly because of this, children make up a large portion of the poor, with well over a third of the poor in the U.S. being children under 18 years. A large proportion of the poor also come from the other end of the age distribution; the elderly constitute over 10% of the poor. There are also disproportionate numbers of visible minorities, largely blacks and Hispanics, among the poor even though in terms of absolute numbers, whites constitute approximately two-thirds of America's poor. Finally, it can be noted that particular states and regions have disproportionately large numbers of poor, and while there are many rural poor, a vast number of the poor are found in urban areas, even in the wealthiest states.

The Global Distribution of Income

If we were to represent an average American's income by a person of average height, say, six feet, and we represented the incomes of the rest of mankind on this same scale, the very poorest would be shorter than mice. Indeed, we would find the vast majority of the Earth's population below the knees of the average American. Yet on this same scale, we would find some industrial tycoons taller than the world's highest buildings. Perhaps more troubling than the disparities of living standards that exist is the fact that the poor show little sign of ever breaking out of their dismal situation.

Poverty versus Population: The Malthusian Trap

The vicious cycle of poverty in the desperately poor lands where meager incomes preclude surpluses for investing in the future is not helped by the tendency for the poorest of the poor to have many children. With odds heavily stacked against children surviving, and with no social assistance from the government for the aged, the desperately poor see their only hope for survival into old age in having a large family. This may indeed improve the prospects for those having the children, but paradoxically puts an increasing strain on the already meager resources available to the nation. That is, there is a conflict between what makes sense for individual families and what makes sense for nations that are the collectivity of individual families.

The tendency for the poor to have large families even though this pushes nations beyond their ability to feed their populations is well documented and accepted by demographers and economists specializing in economic development. Recognition of the virtual inevitability of the problem has also revived interest in the argument advanced in the early 19th century by Thomas Malthus. Taking note of the natural tendency for populations of plants, insects and animals to expand to the limits of subsistence, Malthus was led to the conclusion that the fecundity of humans would push their numbers to the same subsistence limit. That is, given time, human populations would expand until competition for the Earth's limited resources pushed mankind to the bare minimum level of subsistence, a conclusion which led Thomas Carlyle to dub economics the "dismal science." Counterarguments can be made against Malthus' reasoning, including the criticism that it overlooks the choice towards smaller families that typically accompanies economic progress. Furthermore, the evidence on per capita food output, especially in the richer nations, so far casts doubt on Malthus' projections. Nevertheless, in the poorest parts of the globe, the occurrence of famine and the persistence of conditions bordering on subsistence have given Neo-Malthusians reinforcement for their views.

Guns versus Butter and the Poverty Problem

It has been observed that if military budgets, which globally exceed several trillion dollars per year, were turned to fighting poverty instead of preparing for war we could overcome the poverty problem and still have plenty left over. For example, $600 billion from the U.S. defense budget would translate into approximately $10,000 per year for the poorest 20% of Americans. With the ending of the Cold War at the end of the 20th century, conditions seem right for dealing with the poverty problem which, if the translation from "guns" to "butter" using the type of calculation just made were correct, would be solved in the U.S. and greatly reduced worldwide. Unfortunately, the answer is not that simple.

The problem is that most of the *resources* used to produce military hardware cannot produce food or other basic necessities. For example, food production requires land and water for irrigation, and not much of this is released by curtailing armaments output. Saying, e.g., that each $1 billion transferred from military to welfare budgets will buy, e.g., 250 million bushels of wheat at $4 per bushel, overlooks this fact. It is not money transfers that produce wheat instead of rockets, but transfers of resources such as labor and fertile land. The consequences of transfers of resources

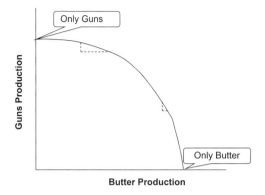

Fig. 1A.3. The production possibilities curve.

for outputs of final products are described by the **production possibilities curve** that is illustrated in Fig. 1A.3.

The production possibilities curve shows the combinations of outputs that are possible if all the inputs of resources that are available are fully employed. Each end of the curve shows the outputs of the final goods that are possible if only one of the goods is being produced. Interior points show potential outputs of alternative possible combinations of the two products. There is a tradeoff of one good for the other. The curvature of the production possibilities curve tells us that we gain less and less food for each unit of reduced output of military hardware, the more food and less military hardware we are already producing: movements along the curve from top left to bottom right result in smaller gains in butter output for the same declines in guns output, the further we are along the curve to producing only butter.

Unfortunately for solving the poverty problem, different resources are employed in producing armaments than in producing food. Therefore, as more and more resources are transferred from producing guns to producing butter, we gain less and less butter. This is not to say that we cannot go some way towards correcting the poverty problem, especially in the long run when we can shift research and development efforts away from military to civilian objectives. Rather, we are cautioning against the view that transfers of money are equivalent to transfers of resources between alternative possible outputs.

SUMMARY OF APPENDIX

(1) There are massive disparities of per capita incomes among countries. U.S. family incomes vary less than incomes between countries, but there are nevertheless large differences.

(2) Poverty can be defined relatively, as being at the bottom end of the distribution of income, but while this does allow an analysis of who is likely to be poor and how long people remain poor, it does not permit the measurement of progress. The alternative of defining poverty absolutely in terms of being able to afford the necessities of life, while allowing a measure of progress, raises the question of what are the basic necessities.

(3) Internationally, the poor countries do not necessarily suffer from low factor endowments. Other factors like the levels of political stability, education, motivation, savings and investment, and willingness to accept the market mechanism appear to play a role.

(4) In the United States the poor tend to be in families headed by a female without a husband present, under 18, elderly and from regions of chronic unemployment. Most of the poor are white, but blacks and Hispanics are disproportionately numerous among the poor.

(5) The need to save and invest in order to enjoy economic progress means that those who are so close to subsistence that they have no surplus to save or invest are trapped in the poverty cycle.

(6) The poorest of poor countries often have a population problem because parents choose large families to compensate for the low survival rates of children and the absence of government help for the aged.

(7) Thomas Malthus believed that population expands to the point of subsistence, at least in poor countries.

(8) While it is possible to increase food production and provide other peacetime necessities when military budgets are trimmed, it is not money that needs to be transferred, but the resource inputs. The shifting of resources provides a transformation of outputs between "guns" and "butter," but this transformation is subject to the limitations of the production possibilities curve.

QUESTIONS ON APPENDIX

(1) Why is most of Africa so poor when the African Continent is relatively rich in resources?

(2) Do dollar-equivalent income levels in different countries accurately reflect differences in their economic standard of living?

CONNECTIONS

ACCOUNTING FOR NATIONAL ECONOMIC PERFORMANCE

Mankind's interest in "keeping score" has a long history. Of course, keeping score requires a consistent numerical system and a framework for keeping records, and it can be argued that it was the needs of business and commerce for a numerical recording system that led to the early development of mathematics. Certainly, the commercial uses of mathematics arose early on for quoting prices, calculating revenues and costs, and recording debts. Accounting principles had emerged for reporting the performance and financial status of commercial enterprises well before they were written down by the Italian mathematician Luca Paciolo, whose *Summa de Arithemetica, Geometria, Proportioni et Proportionalita* was published in 1494. While Paciolo wrote about accounting for commercial enterprises, it was only a natural and short step before Sir William Petty and Gregory King in Britain were formulating rules on the recording of national economic performance in national income and product accounts. The principal purpose of the national accounts was to keep score on how well a nation was doing in providing for the economic well-being of its citizens.

The national accounts have been refined and elaborated to a point where they do far more than just record overall national economic performance. The national income and product accounts today provide data of interest to political scientists, geographers and public policy makers, as well as to economists, historians and others. They are also of value to business when deciding on business expansion or on business contraction. While an individual company may do well in a weak economy or do poorly in a strong economy, on average a rising or ebbing tide carries most businesses in the same direction. (There are always some exceptions. For example, lawyers specializing with bankruptcy and sellers of bulk foods such as potatoes may enjoy better times during recessions and worse times during economic expansions.)

The national income estimates show the division of income between wages, salaries, profits, interest and rent. These data provide evidence on the behavior of the functional distribution of income over time, as well as during the ups and downs of the business cycle. The functional distribution of income is of interest to social scientists who are concerned with the division of income between providers of labor, land and capital. Statistics on the income on capital, i.e., profits, are also of interest to financial analysts.

The Gross Domestic Product (GDP) estimates in the national accounts are not only divided into consumption, investment, government and net exports as explained in this chapter, but also according to the industries responsible for the product, and the regions of the country generating the product. These data are of interest to business economists trying to forecast changes in industrial structure over time, to geographers interested in shifts between rural and urban areas and between different parts of the country, and especially to economic historians.

Sociologists have an interest in the national income and product accounts, not only because many social problems vary with the state of the economy — family violence, child abuse, depression, alienation and so on increasing during economic downturns — but because the accounts are affected by and reflect social trends. For example, the national income has been increased in recent decades by the movement of women into the labor force. Sociologists and economists have recognized that this social change has moved many previously non-market activities such as child-care and home-care into the market; home-makers whose work in the home is not included in the GDP are today paying others for what they used to do, without payment, themselves. For this reason, economists have realized that the growth of GDP has been exaggerated; earlier GDP statistics understated the value of work done to the extent more unrecorded work was performed in the home.

Other social trends have affected the amounts recorded in the national accounts. For example, increases in the proportion of a cohort attending college temporarily reduce income and production because there are fewer people working, although *future* income and production are higher. This is because the national income and product accounts do not include in the investment category, investment in human capital, although education costs are included. At the other end of the age distribution, changes in retirement age also affect production; in a fully employed economy, the earlier people retire, the lower is the national income and product because there are fewer people producing goods and services and earning incomes. Again we see a link between social trends and economics via the national accounts.

Some social trends affect national income and product indirectly. For example, while trade in illicit drugs is not part of the GDP even though it involves market transactions, the consumption of drugs does influence GDP. In particular, lost output from drug addiction reduces output, although extra policing because of drug-related crime may ironically increase 'output'. (As mentioned in the chapter, police costs paid by the government or consumers are a final output, and part of the GDP. However, police costs paid by business are an intermediate product and not part of the GDP). Other examples where GDP is affected by social trends include attitudes to work-related stress — more time off reduces GDP — willingness to perform volunteer public service — more volunteer versus paid work reduces recorded GDP — and so on.

As well as *affecting* GDP, social trends are themselves sometimes the *result* of changes in GDP. For example, the need for two-incomes to pay for housing may at least in part be due to average incomes advancing more slowly than people expected. Crime rates and mental illness may also be affected by GDP, both increasing as economic conditions fall behind what people expected. Again, we see that interests of psychologists as well as sociologists overlap with those of economists.

We mentioned in this chapter that there are many dimensions to human well-being other than the size of the average per capita real NNP, the way economic well-being is measured. As we explained, broader indexes have been constructed which factor in the amount of park space, the number of social problems and so on, to judge whether progress is being made and which countries offer their citizens the best living conditions. But what about such immeasurables as freedom, security, compassion, respect, leisure and so on? When it comes to such matters and the roles they play vis-à-vis economic performance as measured by the GDP, theologians may have more to say than economists.

All religions have warned against excessive emphasis on economic measures of reward. For example, Psalm (62:10) advises, "If riches increase, set not your heart upon them". Similarly, the New Testament teaches "Man shall not live by bread alone" (Mathew 4:4), and warns, "for what is a man advantaged if he gain the whole world, and lose himself, or be cast away?" (Luke 9:25). The Hindu *Bhagavad-Gita* in the *Mahabharata* warns "Pondering on objects of the senses gives rise to attraction ... till purpose, mind and man are all undone." The Buddhist *Dhamapada* likewise warns "Cut down the whole forest of desire, not just one tree only". Similarly, in the *Chapter of the Night*, the *Koran* cautions "his wealth shall not avail him when he falls down (into hell)!"

Attitudes to materialism, which manifest themselves in national consumption and product statistics, differ fundamentally between cultures as well as religions, and have undergone major transformations over the centuries. For example, sociologist Max Weber has attributed much of what occurred in the Industrial Revolution to the sanctification of industriousness in the teachings of John Calvin and his followers. The changes in attitudes that have occurred are, however, due to more than shifts in views of religious leaders. Attitudes to hard work, investment and the enjoyment of the economic fruits of these have been part of the evolving cultural picture of modern-day Japan, other rapidly growing newly industrialized countries (NICs), the U.S., and more recently, Eastern Europe and the independent states of the former U.S.S.R. Economics is inextricably tied to many aspects of culture and to secular attitudes, with the culture and attitudes having important long-run implications for the national accounts and the satisfaction taken from progress reflected in these accounts.

CHAPTER 2

NATIONAL DEBT

"The government is the only organization that can run a deficit and still make money."

Anonymous

Key Concepts: National debt; fiscal deficit; public debt; gross debt; national debt relative to national product; national debt versus corporate and personal debt; foreign debt versus domestic debt; debt growth and pensions; debt retirement and inflation; debt incurred for infrastructure and human capital.

NATIONAL DEBT AND FISCAL DEFICITS

An economic magnitude which has attracted increased attention in recent years is the **national debt**, also sometimes referred to as the **public debt**. The national debt is the amount owed by the national government and is represented by the value of government bonds that lenders to the national government hold. The debt represents the accumulation of government borrowing that has occurred over past years to finance **fiscal deficits**. Just as the debt increases when the government runs fiscal deficits — spending more than it receives in tax revenue — it is reduced when there are fiscal surpluses, i.e., when tax revenue exceeds what the government spends. If we include intergovernmental debt and debt obligations such as social security we then have **gross debt**. The top part of Fig. 2.1 shows vividly why the national debt has become a focus of attention; between 1980 and 2010 the U.S. national debt increased by several hundred percent.

A commonly-expressed concern is that national debt represents a burden on future generations, and indeed, at the extremely rapid rate at which the debt is growing, it represents a future burden on people working today.

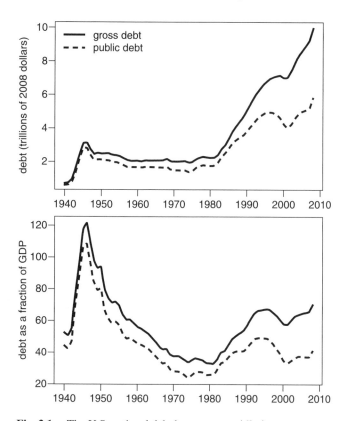

Fig. 2.1. The U.S. national debt has grown rapidly in recent years.

Source: http://upload.wikimedia.org/wikipedia/en/3/3b/USDebt.png.

While U.S. national debt and public debt have both grown rapidly in the last three decades, their importance relative to the size of the economy is not greater than it was at the end of the Second World War.

For example, the need to find the money to make interest payments is forcing the U.S. government to carefully consider its spending on public health, education, research and development, infrastructure including transportation systems, and other programs which contribute to current as well as future well-being; a healthy, educated workforce with sophisticated capital equipment and rapid transportation links is more productive than a workforce that is denied crucial efficiently operating infrastructure and other productive inputs.

Unfortunately, judgment of the extent to which the national debt represents a burden on current and future generations cannot be based simply on the dollar size of the debt. Depending on the circumstances, a rapidly growing debt might be little or even no problem at all. Several circumstances need to be considered, specifically:

(1) The size of the national debt relative to the size of the national economy, and the growth rate of the economy and hence the future tax base.
(2) The effect of high personal and corporate income taxes, collected to service interest and principal payments, on the willingness of people to work hard and invest in human and physical capital.
(3) The amount of debt owed to domestic residents versus foreigners.
(4) Whether the debt is denominated in the country's own currency or in foreign currency.
(5) Whether the national government is *de facto* the guarantor of debt incurred by other entities such as agencies, corporations, state/provincial governments, municipalities and so on.
(6) The fraction of overall government spending directed towards the improvement of infrastructure essential for future economic development.
(7) Whether inflation is "retiring" the real value of national debt.
(8) Whether the government can look forward to growing tax receipts from growing corporate and individuals' incomes, including tax receipts on savings that enjoy a temporary sheltering from income tax.

Let us consider each of these in turn.

National Debt Relative to GDP

When a *company's* debt grows there is not necessarily widespread concern among shareholders. For example, debt incurred for new plant and equipment, corporate acquisitions, marketing programs or employee training could mean a very healthy future. What matters is whether the company's income is currently sufficient and growing fast enough for it to meet all interest payments and scheduled repayments of principal. Similarly, in the case of national debt, what matters is whether the government's income is large enough and growing sufficiently rapidly for it to meet all of its debt obligations.

The parallel between corporate debt and national debt is a good one not only when it comes to common factors influencing the ability to pay — debt size versus company/economy size, and growth in the corporation/economy. Another important parallel is that governments, like corporations, are in principle immortal. They do not have to pay back all their debt by some future stipulated time. This is often forgotten when we hear alarming rhetoric that "at such and such a rate of borrowing we will never be able to repay this debt!" While individuals do have to pay back their debt by some point in time or else default, corporations and governments can indefinitely remain in debt.

The base on which the government collects taxes which can be used to meet debt obligations is the national product. *Ceteris paribus*, the higher is the national product the higher is the government's total tax revenue; since national product is also approximately national income, and because tax collections, for given tax rates, depend on the size of personal and corporate incomes, government tax revenue depends on the national product. Therefore, the level of concern about the national debt depends on how large it currently is and how rapidly it is growing relative to the size and growth of the national product. This can be judged by looking at the ratio of debt to Gross National Product (GNP) or Gross Domestic Product (GDP).[1] The lower part of Fig. 2.1 indicates that U.S. national debt grew more slowly than the U.S. GNP from the end of World War II until the mid 1970s. However, since the mid 1970s the national debt has grown faster than the GNP or GDP, making it increasingly difficult for the U.S. government to meet scheduled debt repayments.

The United States is by no means alone in facing a formidable debt in relation to the size of its economy. Table 2.1 shows that some countries have debts substantially larger than their GDP. Even Japan and Singapore, countries that at times have been economic success stories, have national debts larger than one year of national product. At the other extreme, some countries owe as little as one month of their national product. It is not necessarily that poor countries owe more than rich ones. Clearly, there must be numerous factors influencing debt-to-product ratios.

---

[1]To the extent that foreign factor income earned by residents of a nation generates tax revenue for that nation, tax revenue is more closely related to GNP than GDP: recall that GNP = GDP + Net Foreign Factor Income.

Table 2.1. National debt burdens vary substantially from country to country.

Rank	Country	Public debt (% of GDP)
1	Zimbabwe	241.20
2	Japan	170.40
3	Lebanon	163.50
4	Jamaica	124.10
5	Singapore	113.70
6	Italy	103.70
7	Seychelles	92.60
8	Greece	90.10
9	Sudan	86.10
10	Egypt	84.70
11	Bhutan	81.40
12	Belgium	80.80
13	Sri Lanka	78.00
14	India	78.00
15	Israel	75.70
16	Hungary	73.80
17	France	67.00
18	Ghana	66.50
19	Portugal	64.20
20	Germany	62.60
21	Canada	62.30
22	United States	60.80
23	Morocco	60.20
24	Austria	58.80
25	Cote d'Ivoire	58.30
26	Jordan	58.30
27	Mauritius	57.20
28	Uruguay	57.00
29	Philippines	56.50
30	Nicaragua	53.60
31	Tunisia	53.10
32	Bolivia	52.70
33	Kenya	52.70
34	Norway	52.00
35	Albania	51.20
36	Argentina	51.00
37	Pakistan	49.80
38	Malawi	49.10
39	Cyprus	49.00

(*Continued*)

Table 2.1. (*Continued*)

Rank	Country	Public debt (% of GDP)
40	Croatia	48.90
41	Colombia	48.00
42	United Kingdom	47.20
43	Panama	46.40
44	Aruba	46.30
45	Switzerland	44.00
46	Netherlands	43.00
47	Malaysia	42.70
48	Thailand	42.00
49	Poland	41.60
50	Syria	41.20
51	Brazil	40.70
52	Bosnia and Herzegovina	40.00
53	Dominican Republic	39.10
54	Vietnam	38.60
55	Costa Rica	38.40
56	Montenegro	38.00
57	Spain	37.50
58	Turkey	37.10
59	Serbia	37.00
60	Sweden	36.50
61	Macedonia	35.90
62	Slovakia	35.00
63	Bangladesh	34.60
64	Ethiopia	34.40
65	Papua New Guinea	34.00
66	Bahrain	33.20
67	Finland	33.00
68	Cuba	32.80
69	Korea, South	32.70
70	Yemen	31.80
71	Ireland	31.50
72	Taiwan	30.90
73	Indonesia	30.10
74	South Africa	29.90
75	Czech Republic	29.40
76	Ecuador	29.20
77	Trinidad and Tobago	28.00
78	El Salvador	26.70
79	Gabon	26.30

(*Continued*)

Table 2.1. (*Continued*)

Rank	Country	Public debt (% of GDP)
80	Zambia	25.70
81	Iran	25.00
82	Namibia	24.80
83	Peru	24.10
84	Guatemala	23.70
85	Iceland	23.00
86	New Zealand	22.90
87	United Arab Emirates	22.40
88	Paraguay	22.20
89	Slovenia	22.00
90	Tanzania	22.00
91	Denmark	21.80
92	Mozambique	21.40
93	Senegal	21.40
94	Moldova	21.30
95	Honduras	21.00
96	Mexico	20.30
97	Uganda	19.50
98	Venezuela	17.40
99	Latvia	17.00
100	Bulgaria	16.70
101	China	15.70
102	Gibraltar	15.70
103	Australia	15.40
104	Hong Kong	14.50
105	Romania	14.10
106	Algeria	13.80
107	Uzbekistan	13.60
108	Saudi Arabia	13.50
109	Nigeria	12.20
110	Cameroon	11.90
111	Lithuania	11.90
112	Ukraine	10.00
113	Equatorial Guinea	9.30
114	Kazakhstan	9.10
115	Angola	8.70
116	Kuwait	7.20
117	Luxembourg	7.20
118	Russia	6.80
119	Qatar	6.00

(*Continued*)

Table 2.1.   *(Continued)*

Rank	Country	Public debt (% of GDP)
120	Wallis and Futuna	5.60
121	Azerbaijan	5.20
122	Botswana	5.10
123	Chile	3.80
124	Estonia	3.80
125	Libya	3.60
126	Oman	2.40

Source: The *CIA* Fact Book @: https://www.cia.gov/library/
publications/the-world-factbook/rankorder/2186rank.html.

Note that in evaluating the ratio of national debt versus national product we are comparing debt levels, which have the magnitude of "stocks" — so much at a moment in time — with national products which have the magnitude of "flows" — so much during an interval of time. The ratio of national debt to GNP is the number of months or years of national product it would take to pay back the debt if every dollar was used to pay the country's creditors. Of course, such an action would make no sense, but the ratio does give an indication of the severity of a country's debt problem, particularly when evaluating the relative debt burden of one country versus another or when judging the trend in the debt burden.

It should be clear that the seriousness of any given level of debt versus GDP depends on how rapidly the economy of a country is growing. A static or declining income would indicate a poorer prognostication than would an environment of continuous healthy economic growth and accompanying expansion of the tax base.

> *The seriousness of a county's national debt depends on the debt relative to the country's national product, and the country's rate of economic growth.*

Taxes and the Willingness to Work and Invest

To the extent that the outstanding Treasury bills and bonds are owned by citizens, payments on the debt are **transfers** from one group–the taxpayers–to another group–the bond holders — within the same country. Of course, many people are members of both groups, so they pay tax, such as income tax, and receive interest payments. For example, if all U.S. Treasury bills and bonds were owned by Americans, payments on the U.S. national debt would simply be transfers from U.S. taxpayers to U.S. Treasury bill and bond holders. Therefore, it might seem that the national debt imposes no cost to the nation considered as a whole: the Treasury bills and bonds are assets for some and liabilities for others. However, even when all the national debt is held by citizens, there may still be a cost to the nation from the effect of taxes on incentives to work and invest.

Those who pay the taxes that are used by the government to make interest payments on the national debt find their after-tax earnings reduced. If the taxes are on wages, workers may reduce their effort; the willingness to work overtime might, e.g., be reduced because there is less reward in terms of after-tax earnings. If the taxes are on interest earned on savings, people may reduce the amount saved. Lower rates of savings means banks and other financial intermediaries have less to lend. Furthermore, to the extent that there are taxes on income from investment, e.g., on research and development or on profits earned from new plant and equipment, companies may reduce investment. With less investment there will *ceteris paribus* be slower economic growth. We see that even if all debt is held by citizens, the debt represents a burden on current and future generations.

> *Even when payments on the national debt are transfers within the country, there may still be a cost of larger debts to the nation from higher taxes which can reduce effort, savings, and investment, and thereby current and future national income.*

External Debt

In fact, payments on the national debt are generally not merely transfers from some citizens, the taxpayers, to others, the Treasury bill and bond holders.[2] Rather, part of the national debt is held by foreigners, while at the same time citizens own foreign countries' Treasury bills and bonds. For example, as is indicated in Fig. 2.2, more than a quarter of the U.S. national debt is foreign owned. Interest payments to foreigners are a drain of income from the domestic economy. The extent to which this drain is

---

[2] By convention, Treasury bills have maturity of less than one year, whereas bonds have maturities of a year or longer. Some generally small countries also have bank debt.

Estimated Ownership of all U.S. Treasury Securities (June 2008)

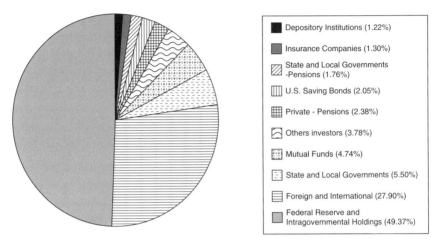

Fig. 2.2.   Holders of United States' national debt.

Source: http://en.wikipedia.org/wiki/File:Estimated_ownership_of_US_Treasury_securities_by_category_0608.jpg.

offset by earnings on holdings of foreign countries' bills and bonds depends on the net investment position of the country. To the extent that a growing debt means more money that is collected from taxpayers is sent abroad, a growing national debt represents a growing burden, one that could result in future generations working in order to meet obligations incurred on their behalf but without their consent.

Foreign held debt is a burden on a country's taxpayers.

The consequence of foreign held debt, not just that of the government but including consumer and corporate debt, can be viewed in terms of the national income and product accounts discussed in the previous chapter. In particular, the need to pay foreigners interest on debt that they hold affects GNP versus GDP. We saw this Eq. (1.2) in Chapter 1:

$$\text{GNP} \equiv \text{GDP} + \text{Net Foreign Factor Income.} \qquad (1.2)$$

The larger are the payments to foreigners, the smaller is the GNP relative to the GDP. As indicated in the previous chapter, the GNP, which includes

Foreign Holders of U.S. Treasury Securities (Jan 2009)
(percentage of total foreign ownership)

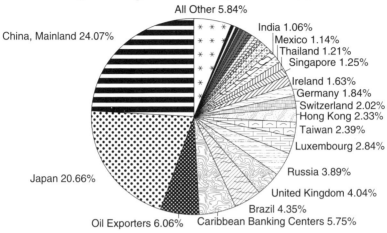

All Other 5.84%

China, Mainland 24.07%

India 1.06%
Mexico 1.14%
Thailand 1.21%
Singapore 1.25%
Ireland 1.63%
Germany 1.84%
Switzerland 2.02%
Hong Kong 2.33%
Taiwan 2.39%
Luxembourg 2.84%
Russia 3.89%
United Kingdom 4.04%
Brazil 4.35%
Caribbean Banking Centers 5.75%

Japan 20.66%

Oil Exporters 6.06%

Fig. 2.3. A major proportion of externally-held U.S. Federal Government debt is held by either Japan or China.

Source: http://en.wikipedia.org/wiki/File:Foreign_Holders_of_United_States_Treasury_Securities-percent_share.gif.

incomes on labor and capital received from abroad minus payments made abroad, is more closely related to a country's standard of living than is the GDP. When a country has large debts to foreigners, some of the income and production within the country is for others to spend and enjoy. It should be remembered, however, that if the foreign borrowing has been used to finance investment projects that have boosted the borrowing country's GDP, there is an offset to the negative effect of interest payments going abroad. Indeed, if the borrowed money is invested in very high return projects, the extra tax base available to the taxman could exceed the interest payments and reduce fiscal deficits. A similar conclusion can be reached when considering *domestic* borrowing as is explained later.

Currency of Denomination of Debt

Countries issue bonds denominated in foreign currencies as well as their own currency. Not all countries are like the United States that issues almost exclusively bonds denominated in its own currency, the U.S. dollar. Small developing countries in particular issue bonds denominated in what are to them foreign currencies, typically those that are widely traded such as the U.S. dollar or the euro. The presence of foreign currency debt is not particularly problematic when making judgments such as the size of the debt-to-GDP ratio: the foreign currency debts can be added to domestically denominated debt at the prevailing exchange rate(s). The main distinction between foreign versus domestically denominated debt concerns the risk of the debt and the possibility of borrower default.

A risk of foreign-currency denominated debt is due to the fact that changes in exchange rates affect the size of the debt in terms of the borrower's currency. For example, if a country borrows U.S. dollars and then the dollar goes up substantially, so does the size of the country's debt converted into the borrower's currency, making it harder to meet the interest and principal payments.

The possibility of default distinction between domestic-currency and foreign-currency debt is a very sharp one: while a country can default on its debt denominated in foreign currency it can never default on debt in its own currency. If a country such as Russia borrows by issuing U.S. dollar-denominated bonds, when the debt is spinning out of control it cannot make more dollars. If it runs out of dollars or the ability to borrow them, it is forced into default. However, Russia can make more rubles without limit. All it needs for rubles is more ink. (Paper is not the problem as more zeros can always be added, and with money mostly being data entries in electronic ledgers the only constraint is disc storage which in reality is essentially unlimited.) Of course, if the country were to resort to making more rubles to repay the debt, the value of the ruble would decline. For example, if Russia doubled the supply of rubles it could count on the value of these rubles falling roughly in half. What this means from the bond-holder's perspective is that they lose from currency **depreciation** if the debt is in a country's own currency, and by default if it is in foreign currency.

Default can occur on foreign-currency denominated debt. Depreciation rather than default can occur on domestic-currency denominated debt.

Other Claims against the Government

Not all the debt obligations of a national government necessarily appear on the national government's books. For example, in some countries agencies such as housing, energy and transportation agencies issue debt that is explicitly underwritten by the national government. Also, when state or local governments can borrow by selling bonds, whether there is or is not a specific guarantee on these bonds, the national government may not want to allow a default. This helps explain why in the United States there are restrictions on the ability of the states to borrow. On the other hand, Canadian provinces can borrow by selling their own bonds, and while the provincial debt is not guaranteed by the federal government, there is reason to believe that default on these bonds would not be allowed. Depending on the likelihood that debt responsibilities might ultimately fall on the national government, by failing to include these responsibilities there is an underestimation of the national debt.

The national debt as normally measured may exclude debt obligations incurred by agencies and lower levels of government.

The Form of Government Expenditures: Infrastructure

To the extent that a government borrows money to increase the productive capacity of its economy, whether borrowed at home or abroad, the debt that is incurred does not necessarily represent a burden; interest and principal payments on the debt can be paid out of the additional income generated in the economy. For example, if much of what is done with borrowed money involves improvements in infrastructure such as transportation systems, education, research and development, telecommunications and so on, the payoff from the spending by the government could make people better off, even though there is a need to make payments on the debt which financed the investment. On the other hand, if borrowed money is used in ways that does not enhance future productive capacity, e.g., on unwarranted perks to politicians and civil servants, then the debt represents a burden.

The burden of debt faced by future generations depends on whether or not borrowed money is used to enhance the future productive capacity of an economy.

National Debt and (Unanticipated) Inflation

The *real value* of the national debt, indeed, the real value of any debt including personal and corporate debt, is reduced by inflation. For example, suppose the national debt is $10 trillion at the beginning of a year, and that during the course of the rest of that year there is 2% inflation. By the end of the year, with prices 2% higher than at the beginning of the year, the real debt, as measured by how much it represents in terms of buying power over goods and services, is 2% smaller than at the beginning of the year. What this means is that if the nominal debt by year end is approximately $10.2 trillion, in inflation adjusted terms it is really equivalent to $10 trillion at the beginning of the year. That is, with 2% inflation, a nominal debt of $10.2 trillion at the end of the year is the same real debt as $10 trillion at the beginning of the year: both would buy the same amount of goods and services. Alternatively, if the nominal debt is the same at year end as at the beginning when there is 2% inflation, the real value of the debt at the end of the year is 2% smaller than at the beginning. We can say that inflation reduces the real value of the national debt.

Inflation reduces the national debt in real terms.

Given the effect of inflation on the real value of the national debt, it might seem that governments have an easy way out of debt: inflate the economy by such means as public spending or facilitating an expansion of the money supply. (Possible causes of inflation are discussed in Chapter 4). However, it is not that simple. The problem is that interest rates tend to reflect the rate of inflation that is generally expected to occur. (The effect of expected inflation on interest rates is discussed in more detail in Chapter 7). For example, suppose that when inflation is zero and widely expected to remain at zero, the interest rate is 2%. Then imagine that there is an increase in widely held expectations of inflation to 5%. A lender realizes that with 5% expected inflation they need to earn a 5% interest rate to expect to be able to buy the same amount of goods and services at year end as they can at the beginning: $105 at year end buys what $100 do at the beginning of the year. If lenders are to be rewarded 2% per year for their patience in waiting while the borrower has the use of their money, with 5% expected inflation they need approximately 7% interest: 5% of this compensates for inflation and 2% is the **real interest rate**. We can think of lenders demanding a **nominal interest rate** consisting of two parts: the real rate, which in our example is 2% — what the interest rate would be with zero expected inflation — and the expected rate of inflation, which we have assumed is 5%. But will borrowers be prepared to pay this nominal interest rate? That is, will they pay the real rate plus the expected inflation?

The answer is that they should. This is because what they buy with the borrowed money — real estate, business equipment, consumer durables, etc. — should on average be expected to be inflating at the 5% rate. A 7% nominal rate is therefore only a 2% real rate to the borrower as well as the lender. We can think of the real value of the debt repayment being reduced by inflation. With lenders demanding to be compensated for expected inflation, and borrowers willing to pay, we conclude:

Nominal Interest Rate = Real Interest Rate + Expected Inflation.

(2.1)

Equation (2.1), which is called the **Fisher Equation** and is discussed in Chapter 7, helps us understand why a country cannot just reduce — or "retire" — its national debt simply by inflating. It also helps us understand why, when there is inflation, we have to be careful comparing the severity of the debt problem over time from simply comparing the progress of the dollar value of the debt: a growing nominal value of debt could represent a declining real debt when there is inflation.

In order to see why inflation is not a simple tool for retiring the national debt, suppose there is 5% inflation and that this 5% inflation had been correctly anticipated by the financial markets. This means that the interest rate contains a 5% component to compensate lenders for the expected decline in the buying power of money. Also, the realized inflation is retiring the real value of the national debt by 5%, so if the debt at the beginning of the year is $10 trillion, by year end the *real* value of the $10 trillion is $9.5 trillion. However, at the same time, the interest rate that is paid by the government on the debt includes the 5% component for expected inflation. This adds $0.5 trillion to the interest bill, leaving the real debt at $10 trillion. What we find is that in this case, when actual inflation is equal to expected inflation, the real debt has not been reduced by inflation because it has added the same amount to the interest bill as it has reduced the real, inflation adjusted debt, in both cases by 5% or $0.5 trillion.

When expected and actual inflation are equal, inflation does not reduce the real value of the national debt.

Let us now drop the assumption that the expected inflation is equal to the actual inflation, and suppose expected inflation is 5% as before, but by year's end it turns out that actual inflation is 7%. In this case, the interest rate goes up by the expected rate of inflation, i.e., by 5%, as before. This adds $0.5 trillion to the interest bill that the government must pay on the debt. However, with the actual inflation of 7%, the real value of the $10 trillion debt at the beginning of the year is reduced during the year by $0.7 trillion. The net effect of extra interest payments from the expected inflation and the debt retirement from actual inflation is ($0.7 − $0.5) = $0.2 trillion. Therefore, by year end the real debt is reduced to $9.8 trillion.

> *When actual inflation is higher than was generally expected the real national debt declines because the interest paid is more than offset by the extent the real debt is reduced by inflation.*

It can just as easily be the case that actual inflation is less than what had been widely expected. In this case, inflation is associated with an increase in the real national debt. For example, if expected inflation is 5% but turns out to be 3%, interest payments are increased by 5% or $0.5 trillion as before. However, there is only a $0.3 trillion decline in the real value of the debt. The net effect is that the real debt ends up $0.2 trillion higher by year end than at the beginning.

What we have found is that using inflation to reduce the real value of the national debt requires that actual inflation is higher than it was expected to be at the time that interest rates were being determined. More generally, we have learned that a proper picture of what is happening to the national debt requires considering inflation, both in terms of expectations and realizations.

Deferred Taxes and Pension Plans

Many countries offer pension plans, such as the 401(K) plan in the United States, designed to encourage citizens, often with the help of their employers, to save for retirement. The basic form of pension plans is that contributions up to some limit can be deducted against the income subject to income tax. The relevance of pension plans for the national debt can best be described according to their effect on current and future fiscal deficits. Let us explain how this works.

Suppose there is a contribution to a taxpayer's pension plan of $1,000 when the taxpayer has a marginal income tax rate of 20%. Suppose the value of the pension contribution is deductible against the contributor's income when computing the tax they are required to pay. Then the taxpayer will reduce their current income tax bill by $200 and thereby decrease the government's tax receipts by $200. With reduced tax receipts, if government spending is maintained the fiscal deficit is increased by $200, or if the government has a fiscal surplus, the surplus is reduced by $200. When this $200 is borrowed the national debt is increased by $200. And, so it would seem that the presence of pension plans increases national debts. However, such a conclusion ignores what happens in the future.

It is true in our example that, *ceteris paribus*, the current year's national debt is increased when pension plan contributions are deductible against income in the assessment of income taxes: the lost tax revenue means a need to borrow $200 if government spending is to be unchanged. But this is not the end of the story. After retirement, beneficiaries of pension plans withdraw what they have saved, including earnings on their investments. This becomes subject to income tax. In this sense, from the taxpayers' point of view, pension plan contributions are a means of deferring, i.e., delaying payment of income tax. From the government's perspective pension plan contributions mean postponement of tax revenue. To understand the implications of tax deferment we need to consider the **time value of money**.[3] Let us do this in the context of our example of contributing $1,000 to a pension plan and the government losing $200 of current tax revenue.

Suppose the pension plan contributor's $1,000 is invested for 10 years, which is when the contributor retires. Let us also suppose there is an annual average compound rate of return on the original $1,000 investment of approximately 7.3%, with the annual returns sheltered from income tax by virtue of being in the pension plan. Under such circumstances the $1,000 will become $2,000 after 10 years. Let us assume the $2,000 is counted as taxable income in the year it is withdrawn, and that the income tax rate that applies at the time of withdrawal is 20%, so that the new retiree pays, and the government receives, $400. What we then have is that the effect of

---

[3]This concept is described in the Background Table B2.1 and associated discussion for those readers who have not come across it before.

the pension plan is a tax deferment: the contributor saves $200 of income tax when the original contribution is made, but 10 years later pays $400, at least under the assumptions we have made.[4]

From the government's perspective, the $400 received at the end of 10 years when the pension plan contributor retires is an **account receivable**. If a balance sheet were constructed at the beginning when the original pension plan contribution is made, this account receivable would show as a government asset. What is the true economic value of this asset? Since the $400 is not going to be available for 10 years when the investment — which has grown to $2,000 — is withdrawn from the pension plan, we need to find the **present value** of $400 due in 10 years. It turns out that if we use the same rate of return for calculating the present value of the $400 as we used for the return on the original investment of $1,000 in the pension plan — a compound return of 7.3% — the $400 is worth $200! This is because $200 invested at 7.3% for 10 years becomes $400. (The student who is unfamiliar with computation of present value can read the Background Table B2.1 placed at the end of this chapter.) Therefore, what we find is that the government's budget is reduced currently by $200 from the lower tax receipts caused by the presence of the pension plan, but at the same time, it gains $200 in terms of present value from the taxes it will collect when the pension funds are withdrawn. These two effects offset each other, and so we might want to ignore the current tax revenue loss due to pension plans when computing the fiscal deficit or surplus: extra debt, a liability, is offset by an asset, an increase in accounts receivable. Alternatively, when calculating national debt, we might compute it net of national assets, including any accounts receivable.

An implication of the preceding argument is that if two countries have the same size national debt, but in one country the citizens have very large pension plans that represent deferred taxes for the government, the debt of that country is in some sense less serious than the debt of the other country. Another way of viewing the situation is that when considering a nation's debt we are considering only one side of the ledger, that of liabilities. A more meaningful view would be the net debt which deducts

---

[4]We will consider the assumptions later.

assets from the liabilities. The impression given by considering the path of gross liabilities over time or comparing gross liabilities between countries may be very different from the real situation.

It should be noted in the preceding discussion that delay in collecting tax does not enter the picture because while the present value is lower the further into the future the government collects the tax — the effect of the time value of money — the amount subject to tax is growing at the same rate as present value declines. This means that it does not matter how many years it is before the pension money is withdrawn from the pension plan.

Deductibility of pension contributions against income tax is not lost tax revenue, but rather deferred tax revenue. The accounts receivable from taxes paid on withdrawal of funds is an asset of the government's that should be considered when comparing national debts over time or between countries.

We have purposely simplified the example used above. For example, the income tax rate is assumed to be the same when the contribution is made to the pension plan and when the funds are eventually withdrawn. In the event that the pensioner's income is lower when retired than it was while working, the tax rate while withdrawing the funds may well be smaller than at the time of contributing to the pension plan. Hence, the account receivable to the government will be smaller in face value, and hence in present value, than the tax lost from the deductibility of the contribution. Another simplification in our discussion is that we ignored possible "accounts payable" by the government from commitments it has made to provide such things as social security. The bottom line is that in judging the significance of the national debt and the trend of that debt, a lot of complications need to be addressed.

SUMMARY

(1) The national or public debt is the amount owed by the national government. It results from the accumulation of government borrowing to finance fiscal deficits.

(2) The implications of the national debt are more similar to those of corporate debt than to an individual's debt. For example, in principle, national debt, like corporate debt, is not subject to a date by which time it must be reduced to zero.

(3) It is generally believed that the national debt is a burden on current and future generations. In fact the extent of any burden cannot accurately be inferred from the dollar size of the debt.

(4) What matters is that the debt does not grow faster than the ability of the country to service it — meet all due interest and principal payments — which in turn depends on the level and growth of the national income or product. Judgment of the seriousness of debt can be made by considering the ratio of debt to GDP.

(5) Even if all the national debt is held by citizens, so that payments are transfers from some citizens–the taxpayers–to other citizens–the bondholders — there can still be real negative effects of the national debt. This is because, *ceteris paribus*, the larger are debt payments, the higher are tax rates, and taxes reduce incentives to work and invest.

(6) When a nation's debts are held by foreigners, *ceteris paribus*, a nation's GNP shrinks relative to its GDP. The GNP is more closely related to a country's standard of living than is its GDP.

(7) Default is possible when a country denominates its debt in foreign currency. In the case of domestic-currency denomination of debt, investors lose from depreciation rather than default: the debtor country can create its own currency to repay debts, but *ceteris paribus*, this will cause depreciation of the country's money.

(8) Government obligations may well extend beyond its bills, bonds and bank debt. It may have guaranteed debts incurred by agencies or other levels of government.

(9) Debts incurred to expand the productive capacity of a country may generate an increase in the tax base and tax collections that readily pays back the debt. Examples would include essential infrastructure projects and educational programs.

(10) Inflation reduces the real value of the national debt. However, a government cannot simply create inflation to reduce its debt because expected inflation raises interest rates, adding to government spending on debt service.

(11) Pension plans with tax-deductible contributions do not cause an indefinite loss of revenue for the government, but rather defer tax revenue. The value of the deferral of tax revenue is an account receivable of the government. If the pension value grows from investment at the same

rate as it is converted into its present value there is no loss due to the time value of money. A case can be made for including tax deferrals, which are an account receivable, in the government's deficit and debt calculations.

QUESTIONS

(1) How does national debt differ from gross debt?

(2) Why is the ratio of national debt to national income a better measure of the seriousness of the debt problem than the dollar size of the debt regardless of the size of the economy?

(3) Why is a country unlikely to default if its national debt is denominated in its own currency? What would likely happen instead of default when debt grows to unmanageable levels?

(4) How does the difference between GNP and GDP depend on whether citizens or foreigners hold the debt?

(5) Is there a burden of debt if it is all held by citizens?

(6) How does the seriousness of national debt depend on why the debt is incurred?

(7) Does inflation necessarily reduce the real value of national debt?

(8) What assumptions are relevant when considering how pension plans influence the size of the national debt?

BACKGROUND: THE TIME VALUE OF MONEY

If you were forced to choose between an offer of $1 to be received imme-
diately, and an offer of $1 to be received in one year's time, there is little
doubt you would choose the $1 immediately, even if the offer of $1 for next
year was iron-clad and could not be revoked. After all, even if you intended
spending the $1 next year you could still take it immediately and invest it
for one year. You would then have more than $1 next year. If the one-year
interest rate is, for example, 5%, then by taking $1 immediately you could
have $1.05 next year. But what if you were offered a choice between $1
immediately versus $1.05 next year?

Most people would have a difficult time making a choice between $1
immediately versus $1.05 in one year if the interest rate is 5%. This is
because they would consider the two alternatives as being of equal value.

The value **today** of $1.05 which is to be received in one year's time is
called the **current value** or **present value** of this amount. For example,
when the interest rate is 5% the present value of $1.05 to be received
next year is $1. This provides us with a procedure for valuing income
to be received, or costs to be incurred, at some future date. Each $1.05 to
be received or paid in one year has a present value of $1, so each $1 to be
received or paid in one year has a present value of ($1 ÷ 1.05 =) $0.9524.
(If you invest $0.9524 for one year at 5% you will receive $1.) But what
is the present value of income to be received or costs to be paid, not next
year, but in the more distant future?

If for each year money is invested you can earn 5% compounded —
which means you earn interest on the full amount you have, including
accumulated interest — then you can take $1 today and turn it into $1.05
next year, and then take the $1.05 next year and invest this for a further year
at 5%, turning it into (1.05 × $1.05 =) $1.1025. Therefore, a person facing
an interest rate of 5% would consider an offer of $1.1025 in two-years'
time as having a present value of $1. It follows that they would consider
$1 in two-years' time as having a present value of $0.9070 (= 1 ÷ 1.1025).
Similarly, they would consider $1.1576 (= $1.05 × 1.05 × 1.05) in three-
years' time as having a present value of $1, and therefore, $1 in three-years'
time as having a present value of $0.8638 (= $1 ÷ 1.1576), and so on. These

values allow us to compute the present values of each $1 in each future year shown in Table B2.1.

The present value of a given amount to be received in the future is the amount that would have to be invested today to provide the given amount in the future. Present value depends on the interest rate.

Table B2.1. The longer the period before a receipt or payment, the lower is its present value.

Years ahead before $1 is received	Present value (@5%)
0	$1
1	$0.9524 (= $1 ÷ 1.0500)
2	$0.9070 (= $1 ÷ 1.1025)
3	$0.8638 (= $1 ÷ 1.1576)
4	$0.8227 (= $1 ÷ 1.2155)
5	$0.7835 (= $1 ÷ 1.2753)
6	$0.7462 (= $1 ÷ 1.3401)
7	$0.7107 (= $1 ÷ 1.4071)
8	$0.6768 (= $1 ÷ 1.4775)
9	$0.6446 (= $1 ÷ 1.5513)
10	$0.6139 (= $1 ÷ 1.6289)
.	.
20	$0.3769 (= $1 ÷ 2.6533)
.	.
30	$0.2314 (= $1 ÷ 4.3219)
.	.
40	$0.1420 (= $1 ÷ 7.0400)

CONNECTIONS

NATURAL ECONOMY

Microeconomics, like microbiology, is concerned with the smaller elements of life. Rather than describe the economy as whole, it looks at the behavior of consumers and firms that together make up the economy, and at the way prices of individual products are determined. It asks how consumers respond to changes in prices of what they buy, and how producers respond to changes in prices of what they sell. Microeconomics also shows how firms respond to changes in the wages and raw material prices they must pay. The principles of microeconomics can even be used to show what economic measures can reduce environmental pollution, and why some needed services would not be provided without the government.

Macroeconomics is concerned with the entire body of economic life and not the living cells of which it is made. It is concerned with the level of unemployment, the rate of inflation, the size of the total national output, the balance of payments, and other big economic issues of that kind. Of course, the level of unemployment is made up of all the separate living individuals who do not have a job, and the rate of inflation is composed of the rising prices of bread, meat, apples, gasoline, textbooks, and other individual goods and services. But macroeconomics ignores the special causes of particular people being unemployed, and why bread prices went up. These are considered in the realm of the other part of economics, namely microeconomics.

The basic organizational units of study in microeconomics, the firms that produce the goods and services and the consumers who buy them, are analogous to the cells that form the basic organizational units of study in biology. Indeed, there are strong parallels between the two disciplines also at the sub-cellular as well as the more aggregate levels of study in biology.

The cell consists of a number of components — the nucleus and its nucleolus, the ribosome, and so on. In the same way, the firm consists of some finer divisions — the senior and middle managers, quality controllers, line workers and so on. Similarly, the family, which is the basic unit of study of consumer demand, consists of a head of household and other family members. The subcomponents of firms and families perform specialized tasks just as do the subcomponents of living cells. Indeed, the **division of labor** is used to describe the specialization that occurs inside cells as well as the specialization in the firm or family.

Divisions of labor operate not only within cells, firms, and consumers, but between them. Let us illustrate this by concentrating on the parallels between the structure of the cell and the firm.

Tissues such as the epidermis and bone in animals, and the pith or pheom in plants, are aggregates of cells of one type or of only a few types.[1] In a similar way, **industries**, a principal unit of study in economics, are made up of aggregates of firms of a common or similar kind. A major topic of interest in biology is how the cells which constitute tissues are organized; do they attach to each other or float freely, and when they attach, do they line up vertically or horizontally, and so on. In the same way, economists are interested in the organization of firms in an industry; to what extent are the firms **vertically** or **horizontally integrated**, do firms cooperate by forming cartels or do they compete, and so on?[2] Indeed, there is a growing branch of economics with its own specialized courses, research journals and textbooks, known as **industrial organization**.

Several tissues grouped together constitute organs. The heart, lungs, stomach, brain and skin are examples of organs in animals, while roots, leaves, flowers and stems are examples of organs in plants. Organs are analogous to **sectors** of an economy. Energy, resource extraction, manu-facturing, financial services, transportation and retailing are examples of economic sectors. Just as the tissues which are components of an organ interact and are highly dependent on each other, so are an economy's sectors. We could not have a heart without the supply of oxygen and fuel from other organs, any more than we could have a manufacturing sector without the supply of raw materials from mining and other extractive firms, and without sectors for distributing and selling the products. Just as biologists

---

[1]The pith and pheom are components of stems, holding up the plant and carrying nutrients.
[2]Vertically integrated firms deal with many different stages of production. Horizontally integrated firms deal with different products, concentrating on only one stage of production such as extraction, fabrication, marketing and so on.

specialize in the study of organs so do economists specialize in finance, energy, transportation, education and so on.

Biologists consider larger aggregates than individual organs. The next level up from organs is systems. For example, the brain and nerves make up the nervous system, while the heart and blood vessels make up the circulatory system. Economists also sometimes deal with a level of aggregation above that of sectors. In moving to form the larger aggregates from sectors the economist moves from microeconomics to macroeconomics. The important aggregates of consumption and investment are of particular interest to the macroeconomist.

Organs, grouped together into their larger aggregates, systems, work together to form an organism just as economic sectors grouped into their larger aggregates work together to form an economy. The organism is the animal or plant that can be considered as having an independence, just as can an economy.

As we have become patently aware in recent years, all plants and animals, the organisms that are the large organizational units of study in biology, are highly dependent on each other. This growing awareness of the interdependence of organisms has resulted in increased attention to the higher-level biological study, ecology. Most of the work in ecology involves showing how, without an appreciation of the fundamental interdependence between everything on this Earth, we run the risk of damaging the entire biosystem of which we humans are part. In a strikingly similar way, economists have become increasingly aware in recent years that different economies, those of the United States, Europe, Canada, Japan, China, South Korea and so on, are highly dependent on each other. **Contagion** that can cross borders like a communicable disease is the price countries pay for being economically interdependent and is an aspect of the **globalization** that has taken place. Globalization is manifest in the growing importance of international versus domestic trade. It has also been manifest in the way financial panics have spread around the globe, and in how problems in one country such as huge fiscal deficits or imbalances between imports and exports have had repercussions for other countries. That is, the growing importance of the biological field of ecology has a strong parallel in the growing importance of international economics.

CHAPTER 3
MONEY, BANKING, AND FINANCIAL INTERMEDIATION

"It would be too ridiculous to go about seriously to prove that wealth does not consist in money, or in gold and silver; but in what money purchases, and is valuable only for purchasing."

Adam Smith

Key Concepts: Advantages of money versus barter; value of money to an individual versus society; money defined; M1, M2; money versus liquidity; money versus credit; money versus income; history of fractional reserve banking; money and the central bank; the money multiplier; open market operations; discount rate; role of financial intermediaries; stocks and bonds; credit cards; debit cards.

WHAT MONEY IS AND DOES

Confusions Surrounding Money

As simple a matter as it may appear to be, there is probably more confusion about money than any other topic in macroeconomics. For example, while many people believe everybody would be better off if they were all given more money, in fact it is only if *some* people were given more money that they would be better off — and others would be correspondingly worse off! In this and the next chapter, we consider such issues as this and many other matters surrounding money. However, before we turn to these interesting issues, we should explain what money is, and the role it plays in an economy.

The Nature and Role of Money

Money is what we receive for what we sell and pay for what we buy. What is bought and sold with the use of money includes final products, intermediate products, capital equipment, land, houses, raw materials, stocks, bonds, and the services of labor. For example, workers sell their labor for wages which are paid in money, and then use the money to pay rent and buy groceries. People are willing to accept money because they know others in turn are willing to accept it from them. It is only because there is a generally acceptable medium for use in trade that we can avoid **barter**, which is the exchange of one good or service directly for another good or service.

Money is not something with value in and of itself; we cannot eat money, wear it, and so on. However, while money does not have intrinsic value, by allowing us to avoid the use of barter money performs a fundamental and unparalleled role in an economy. Without something serving as money we would be much poorer because the alternative of barter has a number of serious disadvantages. Let us consider some of these.

Money allows us to avoid barter, which is the direct exchange of one good or service for another.

The Disadvantages of Barter Exchange

Having all grown up using money, it is difficult to imagine ourselves functioning without it. However, let us put the power of our imaginations to the test, and think of some of the difficult problems we would face if there was no money.

Finding Others with Coincident or Mutually Compatible Wants: Suppose you had a used car to sell, and needed to pay your college tuition. It would be unlikely a college would accept your car to cover your tuition. People often do not want what others are supplying in a barter exchange. However, if you could sell your car for money to somebody who likes the car, you could then pay your tuition with the money you received. Therefore, money avoids the need to find a party with mutually compatible wants. That is, it avoids the need for a double coincidence of wants. It does this by serving as a **medium of indirect exchange**; you exchange something for money, and then exchange the money for something else.

Supplying and Buying Indivisible Products: Even when wants are coincident there is a problem if the mutually desired items are of unequal value. In the context of the example of a car being used to pay for tuition, the car could be worth more than the tuition. Therefore, even if the college could find a use for your car, it is unlikely to accept only part of it. However, if you could sell the car for money, you could use part of the money for tuition and the remainder to cover living expenses. Money can be divided up or gathered into larger amounts, thereby making exchange much easier.

Supplying and Buying Perishable Products: Barter requires that the two sides of the double coincidence of wants occur at the same time. However, it might be, e.g., that a farmer has crops available only at harvest time but needs to make purchases all year long. If the crops are perishable and therefore cannot be stored, it is not possible for the farmer to use barter. But if the crops can be sold for money at the time of harvest, the money can subsequently be used as it is required. Therefore, money serves as a **standard of deferred payment** between the times when it is received and the times of subsequent purchases.

Saving: Even setting aside the problem of perishability, under a barter system it is difficult to save for the future. Holding every product that might be needed, or holding products to exchange for what might be needed, represents a major storage problem. Money serves the role of a **store of value**. In the absence of inflation, money saved today helps provide buying power in the future.

Transporting Bulky or Heavy Products: Even if we could overcome the problems of coincidence of wants and of dealing in perishable products, we would still face the problem of transporting items used in barter. Most monies offer the advantage of being compact and easy to move around. Indeed, it can take no more than the pressing of a few keystrokes to make a payment with money held in a bank account.[1]

---

[1] In fact, while money is typically easy to move around, as Example 3.1 explains, there are some extremely bulky monies.

Example 3.1. All You Need is Trust

Perhaps one of the strangest monies described by anthropologists is the stone money of Uap Island, also commonly written as "Yap". The following account of Uap money explains how important faith is to the functioning of any medium of exchange.

"On the island of Uap (one of the Caroline Islands), the medium of exchange is called Fei. This currency consists of large, solid, thick stone wheels ranging in diameter from a foot to 12 feet, and in the center a hole varying in size with the diameter of the stone, so that the stones may be slung on poles and carried. They are not found on Uap itself, but are quarried in Babelthuap, some 400 miles away to the south. Size is the most important factor, but also the fei must be of a certain fine, white, close-grained limestone. A traveler to Uap described the fei as follows:

'A feature of this stone currency, which is also an equally noteworthy tribute to Uap honesty, is that it is not necessary for its owner to reduce it to possession. After concluding a bargain which involves the price of a fei too large to be conveniently moved, its new owner is quite content to accept the bare acknowledgement of ownership; and without so much as a mark to indicate the exchange, the coin remains undisturbed on the former owner's premises.

My faithful old friend Fatumak assured me that there was in a village near by a family whose wealth was unquestioned — acknowledged by every one, and yet no one, not even the family itself, had ever laid eye or hand on this wealth; it consisted of an enormous fei, where of the size is known only by tradition: for the past two or three generations it had been, and at that very time it was lying at the bottom of the sea! Many years ago an ancestor of this family, on an expedition after fei, secured this remarkably valuable stone, which was placed on a raft to be towed homeward. A violent storm arose and the party, to save their lives, were obliged to cut the raft adrift, and the stone sank out of sight. When they reached home, they all testified that the fei was of magnificent proportions and of extraordinary quality, and that it was lost through no fault of the owners. Thereupon it was universally considered in their simple faith that the mere accident of its loss overboard was too trifling to mention, and that a few hundred feet of water offshore ought not to affect its marketable value, since it was all chipped out in proper form. The purchasing power of that stone remained, therefore, as valid as if it were leaning visibly against the side of its owner's house.'

When the German Government purchased the Caroline Islands from Spain in 1898 there were no wheeled vehicles on Uap, and hence no roads. The paths, too, were in poor shape, and the Government ordered the natives to put them into better condition. Somehow or other the natives were quite happy with the paths as they were; the job did not get done. The Government was in a dilemma. It would be rather difficult to fine the natives and carry off the fei to Germany. In the first place, German shopkeepers might have been a little doubtful about exchanging their wares for fei, and then in the second place, it would have taken the labors of every available native to get the fei off the island, and the repairing of the paths would have had to wait while the natives paid up. Finally the Government hit on a sound scheme. They simply sent a man round to mark some of the most valuable stones with a cross in black paint to show the Government claim. The impoverished natives immediately fell to work, and the paths were soon in good order. Then a second man went round for the Government to remove the crosses; and there was great rejoicing on the island of Uap."

Source: Norman Angell, *The Story of Money* (Garden City Publishing Co., New York, 1929), pp. 88–89.

Measuring Prices and Keeping Records: If money did not exist, just imagine all the different prices that would be faced. For example, there would be a price of economics books in terms of everything that might be traded for the books, such as political science books, hours of help in the college library and so on. Each item would have a price in terms of every item for which it might be exchanged. Money allows us to state all prices in terms of a common unit, as so many dollars, euros, or whatever. It is a **numeraire**, allowing us to avoid the need to state the price of everything against the price of everything else. Money also allows us to add up values for accounting purposes because all prices and values are measured in the same unit, dollars. That is, money is also a **unit of account**.

Enjoying Gains from the Division of Labor: Because barter is so inconvenient and inefficient, if we did not have money as a medium of exchange, people would be led to be more self-sufficient; the cost in terms of time and effort of finding others with whom to make direct exchanges would be so high, people would concentrate on supplying their needs themselves. While this may sound romantic, we would lose the advantages of the division of labor on which much of prosperity is based.[2] These gains come from a number of sources. They come from the ability to acquire expertise in the specific task each worker performs; from not having to continually change tools with consequent loss of time as each task is finished; from making it worthwhile developing new machines which help in just one task; and from making it easier to innovate because a specialized task can be replicated more easily by a machine.

> *Money serves as a medium of exchange, a standard of deferred payment, a store of value and a unit of account. Most importantly, money frees up time and resources otherwise devoted to barter, and in this way it facilitates the division of labor.*

The role of money in allowing a division of labor is similar to the role played by a network of roads. Without roads we would be forced to be more self-sufficient and to make do with a reduced standard of living. Like money, roads are useful for what they allow us to do, not because they have intrinsic value. Both money and roads keep the economy moving by serving as an important lubricant of the economic system. Of course, money also confers the benefits of offering a unit of account and store of value, in addition to the medium of exchange role by which it facilitates the division of labor.

> *Money plays an important role in keeping the economy moving.*

The Value of Money: The Individual versus Society

To an individual who is holding money, the value of that money is equal to the value of goods and services it can buy. For example, if a dollar bill will buy a hamburger or newspaper, the dollar is worth a hamburger or newspaper. It follows that if an individual has twice as much money, he or she can enjoy twice as many goods and services. However, society as a whole cannot enjoy more goods and services just by having more money.

---

[2]Many movies project an appealing image of pioneers able to supply their many needs independently, and ignore the hardships. In reality, life of the early pioneers was tough, and they were rarely entirely self-sufficient.

For example, if a helicopter were to drop money so that everybody had twice as much as before, there would still be the same output of goods and services for people to share. It is this output, measured as we have seen by the real per capita NNP, that is the basis of peoples' well-being, not the number of pieces of paper in their wallets or pocketbooks or amounts in their bank accounts. The value of money to society derives not from what it will buy, but from the avoidance of the inconveniences and inefficiencies of barter that would be faced in a world without money. This distinction between the value of money to an individual versus the value to society is the subject of Example 3.2.

To an individual the value of money is what it will purchase. However, to society as a whole, the value of money derives from its role in avoiding the inconveniences and inefficiencies of barter.

Example 3.2. Losing Money

The value of money to society is very different from the value to an individual. One of the clearest statements that this is so, is the following by Sir Denis H. Robertson.

"If one unit of money were suddenly abolished, the possessor of the particular unit selected for abolition would clearly be the poorer. Nobody who has ever lost a sixpence through a crack in the floor will dispute this. But it is by no means obvious that the world as a whole would be impoverished in the same degree: for the command over real things surrendered by the loser of the sixpence is not abolished, but passes automatically to the rest of the community whose sixpences will now buy more. If indeed there were a large and simultaneous loss or destruction of money, society might easily find itself hampered in the conduct of its business, and the consequent check to exchange and production might lead to a serious decrease in its real economic welfare. But the fact remains that the value of money is (within limits) a measure of the usefulness of any one unit of money to its possessor, but not to society as a whole: while the value of bread is also a measure (within limits) of the social usefulness of any one loaf of bread. And the reason for this peculiarity about money is the fact that nobody generally speaking wants it except for the sake of the control which it gives over other things."

Source: Sir Denis H. Robertson, Money (University of Chicago Press, Chicago, 1959), pp. 25–26.

Defining Money

One way of determining what to consider as money is to identify what simultaneously serves as a medium of exchange, standard of deferred payment, unit of account and store of value: these are the attributes of money we described earlier. However, it is simpler to ask what is a generally acceptable medium of exchange, and then check afterwards whether what serves as a medium of exchange also serves the other functions.

Because we know that others will accept coins and paper currency — the bills with pictures of current or former heads of state — from us, we are in turn willing to accept them from others. Therefore, coins and paper currency are generally acceptable means of payment. Coins and paper currency also serve as a standard of deferred payment; they can be accepted today and spent later. They also serve as a unit of account and a store of value. Therefore, coins and currency are quite obviously money.

Relatively few payments are made with coins and paper currency. Far more payments are made by using a check, or by swiping a debit card and providing a PIN. Checks and debit cards are authorizations for the transfer of funds held in bank accounts from the account of the payer to the account of the payee. Checks and debit cards do the same job as coins and paper currency and indeed, are sometimes more convenient: paper currency might be stolen and not easily retraced, whereas checks require a signature and debit cards require a PIN, and both can be cancelled if they are stolen. Because of the close similarity of the functions of checks/debit cards and paper currency, money consists at least of coins and paper currency, plus the sum total of readily accessible (**liquid**) bank deposits from which payments can be made. These bank deposits are held at **financial institutions** such as commercial banks, savings banks and credit unions.

The sum of coin and currency held by the public, plus readily accessible deposits at financial institutions, constitutes the major share of the money supply referred to as **M1**. This particular monetary aggregate also includes travelers' checks, such as those issued by American Express, which can readily be used when making payments. M1 also includes deposits at financial institutions which can be withdrawn or transferred at short notice. This money supply aggregate is the most restrictive, or narrow, definition of money which is commonly used when discussing the macroeconomic influences of the money supply.

The money supply called M1 consists of currency, readily accessible deposits at financial institutions, travelers' checks, and deposits that can be transferred at short notice.

Banks and other financial institutions have been innovative in offering different types of deposits. For example, there are numerous varieties of savings accounts and **time deposits** — deposits with a stated maturity — which offer a higher interest rate than checkable and debit card accessible deposits. However, there may be penalties if the funds are withdrawn without sufficient notice in the case of savings accounts, or before the maturity date in the case of time deposits. Therefore, savings accounts and time deposits are not as liquid as currency or checkable deposits. Nevertheless, savings and time deposits are sufficiently similar to some of the deposits included in M1 that they cannot be ignored when calculating the money supply. The same is true of funds held in banks' **money market funds**. A money market fund is a pool of interest-bearing securities such as Treasury bills held by a bank against which the bank's customers hold claims. Because the savings accounts, time deposits, money market funds and even some U.S. dollar deposits held abroad can quickly become a medium of exchange, a broader money supply aggregate is computed and published called **M2**. As of September 2012, the seasonally adjusted values of M1 and M2 of the United States were $2,379.1 billion and $10,128.0 billion respectively.[3]

The broader money supply aggregate M2 consists of M1 plus a variety of other deposits at financial institutions.

The Money Supply versus Liquidity

You might be thinking, "Why stop our definition of money after including coin, currency, checking and savings accounts, time deposits, money market funds, and the other items in M2? If people want to make payments they can sell off short-term securities such as Treasury bills. Indeed, they can sell off stocks, bonds, or even their cars or houses. Why then are not all these other parts of wealth considered to be money?

One way of answering this question is that while people can sell these other assets, they do not know precisely how much they will receive.

---

[3]Data obtained from http://www.federalreserve.gov/releases/h6/Current/.

If somebody has a one-dollar bill it can be used to settle one dollar in payments. So can a one-dollar check or debit card payment be drawn on a bank account. However, assets such as stocks and bonds have uncertain value, changing in price from day to day or even from minute to minute, and involve a brokerage cost to convert into money; stockbrokers have to be paid. Furthermore, many assets, such as automobiles and houses, are not readily marketable; it might be necessary to considerably lower the price of an automobile to sell it quickly enough to pay the rent. We therefore say that stocks and automobiles and other such assets are not money because they are not significantly liquid. Liquidity refers to the costs and uncertainties when converting assets into other goods and services. Money as we have defined it, consists of the most liquid of assets, those which can be converted into goods or services without uncertainty of value and without incurring cost; "a dollar is a dollar" in the case of money, but not for other assets. Indeed, it is because money is liquid that it has become accepted as the medium of exchange, just as its acceptance as a medium of exchange has made it liquid.

> *Money is the most liquid asset, where liquidity refers to the uncertainties and costs of converting an asset into other goods and services.*

The Money Supply versus Credit

A considerable number of payments are made with credit cards. We might as well ask how these credit cards should be treated in our definition of money, since many of the cards are quite generally acceptable as a means of making payments.

Credit cards give their holders the right to what their name suggests, specifically, pre-approved **credit**. This means that cardholders can make purchases up to some pre-approved limit, making no payment until the settlement date on the next billing statement. The credit is usually provided with zero interest up to the settlement date, with interest applying after that point, generally charged from the date of purchase, not from the settlement date. Even if cardholders do not pay by the due date, and therefore use their credit, they must eventually pay with money. In other words, they must use money in their bank accounts to pay the card issuer. In this sense, credit cards are not money, and so the credit limits on them should not be included in addition to bank accounts and other items that are included in the definition of the money supply. (This does not mean that credit cards are irrelevant. They can affect spending via providing pre-approved credit, and allow the public to economize on holding money, especially in the form of currency. That is, while credit cards do not increase the *supply* of money, they can reduce the *demand* for money, particularly the demand for currency. For example, if you have a credit card in your wallet or purse you don't need to carry as much cash.)

> *Credit cards allow people to spend now and pay later, with money. Therefore, credit cards are not part of the money supply, although they may affect money demand.*

The Money Supply versus Income

Income, as we observed in our discussion of national income and national product in Chapter 1, is a flow. It is so much *per period of time*. The money supply, on the other hand, is a **stock**. Money is so many dollars *at a point in time*. This is true whether we are speaking about a nation's or an individual's supply of money. The currency and bank deposits you hold on a particular date do not sum to $1,000 per month. They sum to $1,000, period. Your income might be $2,000 per month while your money holdings are $10,000, $100, or any other amount.

With the distinction between money and income being so important, it is remarkable how common it is to hear sloppy use of these terms. For example, the question "How much money do you earn?" is poorly expressed. It would be better to ask, "What is your income?" We can correctly ask, "How much money do you *have*?" It is true that we generally receive our income in the form of money, but holdings of money and income are completely different, even in terms of dimension. To make our distinction between money and income even clearer, we can observe that people can consider themselves to have too much money, but are never likely to consider their incomes to be too high. Let us consider this further.

> *Money is a stock while income is a flow.*

The Limited Demand for Money

As we have indicated, the amount we hold in coins, currency or bank deposits is only part of our wealth. We also hold wealth as stocks and bonds, automobiles, houses, furniture, and university degrees. (A university degree is human capital and is therefore a component of wealth, and like other components such as stocks and bonds, provides income in the future.)

When we hold a dollar in the form of currency or in a non-interest-bearing bank deposit — both components of M1 — we give up the interest we could otherwise have earned if instead the funds had been put in a bond. This foregone interest is the **opportunity cost** of holding money. Because money is convenient for buying lunch, paying rent, and so on — that is, it is liquid — we hold some money despite the interest we might otherwise have received. But suppose we had decided on holding a given amount of money for its convenience when bonds offered 4% interest, and the bond interest rate then rose to 8%. How would we feel about the amount of money we are holding *vis-à-vis* wealth?

When the convenience of money costs us more in forgone interest on bonds we generally want to hold a smaller proportion of our wealth in the form of money. That is, the quantity of money demanded declines when there is an increase in the opportunity cost of holding money rather than bonds. For example, what was considered as the correct amount of money vis-à-vis other assets at an interest rate of 4%, is too much when the interest rate increases to 8%. It would be better to hold more bonds. We find that we can have too much money vis-à-vis the other components of our wealth. However, very few people would ever consider themselves to earn too much income. Money and income are clearly quite different.

The quantity of money demanded declines with an increase in the opportunity cost of holding money which is the interest rate.

THE CREATION AND HISTORY OF MONEY

Banks as Creators of Money: An Historical Perspective

Currency makes up a small part of even the narrow definition of the money supply, M1, and is only a miniscule part of the broader monetary aggregate, M2. The major component of the money supply, deposits of various kinds, is "created" by commercial banks and other financial institutions. The process of creating money dates back at least to the time of the goldsmiths of Europe. The way the goldsmiths became creators of money serves as an excellent introduction to the discussion of the **fractional reserve banking system** of today.

Before the advent of paper money as we know it today, many payments were made in gold and silver. However, with the values of these metals being high, with assaying of purity being difficult and with insurance and police protection poorly developed, there were risks involved in using precious metals as money.

In pre-banking times, the people who owned the strongest safes in town were the goldsmiths whose work required that they keep a supply of gold and silver on hand. The goldsmiths' safes were known to others who would sometimes ask the goldsmiths if they would take gold in for safekeeping. The goldsmiths might oblige and charge a small fee. They would issue "depositors" receipts which stated that the persons named had deposited so many ounces of gold or silver.

Rather than going to the goldsmith to redeem gold when needs arise, some depositors asked if they could sign over their receipts to whomever they owed money. This helped avoid the risk of theft of the gold in between taking it out and making delivery. The receipts would simply be transferred over from the payer to the payee. Indeed, to facilitate this transfer of title to gold, the goldsmiths often issued a number of receipts, each representing a claim to a small fixed amount of gold. These could easily be made out to "pay the bearer on demand" so as to avoid the need for the receipts to be signed each time they were transferred to new owners. With paper "claims" such a convenient means of making payment, they circulated freely without people demanding their gold from the goldsmiths very often.

It was not uncommon for governments and businesses to ask goldsmiths for loans. The goldsmiths could oblige because they knew that most of the gold they had on deposit sat idly in their vaults, with the holders of the deposit receipts rarely coming in to redeem their bullion: the receipts just circulated from hand to hand. A trustworthy borrower could be loaned a number of paper receipts with the knowledge that they would circulate just like the rest, and only a small fraction would be redeemed at any particular time. Consequently, goldsmiths moved more and more into the lending business, issuing more receipts than they had gold in their vaults. Since they could charge borrowers interest, and would usually eventually be repaid, the more loans the goldsmiths made, the richer they became.

Now of course, there were limits on the volume of paper gold receipts each goldsmith could issue. Even though they would eventually be repaid on their loans, they had less gold on hand than there were paper receipts in circulation. This did not necessarily cause any problem since only a fraction of receipt holders would arrive at any time to demand gold. Furthermore, the loans would eventually be repaid, with interest. However, the amount of gold each goldsmith kept back had to be sufficient to reimburse whatever number of receipt holders might reasonably be expected to turn up. Any fear that the goldsmith might run out of gold might cause a "run on the bank" that the vaults might not bear. To avoid this, each goldsmith had to ensure that they had a prudent volume of bullion in their **gold reserve**. They knew that the more gold they held on reserve, the more loans they could safely grant. And the more loans they granted, the higher the profits they made.

Goldsmiths issued more paper receipts than they had gold in reserve. A prudent amount of gold had to be held to ensure they could deliver on their obligations.

In order to attract more gold into a goldsmith's vaults where it could serve to back up a larger volume of receipts issued, the storage fees on depositors' gold were reduced. Eventually, the goldsmiths paid money to depositors to "interest" them in depositing gold. The value of these interest payments on deposits was determined by a competitive process. Each goldsmith wanted more gold reserves so that they could grant additional loans. In their efforts to attract depositors' gold away from other goldsmiths, each goldsmith raised the rate of interest paid on gold deposits until the profit that remained from interest earned on loans to borrowers was not out of line with profits in other endeavors.

The goldsmiths are the precursor of the banks we know today. In particular, like modern commercial banks, they held a fractional reserve of deposits. The remainder of the goldsmiths' assets were interest-earning loans. They paid interest on deposits, and in return earned interest on their loans. There was a sufficient difference — or **spread** — between the interest charged on loans and the interest paid on deposits for a profit to generally remain. This profit was the return for their enterprise and risk they faced of not being repaid on some of their loans.

The profitability of issuing paper money attracted the attention of governments who decided to go into the business themselves. At first, the governments issued paper money that could be converted into gold on demand, just as were goldsmiths' receipts. The convertibility of money for gold was the **gold standard** system that existed in many parts of the world until the early part of the 20th century. After a while, however, the new issuers of currency, the governments, learned they could ensure the public held their paper currency even if they did not offer to convert it into gold. By making currency **legal tender** by an appropriate legal order the government could make it illegal not to accept its **fiat money** — so named because of the order, or fiat, to accept the currency — in payment for any private or public obligation. This is clearly stated on the top left hand side of United States currency, and on currencies of other countries too.

> *Governments today issue legal tender money. This is money created by declaration, or fiat, of the government.*

With paper and ink relatively cheap, governments found the money-making business to be very profitable. We will discover how profitable it is, when we turn to the topic of inflation in the next chapter. Before doing that we should observe that in the United States, the creator of bank notes is the Federal Reserve System. That is why US dollar bills are headed "Federal Reserve Note". The Federal Reserve is also responsible for controlling other components of the money supply, and as such plays an important role in economic policy.

The U.S. Federal Reserve System

The **Federal Reserve System**, or **"Fed"**, functions as the central bank of the United States. As such, the Fed plays the central role in setting and administering U.S. **monetary policy**. By monetary policy we mean decisions on the availability of money, either in terms of the supply of money such as M1 or M2, or in terms of the price of borrowing money, which is the interest rate.

> *The Federal Reserve System sets U.S. monetary policy which concerns the availability of money, either in terms of the supply of money or the interest rate.*

The Federal Reserve System was established in the Federal Reserve Act of 1913. The Fed consists of a Board of Governors in Washington, D.C. that is headed by a Chairman, and 12 regional Federal Reserve Banks. The regional banks are located in New York, Boston, Chicago, Cleveland, Philadelphia, Richmond, St. Louis, Atlanta, Kansas City, Dallas, Minneapolis, and San Francisco. The circle to the left of center on each one-dollar bill, or Federal Reserve Note, in your wallet or pocketbook reveals the Federal Reserve Bank that issued it: they are identified by the number of the Reserve Bank, and the alphabetic letter corresponding to the number.

Commercial banks that are members of the Federal Reserve System keep their reserves either as cash, i.e., Federal Reserve notes, or as deposits with their regional Federal Reserve Bank. If a customer of one commercial bank writes a check or makes a debit card payment in favor of a customer of a different commercial bank, the banks must settle-up between themselves. Consider, e.g., a payment by check. What happens is that the receiver of the check places it in her or his bank account. The bank **credits** the check receiver's account, and presents the check to the bank against which it was drawn.[4] The latter bank **debits**, i.e., reduces, the deposit of the person who wrote the check. The banks then settle between themselves, with the bank against which the check was drawn paying the bank in which the check was deposited. By the member banks keeping deposits with the Fed, the settlement between commercial banks involves the simple transfer of these deposits from one member bank — the bank against which the check is drawn — to another member bank — the one in which the check is deposited. This is part of the **check-clearing** function of the Federal Reserve System.

Regional Federal Reserve banks clear checks between member commercial banks. This is done by crediting and debiting accounts member banks have at the Fed.

The Fed serves as the U.S. government's bank, handling a considerable volume of government business. This includes the sale and redemption of

---

[4]The term "credit" is used in two ways. As in our discussion of credit cards, the word refers to lending, where a buyer does not have to pay until later. In the context here, the word refers to an addition made to an account. The context determines the meaning of the word.

Treasury bills and bonds — which are issued by the United States Treasury, but handled by the Federal Reserve Bank of New York — as well as much of the day-to-day banking business of government.

Many smaller banks are not members of the Federal Reserve System. However, many of the smaller banks keep accounts at larger banks that are members, and therefore, directly or indirectly, most banking business takes place through the Fed. There are also institutions which offer many of the services of banks, but are actually savings and loan associations or credit unions. The role of these so-called "near banks," and their importance and relationship to the banking system are frequently under review.

The deposits of most banks in the United States, whether they are members of the Federal Reserve System or not, are insured by the **Federal Deposit Insurance Corporation (FDIC)**. This institution was established in 1933 after the failure of many thousands of U.S. banks in the **Great Depression**, 1929–1933. The FDIC provides insurance to depositors on their deposits of up to a prescribed limit against the risk of failure of the bank. The purpose of the FDIC is to reduce the risk of "runs" on banks — where depositors run to the bank to take out their money — due to fear that the bank has more deposit liabilities than it has assets. Because the deposits are insured there is less likelihood that depositors will withdraw their funds on account of rumors.

The FDIC insures deposits to help avoid runs on banks.

The existence of deposit insurance became extremely important in the savings and loan crisis of 1989–1992 and the banking "panic" during 2008–2009, where the public's losses on deposits would otherwise have run into many hundreds of billions, and where the FDIC helped prevent financial collapse. In the case of the bank problems of 2008–2009, numerous U.S. banks did fail following the collapse of Lehman Brothers and the forced sale of Bear Stearns to JPMorgan Chase.

The Reserve Ratio and Money Multiplier

We have mentioned that commercial banks that are members of the Federal Reserve System keep reserves either as currency in their vaults, and as deposits in their regional Federal Reserve Bank.[5] The commercial banks must maintain a minimum fraction of the value of their deposits in the form of reserves. This fraction is called the **minimum reserve ratio**, and is determined by the Board of Governors of the Federal Reserve. The commercial banks prefer not to hold more reserves than they are required to hold because interest rates earned on reserves are low.[6] However, the banks cannot plan on holding less than the minimum required reserve. The effect of this is that in normal circumstances there is a relatively predictable change in the money supply from a given change in banks' reserves. Let us see why this is so by assuming that $100 of currency is deposited by an individual into the First National Bank, thereby increasing that bank's reserves. Let us assume the minimum required reserve ratio on deposits is 5%.

Banks must maintain a minimum ratio of reserves versus deposits.

After the deposit of $100 of currency the bank owes this amount to the depositor. This is the "original deposit" entry of $100 in Table 3.1 that appears as a liability of the bank in the bank's **balance sheet**. (The balance sheet records assets and liabilities at a given point in time.) The currency itself appears on the asset side of the balance sheet. The currency held is divided into $5 of additional required reserves to meet the 5% minimum required reserve ratio on the $100 deposit, and $95 of **excess reserves**.

Table 3.1.   After a deposit of currency a bank has excess reserves.

BALANCE SHEET: FIRST NATIONAL BANK			
Assets		Liabilities	
Required reserve	$5	Original deposit	$100
Excess reserve	$95		
Total	$100	Total	$100

[5]While approximately half of the banks in the United States are members of the Fed, these banks are generally large and therefore account for the majority of deposits. This is why we concentrate on member banks.

[6]Until the banking crisis of 2008–2009 the interest rate of reserves at the Fed was zero. The decision to pay interest on reserves occurred when banks were holding far more reserves than required, resulting in a credit "crunch": commercial banks had the means to lend but chose not to for fear of borrowers defaulting.

Table 3.2.   Banks grant loans by crediting borrowers' bank accounts in return for borrowers signing IOUs.

BALANCE SHEET: FIRST NATIONAL BANK			
Assets		Liabilities	
Required reserve	$9.75	Original deposit	$100
Excess reserve	$90.25	Borrower's deposit	$95
Loan (IOU)	$95		
	$195		$195

(Recall that reserves consist of bank-held currency, plus deposits at the Federal Reserve.)

After setting aside the required reserve of $5, the excess reserves can be put into use by granting a loan and charging interest. Let us suppose someone wishes to borrow $95 to buy a bicycle. The borrower would be required to sign an IOU promising to repay the $95, plus interest, and the borrowed funds would be credited, i.e., added, to the borrower's account. This is shown in Table 3.2.

After granting a loan of $95 by crediting the borrower's account, the First National Bank has a total of $195 of deposits. With a 5% minimum reserve ratio, $9.75 (= 0.05 × $195) is required as a reserve against the deposits of $195. The remaining $90.25 (= $100 − $9.75) of the original deposit of $100 of currency is an excess reserve. The IOU against the $95 loan is an asset of the bank. However, this situation, shown in Table 3.2 is temporary. This is because people do not generally borrow unless they have some purpose for the loan — like our borrower's desire to buy a bicycle. Consequently, the borrowed funds are unlikely to remain in the borrower's bank account.[7] In our example, the payment for the bicycle could be made either by withdrawing the funds in currency, or by writing a check. As we shall show, in either case The First National Bank loses its excess reserves.

Individual bank loan funds they are not required to hold as reserves against deposits.

---

[7]Indeed, because the bank can anticipate the borrowed funds being spent and coming out of the borrower's account, it may not keep reserves against the temporary deposits.

Table 3.3.   One bank's loan becomes another bank's deposit.

THE FIRST NATIONAL BANK			
Assets		Liabilities	
Required reserve	$5	Deposit (original)	$100
Loan (IOU)	$95		
	$100		$100

THE SECOND NATIONAL BANK			
Assets		Liabilities	
Required reserve	$4.75	Deposit	$95
Excess reserve	$90.25		
	$95		$95

If the bicycle is paid for with currency, i.e., cash, the First National Bank's excess reserves will decline as the $95 of currency is withdrawn. However, the receiver of the funds from the sale of the bicycle might then deposit the $95 in his or her own bank account. With thousands of banks in the United States, there is a good chance this is not the original borrower's bank. Let us assume the bicycle seller uses The Second National Bank. The balance sheets for both The First National Bank and The Second National Bank are given in Table 3.3.

The deposit of $95 to the bicycle seller's account results in his account being credited while the buyer's account is debited. With a 5% minimum required reserve ratio the $95 deposit by the bicycle seller requires the holding of $4.75 ($= 0.05 \times \$95$) of reserves, leaving the remaining $90.25 ($= \$95 - \$4.75$) as excess reserves at The Second National Bank.

If payment is made with a check instead of cash, the settlement still follows the lines we have indicated. The bicycle seller deposits the check in his or her bank, The Second National. This bank credits the bicycle seller's account with $95, and then presents the check to The First National Bank for collection. If both banks are members of the Federal Reserve System, this is done through the regional Federal Reserve Banks. The Federal Reserve credits the **reserve account** of The Second National Bank and debits the reserve account of The First National Bank. The check is then returned to The First National Bank which debits $95 from the account of the original borrower. What was an excess reserve for The First National Bank becomes the reserve of The Second National Bank.

One bank's loan is likely to become another bank's deposit.

Unlike The First National Bank, with its actual reserves equal to required reserves, The Second National Bank is holding excess reserves. With only $4.75 required reserves against the $95 of deposits it can loan out the remaining $90.25. Suppose it finds a willing borrower who wants $90.25 to buy a pair of skis. The bank will credit the account of the borrower, which becomes a deposit liability of the bank. The bank will have an offsetting asset, the borrower's IOU. When the borrower pays for his or her skis, the $90.25 of excess reserves is removed from the asset side of The Second National Bank's balance sheet. The payment from the ski-buyer's account also reduces the bank's liabilities: a deposit at a bank is an asset of the depositor but a liability of the bank.

If the seller of the skis deposits the $90.25 in The Third National Bank, this bank needs to keep $4.51 ($= 0.05 \times \$90.25$) to satisfy the 5% minimum reserve ratio. It can create an interest-earning loan for the remaining $85.74 ($= \$90.25 - \$4.51$). This might be spent on something sold by a person banking with The Fourth National Bank, which keeps $4.29 ($= 0.05 \times \$85.74$) and loans the remaining amount, and so on. Four stages of this sequence, which could continue indefinitely, are shown in Table 3.4.

Since we have agreed that the supply of money consists of coin, currency, and commercial bank deposits, the money supply has been increased by the initial deposit of $100 of cash. If our process continues indefinitely, the value of total created bank deposits is

$$\Delta D = \$100 + 95 + 90.25 + 85.74 + \cdots , \qquad (3.1)$$

where ΔD stands for the change in bank deposits. The original deposit of $100 of currency moves through the banking system creating additional deposits at every step. Since these bank deposits are money, the multiple increase in the money supply from extra reserves is the result of the banks creating money. The sum of numbers in Eq. (3.1) has a finite value even if we take it to an infinite number of steps. Let us calculate this value.

Table 3.4.   Deposit creation can continue indefinitely in diminishing amounts.

Assets		Liabilities	
THE FIRST NATIONAL BANK			
Required reserve	$5	Deposit	$100
Loan	$95		
Total	$100	Total	$100
THE SECOND NATIONAL BANK			
Required reserve	$4.75	Deposit	$90
Loan	$90.25		
Total	$95	Total	$95
THE THIRD NATIONAL BANK			
Required reserve	$4.51	Deposit	$90.25
Loan	$85.74		
Total	$90.25	Total	$90.25
THE FOURTH NATIONAL BANK			
Required reserve	$4.29	Deposit	$85.74
Loan	$81.45		
Total	$85.74	Total	$85.74

We begin by multiplying both the left- and right-hand sides of Eq. (3.1) by 0.95, giving:

$$0.95\Delta D = \$95 + 90.25 + 85.74 + 81.45 + \cdots . \qquad (3.2)$$

Equation (3.2) can be subtracted from Eq. (3.1) by subtracting the left-hand sides and the right-hand sides, giving

$$\Delta D - 0.95\Delta D = 0.05\Delta D = \$100 + (95 - 95) + (90.25 - 90.25)$$
$$+ (85.74 - 85.74) + \cdots .$$

All but the $100 on the right-hand side disappears. Therefore,

$$0.05\Delta D = \$100,$$

or

$$\Delta D = \$2{,}000.$$

We find that the deposit of $100 of additional reserves into the banking system has raised bank deposits by a total of $2,000 — a multiple of 20 times the original increase in reserves.[8] This multiple, obtained by dividing the change in the money supply by the change in reserves, is called the **money multiplier**. In our example the money multiplier is 20.[9]

> *The money multiplier is the ratio of new deposits to the original increase in bank reserves.*

Our example shows banks do indeed create money. Without the example, one might have believed that since currency and bank deposits are just two different forms of money, taking currency from your pocket and depositing it in the bank would leave the total money supply unchanged. Yet with fractional reserve banking, we find the money supply is increased. Whichever way new bank reserves are created, the supply of money is increased by a multiple of the increase in bank reserves. Let us consider other ways in which the supply of money can be increased, and focus on the role of the central bank.

> *With fractional reserve banking, commercial banks create money.*

THE CENTRAL BANK AND THE MONEY SUPPLY

There are several ways in which a central bank such as the Fed can change the money supply. The most commonly used procedure in countries where money and capital markets are well developed, as they are in the United States and Europe, is **open market operations**.

Open Market Operations

In the U.S., open market operations involve the purchase and sale of securities by the Federal Reserve Bank of New York, which acts as agent for

---

[8]When, as in our example, the extra bank reserves come out of currency, the currency is no longer held by the public. The currency has hence disappeared from the money supply, which includes only *publically-held* currency, plus deposits. Therefore, the precise increase in the money supply is $2,000 of extra deposits, minus the $100 reduction in circulating currency. That is, the money supply grows by $1,900, slightly less than the increase in bank deposits.

[9]The value of 20 is $1.0 \div 0.05$. More generally, the multiplier is 1.0 divided by the required reserve ratio measured as a decimal.

the Federal Reserve System. The securities that are bought and sold are generally those issued by the government — Treasury bills and Treasury bonds — although the banking crisis of 2008–2009 led to a much wider range of securities being bought by the Fed.

We have seen that an increase in the money supply will occur if there is an increase in bank reserves, and that the money supply increases by a multiple of the reserve increase. The reserves of the banking system are increased when the Federal Reserve *buys* securities in the open market. The converse is true when the Fed *sells* securities. The securities are purchased from or sold to dealers who act on their own behalf or on behalf of their clients.

Open market operations involve central bank purchases and sales of securities.

When the Federal Reserve buys a Treasury bill from a securities dealer it pays by a draft drawn against funds in an account at the Fed: yes, the Fed pays from its own bank account. The securities dealer deposits the draft in its account at a commercial bank, and in turn the commercial bank presents the draft to the Fed. The Fed credits the commercial bank for the value of the draft: the commercial bank's account at the Fed is credited and the Fed's account at the Fed is debited. This means that the commercial bank's reserves have been increased: funds at the Fed have moved from the Fed's account at the Fed to the commercial bank's account at the Fed.[10] The extra reserves the commercial bank then holds allow it to offer loans: commercial bank deposits at the Fed are reserves of the commercial banks. These loans involve crediting the borrowers' bank accounts. The proceeds of the loans, when spent, cause the extra reserves to move through the banking system, resulting in an overall multiple expansion in bank deposits and the money supply.

The reverse pattern occurs from an open market sale of securities by the Fed. In particular, when the Fed sells securities to a securities dealer, the dealer pays with a draft drawn on an account at a commercial bank. When the Fed receives the draft it debits the commercial bank's reserve account. In this way, the Fed's sale of securities in the open market results

---

[10]We assume the commercial bank is a Federal Reserve member. If not, the non-member bank deposits the check with a member bank and the member bank's reserves are increased.

in a shrinking of the commercial bank's reserve account. If the commercial bank is holding minimum required reserves before its reserve account is debited, the bank is forced to reduce its deposits or to try to regain its reserves in order to maintain the minimum required reserve ratio. While an individual commercial bank may be able to increase its reserves by borrowing reserves from another bank with excess reserves in the **federal funds market**, the commercial banking system in general cannot create reserves by itself.[11] The only way reserve ratios can collectively be met after a decrease in reserves is via a decrease in deposits, and hence in bank loans. The effect on the banking system is like that shown earlier as summarized in Table 3.4, only working in reverse.

> *Purchases of securities by the central bank increase commercial bank reserves and thereby allow an increase in the money supply. Sales of securities reduce commercial bank reserves and thereby reduce the money supply.*

Discount Rate

Another way the Fed can influence the money supply is via changes in the **discount rate**. This is the interest rate at which commercial banks can borrow reserves from the Fed if they are short of reserves.

> *The discount rate is the interest rate commercial banks pay to borrow reserves from the central bank.*

Each bank must satisfy the minimum reserve requirement by having average holdings of reserves over a specified period that are sufficient, given the bank's average deposits over the averaging period. If there are sufficient reserves in the banking system as a whole, then even if some banks have insufficient reserves they can borrow from other banks with excess reserves. However, when the banking system as a whole has insufficient reserves it is not possible for all reserve-deficient banks to satisfy their minimum reserve requirements by borrowing from other commercial banks. Then, commercial banks must borrow reserves from the Fed.

---

[11]The interest rate on borrowed reserve by one commercial bank from another commercial bank is called the **federal funds rate**. The Fed sets a target federal funds rate in the setting of the direction of its monetary policy: a lower target means an easier monetary policy and a higher target means a tighter policy.

Today, getting extra reserves involves the commercial banks taking **advances** from the Fed, called **repurchase agreements**, or **repos** for short. The commercial banks are required to hold government securities to guarantee their obligations to repay the advances.

The discount rate influences the risk commercial banks take of having deficient reserves. Specifically, if the discount rate is considered high, banks make fewer loans. This means creation of a smaller amount of deposits and hence smaller money supply, and reduces the chance of having to borrow in the federal funds market or from the Fed because of deficient reserves: smaller deposits mean smaller required reserves. On the other hand, when the discount rate is low, banks worry less about being forced to borrow, and therefore create more deposits via offering more loans. Therefore, *ceteris paribus*, the money supply is larger the lower is the discount rate, and vice versa.

Ceteris paribus, the lower is the central bank's discount rate, the larger is the money supply, and vice versa.

Changes in Reserve Requirements

A highly effective albeit blunt instrument for changing the money supply is via changes in the minimum required reserve ratio, i.e., the minimum fraction of commercial bank deposits that must be held in reserves. If the required reserve ratio is increased, the same bank reserves support a lower level of deposits, i.e., a smaller money supply, while a lower reserve ratio means a larger money supply.[12]

Even a small change in the required reserve ratio can cause an extremely large change in the money supply. This is because a change of only a half or one percent in the required reserve ratio is large vis-à-vis the base of the typical required reserve ratio. As a result, in countries with well-developed markets for buying and selling securities, open market operations are a more commonly employed means of changing the money supply than

---

[12] In fact, there are different reserve requirements on different types of bank deposits. Smaller reserves are required against time (or savings) deposits than against demand (or checkable) deposits. Also, the calculation of required reserves depends on the size of banks. Smaller banks have a different reserve **maintenance cycle** than larger banks. Specifics can change from time to time.

the relatively crude instrument of changes in reserve requirements. For example, in the United States, reserve requirements are often unchanged for decades, with virtually all monetary policy instead being performed via open market operations or changes in the discount rate. In economies with less well developed security markets, open market operations may not be feasible. In such economies, changes in reserve requirements can be relatively frequent.

The lower is the required reserve ratio the higher is the money supply, and vice versa.

FINANCIAL INTERMEDIATION

Commercial Banks as Financial Intermediaries

As well as being the most important providers of the means of payments, banks serve the crucial role of bringing savers and investors together. The banks gather funds that savers — those spending less than they earn — are not yet ready to spend, and make them available to borrowers who wish to invest in new factories, machines, automobiles, houses, and so on. In their performance of this role, banks are serving as **financial intermediaries**. It is well worth pausing to consider what would happen if there were no institutions to bring savers and investors together.

Banks serve as financial intermediaries between savers who deposit funds, and borrowers who invest funds.

If there were no banks or other financial intermediaries it would be difficult for those wishing to borrow to locate others wishing to lend. Borrowers would have to incur **search costs**, such as payments for advertising, and so on, in order to locate lenders. At the same time, lenders would have to incur search costs to locate borrowers to whom they are prepared to lend. Banks serve to reduce the costs of borrowers locating lenders and of lenders locating borrowers. Borrowers and lenders can both go to banks, and in effect pay for the banks' services in bringing them together and serving as the middleman. In serving as financial intermediaries, banks make profits by charging borrowers higher interest rates than they pay to lenders, i.e., the depositors. We have earlier referred to this difference between the interest rates charged to borrowers and paid to depositors as the spread.

Bank earnings from the spread minus the costs of running the bank is a source of the banks' profits.

Even if lenders and borrowers could locate each other directly without the intermediation of banks there would still be problems to overcome. Savers would have to determine the creditworthiness of borrowers, with this involving the evaluation of information which requires accounting knowledge and other skills. Furthermore, even after lenders had found creditworthy borrowers, it would still be necessary to know how to draw up the conditions of loans according to the correct legal principles. It is a lot easier to take savings to a bank and let the bank's experts determine which borrowers are creditworthy, and let the bank take care of drawing up documents.

A further problem we would have in the absence of banks and other financial intermediaries is that the amounts lenders typically have available are smaller than the amounts borrowers need for their house, automobile purchase, factory expansion, and so on. Banks serve the function of gathering up lots of small deposits to make large loans. Of course, there are sometimes deposits that are larger than small loans. Then the banks can allocate the funds to numerous borrowers. However, typically, the amounts people put in banks at any time are small relative to the size of bank loans.

An additional problem that stems from the small size of what savers have available to lend is that if there were no financial intermediaries, savers would be poorly **diversified**, perhaps with their only asset being a loan to one person or company. Because banks have numerous loans which are unlikely to all turn bad at the same time, banks have diversified portfolios of assets, and therefore banks' depositors indirectly acquire the protection of these diversified portfolios.

Financial intermediaries like banks reduce the cost of savers locating investors, and vice versa. They also provide accounting and legal expertise, gather deposits to make loans to borrowers, and allow savers to indirectly enjoy benefits of diversification of risky assets.

The added costs of savers locating investors, preparing documents and so on, would mean that without financial intermediaries, savers would be tempted to spend more of their earnings or to invest their savings in their own projects. In general, the savers' own projects would not be as profitable as the projects that would otherwise have been pursued. This is because those with large savings are not necessarily those with the best opportunities for investment. Therefore, if we did not have banks and other intermediaries we would have less investment, or else investment that offered lower returns on average. Whether it be lower investment or investment with lower returns, we would have slower economic growth without financial intermediation; economic growth depends on the amount of investment and the rate of return on investment.

> *Financial intermediaries help facilitate more investment or else investment with higher returns, either of which increases economic growth.*

Other Institutions Bringing Savers and Investors Together

Being on so many Main Streets and in so many downtown plazas, banks are the most visible of the financial intermediaries that bring savers and investors together, but they are by no means unique in serving this role. Other links between savers and investors are provided by:

(1) Non-bank deposit-taking institutions, "thrifts,"
(2) non-deposit-taking institutions such as pension funds,
(3) the money and bond markets, and
(4) the stock market.

Thrift Institutions: The work of commercial banks in gathering deposits and extending loans is parallel to the work of the **thrift institutions**. These thrifts are also known as **near banks**. The thrifts consist of **mutual savings banks**, which are largely on the Eastern Seaboard of the United States, **savings and loan associations**, and **credit unions**, both of which are all over the United States, Canada, and other countries. While the thrifts serve the function of bringing savers and borrowers together in the same way as commercial banks do, the nature of the savers and borrowers is a little different.

> *Thrift institutions include the mutual savings banks, savings and loans associations, and credit unions.*

The thrifts specialize in real estate lending and consumer loans. Of course, commercial banks also provide loans to home and automobile buyers. However, commercial banks allocate a substantial part of their funds to business and government lending, the latter involving the purchase of Treasury bills and bonds. For deposits, the thrifts depend almost exclusively on **retail deposits**, which are funds gathered in street-level offices. While commercial banks also depend on retail deposits as a source of funds, large commercial banks also raise funds via the sale of **certificates of deposit** which are interest-bearing negotiable instruments, and via money market funds, mutual funds and other means.

Non-Deposit Institutions: Large amounts of savings are gathered in and invested by **pension funds**. Pension funds do not take in deposits as do banks and thrifts, but rather as their name suggests, collect and invest peoples' savings for retirement. Contributions to the funds may be made monthly from salaries, or perhaps, once each year. Pension funds invest in stocks, mortgages, and corporate and government bonds. In this way, pension funds bring savers and borrowers together. Some pension funds also invest in real estate.

Money and Bond Markets: Large corporate and government borrowers can circumvent banks and other financial institutions and borrow directly from individuals or institutions via the money and bond markets. For example, well-recognized companies with a good track record for repaying debt can borrow by selling **commercial paper** which is purchased by those with surplus funds. Commercial paper is an obligation of a company — a **promissory note** — to pay the holder a certain sum at a particular future date, with the repayment date commonly 30 days or 90 days after the paper is sold. Commercial paper is sold in the **money market** which is where negotiable interest-bearing securities with maturities of up to one year are bought and sold.

> *Commercial paper is an agreement to pay the holder a sum of money at a specified future date. Commercial paper is sold in the money market, which is the financial market in which securities with a maturity of up to one year are bought and sold.*

Companies that are not well-known to potential lenders can pay for commercial banks to guarantee their obligations to repay the holders of their commercial paper. The guarantee takes the form of a bank stamping on a company's paper that the bank is prepared to repay the holder the promised amount on the company's commercial paper, whatever is the financial status of the company when payment is due. A company's commercial paper guaranteed in this way is called a **banker's acceptance**, and by having its paper accepted a company can borrow at an interest rate that reflects the riskiness of the bank offering the guarantee. Banks are prepared to offer their guarantee because they can collect a fee for their service without themselves having to raise the funds required by the borrower. A large number of bankers' acceptances arise from credits granted in international trade; the checks for payment for exports at a future date, called **bills of exchange**, are accepted by banks, i.e., guaranteed, and then sold in the money market.

A banker's acceptance is commercial paper on which payment is guaranteed by a bank.

Those who wish to borrow directly from savers, but who wish to repay after more than one year, can use the **bond market** rather than the money market. Bonds are obligations of a company or a government to pay a sequence of interest payments known as **coupons**, and repay the **principal** that was borrowed at an agreed future date or according to an agreed schedule over a period of more than one year.[13] The bond market where bonds are bought by savers and sold by borrowers is not housed in any specific location. Instead, it consists of an informal linkage of traders who connect through telecommunications. As such it is considered to be an **over the counter (OTC) market**. Most large **brokerage houses** have special bond departments, and for a fee arrange for the issue of bonds for their corporate clients, an activity known as **underwriting**.[14] The informal

---

[13]Not all bonds pay coupons. Some bonds are sold at a price below what is eventually to be paid to the holder, with the appreciation from the issue price to the value at maturity being the way the holder earns "interest". Such bonds are **discount bonds**, and are so-called because they are sold at a discount from their maturity value. However, most bonds pay coupons and are not discount bonds. Money market instruments such as Treasury bills and commercial paper are discount instruments.

[14]The issue of bonds for a corporate client is called underwriting because the brokerage house arranging for the issue of the bonds gives an assurance, setting a floor or minimum selling price of the bonds. This means that if the brokerage house cannot sell the bonds, it purchases them itself.

nature of the bond market contrasts with the **stock market** which is another component of the **capital market**. (The capital market is the collective of all the financial markets and institutions: the banks, the money market, bond market and the stock market.)

> *Bonds are obligations to pay interest and repay the principal amount over a period of more than one year. Bonds, along with stocks and other securities, are sold in the capital market.*

The Stock Market: Stocks are exchanged on a **stock exchange** such as the New York Stock Exchange (NYSE), or the exchanges in Chicago, Los Angeles, San Francisco, Philadelphia, London, Paris, Tokyo, Toronto, and so on. The traders in the stock exchanges are linked to brokerage houses that are in turn in contact with clients. The stock exchanges are, therefore, only the focal points of an informal linkage between savers and those requiring funds. (Most trades in the stock market are exchanges of previously issued stocks rather than new issues. It is only at the time of issue that savers and investors are brought together.)

Unlike bonds, stocks represent claims to the ownership of a company, and any payment to the owners of stocks, the **shareholders**, can be made only after scheduled payments to bondholders and other creditors have been made. The amount left over to pay shareholders after meeting all prior claims to bondholders and other creditors of a company is uncertain, and depends on the company's profitability. In contrast, bondholders receive the agreed amount of interest or principal repayment, provided a company is solvent. Stated somewhat differently, stocks are subordinate to bonds as claims against a company. However, despite this important difference, we should not lose sight of the fact that the stock and bond markets share the role of bringing savers and investors together.

> *Stocks are subordinate to bonds as a financial obligation of a company.*

The sale of stocks, like the sale of bonds, is handled by brokerages. Whereas banks earn their incomes from the spread between borrowing and lending interest rates, brokerages earn their incomes from **brokerage charges** paid by the companies issuing the stocks and bonds, and by the public trading stocks and bonds after they have been issued.

Savers and investors are brought together by commercial banks, thrifts such as mutual savings banks and savings and loan associations, by pension funds, and by the money, bond, and stock markets.

Because the payment to shareholders in the form of **dividends** is uncertain, as is the market value of stocks, savers who place their funds in stocks require a return which compensates them for the risk. Since the return is not known in advance, what is required is that their **expected return** compensates for the risk shareholders take.

Risk is greater on stocks than on bonds.[15] Since it is generally assumed that people are **risk averse**, i.e., they do not like risk, expected returns on stocks must be higher than returns on bonds. The expected return on stocks consists of expected dividends and changes in the stocks' market prices. The extent to which the expected return on a particular stock must exceed the return on bonds depends on the perceived riskiness of the stock. However, while it is not obvious, the riskiness of a stock does not depend only on the amount of possible variation in its market value and variation in its dividends. A stock's riskiness depends on how much more variable it makes the wealth of a person who holds the stock in a portfolio of many stocks and other assets. This is because an individual stock is rarely, if ever, held on its own. Therefore the stock market determines an expected return based on the fact that shareholders hold diversified portfolios. In fact, since all stocks trading in the market must be held by somebody, the return on any individual stock depends on how much risk the stock adds to a portfolio of all stocks and other assets.

Interest rates and expected returns depend on the relevant, associated risks.

SUMMARY

(1) Money is the medium of exchange that we accept for what we sell and then use to make purchases, and which thereby allows exchange to be indirect.

---

[15]In fact, it is only if bonds are held to maturity that the return on them is known, and furthermore, there may be a **default risk** on corporate bonds; default risk is the risk a company goes bankrupt and cannot pay its bondholders. Bonds are, however, normally less risky than stocks.

(2) Money offers a number of advantages over barter. Money overcomes the need for a double coincidence of wants, the problem of exchanging indivisible products, perishable products and products that are difficult to carry around. Money also offers a common unit of measurement of prices and debts. Because money has these advantages, we are able to specialize in economic activities and thereby enjoy the gains from the division of labor.

(3) Money can be defined as whatever is generally acceptable as a medium of exchange, and which also serves as a standard of deferred payment, a store of value, and a unit of account.

(4) The monetary aggregate M1 consists primarily of coin, currency and checkable deposits at banks and near banks, including account balances accessible to debit cards.

(5) While savings accounts, time deposits, money market funds, mutual funds and so on cannot themselves be used to make payments, they can be quickly converted into checkable accounts, and are therefore included in the broader definitions of the money supply, M2.

(6) Money is the most liquid asset. Every asset has some degree of liquidity, but only money avoids all uncertainty and cost when making purchases.

(7) Holding money because of its convenience in making purchases involves forgoing interest that could otherwise be earned. The interest rate is the opportunity cost of holding money. The higher the interest rate forgone by holding money, the lower is the quantity of money demanded.

(8) Paper money arose from the deposit taking activity of goldsmiths who issued paper claims against gold held for safekeeping in their vaults.

(9) The Federal Reserve System is the central bank of the United States. It has a Chairman and Board of Governors in Washington, DC, and 12 regional banks. The Federal Reserve holds member commercial banks' reserves, clears checks between member banks, serves as the government's bank, and manages the supply of money.

(10) Runs on banks are effectively prevented by the Federal Deposit Insurance Corporation (FDIC) which insures deposits at commercial banks.

(11) The fractional reserve system enables commercial banks to create money. The money supply creation process, occurring through

re-depositing and the granting of loans, results in the supply of money increasing by a multiple of the increase in commercial bank reserves.

(12) The Federal Reserve can affect the money supply by open market operations, by changing the discount rate, and by changing reserve requirements.

(13) Commercial banks and other financial institutions gather up funds from those earning more than they spend, and make these funds available to those wishing to spend more than they earn. Members of the former group are savers, and the latter group consists of investors, and consumers who wish to consume today and pay later.

(14) Financial intermediaries reduce the cost of channeling savings to investors, and thereby increase investment and economic growth.

(15) Savers and investors are brought together by commercial banks, thrifts, which consist of mutual savings banks, credit unions, and savings and loan associations, as well as by pension funds, money and bond markets, and the stock market.

(16) Stocks represent a claim to the ownership of a company. Stocks are subordinate to bonds in that bondholders must be paid before a firm can pay anything to shareholders.

(17) Stocks are riskier than bonds, and because people are risk averse, the expected return on stocks must exceed that on bonds.

(18) The degree of riskiness of a stock does not depend on how volatile is its value, but rather, on how much volatility it contributes to a diversified portfolio of stocks and other assets, specifically the market portfolio of all stocks, bonds and other assets.

QUESTIONS

(1) What features of gold have given it such an important historical role as a medium of exchange, unit of account and store of value? How "liquid" are gold and silver?

(2) Should available unused balances on department store-issued credit cards be considered part of the money supply?

(3) What "variables" are relevant for the amount of money a person wants to hold?

(4) Do you think the demand for money would vary more closely with wealth than it does with income?

(5) If many of the customers of a bank gave lengthy advance notice to withdraw their deposits, would the bank be able to meet their demands? What would it sell to obtain currency for its customers?

(6) Why doesn't the government leave insurance of bank deposits to private insurance companies, as it does with most other types of insurance?

(7) An individual bank merely lends money that people deposit, and therefore does not add to the money supply. How, then, does the banking *system* add to the money supply?

(8) How does the interest rate on bank loans versus the central bank discount rate influence commercial bank decisions on how much to lend?

(9) How can financial intermediaries increase economic growth?

(10) Most sales of stocks are "secondary sales" which is the resale of stocks, rather that the original sale of new issues. Why do secondary sales assist the sale of new issues?

(11) What are the differences between the money, bond, and stock markets, and how do these differences affect the nature of the people that raise funds in these different markets?

(12) What is the difference between a credit card and a debit card?

CONNECTIONS

MONEY: A MATTER OF CONSIDERABLE INTEREST

Economists are not the only people who are interested in money. However, economists are more-or-less alone in viewing money so favorably, with their emphasis on money as a means of avoiding the inefficiencies of barter.

Money is a prize sought by archaeologists. This is not because ancient money necessarily has a market value to collectors, but because it tells so much about the lives of its users. For example, discoveries of money provide information on the patterns of international trade and influence two millennia ago when Greek and then Roman coins were used widely in commerce from the Mediterranean to the Baltic. Spanish "pieces of eight" — 8-reales coins — paint a picture of conquest and trade in the 16th century. The imprints on monies provide archaeologists and historians with other information, including who held power at a particular time; coins were frequently issued to commemorate the coronation of rulers and their successes on the battlefield. Mesopotamian coins, which consist of inscribed tablets, even provide information on prices of important items of trade, such as wool and barley.

An amazing array of objects have served as money: bark cloth in Samoa; huge round stones in the Yap Islands; beads in Pelew; feathers in Santa Cruz; fur in Alaska; and shells in the Soloman Islands. Rice, tea, salt, cattle, slaves, silk, cigarettes, wine, and of course, bronze, copper, gold and silver have all served as money.[1] Demands for convenience have recently resulted in the almost universal use of paper currency and magnetic records in bank computers.

Money has long had a ritual significance, and been the object of numerous superstitions. Anthropologists note how in many societies, money has been used to drive off demons, provide cures for illness, protect soldiers in battle, fend off plagues and bring fertility to newly married couples.

---

[1] A fascinating account of different monies and the roles they played is provided by Paul Einzig's penetrating and insightful study, *Primitive Money* (Eyre and Spottiswoode, London, 1948).

Numerous rituals involve the exchange of coins as an appeal to some external power or 'spirit.' Even today we talk of the "high priests of finance," and of people being "obsessed" by money, with misers being obsessed by their own money and thieves by other peoples' money. Money is both revered and feared, viewed as good — when it involves charity — and as evil — when it involves acquisitiveness and single-minded desire. To some, money is viewed as having transformative power, able to turn Cinderella into a princess or a lottery winner's miserable existence into a life of joy.

The ritual significance of money probably predates its use as a medium of exchange, and money still retains a ritual significance. William Desmonde and more recently Russel Belk and Melanie Wallendorf, have claimed that money originated as a ritual symbol, citing the fact that money played a role in societies in which exchange of goods and services outside the family was very limited.[2] Just as the acquisition of food signified special hunting and gathering skills such as endurance, daring and intelligence, so today, the acquisition of money signifies possession of necessary life skills. Certainly, we still see extremely rich people working feverishly to add further to their wealth, perhaps more out of a desire to increase their power, stature, control and prestige than to exchange their money for items to consume. While we must distinguish desires for money from desires for wealth — money is but a narrow component of wealth, being just liquid wealth — it does appear that 'money' is linked to status, serving as a medal of achievement and perhaps giving its owner a sense of immortality and durability.

Money is surrounded by emotions and taboos, the emotions reflected in the use of terms such as "bond" and "security." While bonds and securities are not themselves money, these terms reflect the feelings attached to the ties of indebtedness and the comfort of having money. Reference is also made to *trust* companies, *confidence* crises, bank *panics*, market *optimism* and so on, imbuing institutions relating to money with human emotions.

The taboos associated with money are many. They include the social rules governing money as a gift. For example, it is usually unacceptable to

---

[2]William Desmonde, *Magic, Myth and Money: The Origins of Money in Religious Ritual* (Free Press of Glencoe Inc., New York, 1962), and, Russel W. Belk and Melanie Wallendorf, "The Sacred Meanings of Money," *Journal of Economic Psychology*, Vol. 11, 1990: 35–67.

give money as a gift to non-family members. Money can be given within the family, and indeed, is a sign of devotion, but traditionally money is given down the age ladder from older to younger family members, and not the reverse. In addition, when giving money, new crisp notes are better than old, limp ones, and it is better to give a $100 bill than a bundle of $5 or $10 bills. There are also taboos when making payments with money. For example, payment for the services of a doctor or dentist are made to a receptionist or via a check in the mail, rather than directly. Similarly, it is not acceptable to give money to a neighbor for a friendly gesture such as a gift of produce from their garden. However, a return in kind is considered appropriate — if separated sufficiently in time so as not to seen as a payment. So strong are the taboos surrounding money, and particularly the discussion of money, that David Krueger in his *Last Taboo* notes that some people are more open discussing sex than money.[3]

Marxists have noted that the use of money detaches workers from the objects they make, and puts worker–employer relations on an impersonal footing. On the other hand, it has also been noted how much human interaction revolves around the exchange of money, making money a focus of interpersonal relations; the exchange at the supermarket checkout, with the bus driver, at the gas station or newsstand is a human interaction involving money.

Money relates to the law. In particular, typically a currency is declared to be **legal tender**, meaning that it must be accepted by vendors if they agree to the terms of a sale. (Vendors are not required to sell their goods or services, but once they have agreed to a sale they are required to accept the country's legal tender in exchange). As well as applying to the acceptability of currency, the law also applies to the establishment and management of the banks and other financial institutions whose liabilities represent the major component of the money supply. Federal and state law is rich with legislative enactments and case precedents relating to banking and financial intermediation. Indeed, "liability" is a term spanning law and finance.

The emergence, spread and occasional collapse of banks weave threads in the fabric of history, from the influence and power of the Flemish and

[3]David W. Krueger, *Last Taboo: Money as Symbol and Reality in Psychotherapy and Psychoanalysis* (Brunner/Mazel, New York, 1986).

Lombardian banks, to the turmoil surrounding the collapse of thousands of U.S. banks in the Great Depression, 1929–1933, and more recent failures of banks around the world in 2007–2009. Because of its ramifications for social and political developments, monetary history is an integral part not only of economic history, but of general history.

As we saw in the previous chapter, many religions view money — or more generally, wealth — as corrupting the soul if it becomes regarded with reverence. The need to prevent the desire for money from obfuscating more important "other worldly" objectives is at the core of a large body of liturgical writings. Readers of books in that other "other worldly" discipline, astronomy, might be forgiven for thinking that money is also at the core of a large body of their literature, that relating to the more easily identifiable nebulae and galaxies. This is because according to the classification system of the French astronomer Messier, the most visible blurry patches in the sky are labeled M1, M2, and so on. With the numerous innovations in different kinds of deposits and financial institutions, the pressure is on for more definitions of money than the current M1 and M2, although it is to be hoped that the listing of monies falls short of cosmic proportions.

CHAPTER 4

INFLATION

"If buyers won't fall for prices, prices must fall for buyers."
Evan Esar

Key Concepts: Consumer price index; GDP deflator; difficulties measuring inflation; quantity theory of money; money demand versus money supply; cost-push versus demand-pull inflation; hyperinflation; inflation as a hidden tax; gains and losses from inflation; importance of inflationary anticipations.

UPS AND DOWNS IN INFLATION

At different times and in different countries inflation has been a matter of major concern, of little or no concern, and of just about every level of concern inbetween. That is, inflation has varied greatly over time within countries, and also differs substantially between countries. For example, in the first few years of the 21st century the rate of inflation in Zimbabwe reached 5,000 trillion, trillion percent per year i.e., 5,000,000,000,000,000,000,000,000%. Bank notes were issued for 100 trillion dollars, Zimbabwe dollars. That many dollars, if they were U.S. dollars, could have paid off the U.S. national debt; just one bank note of the millions that were printed! Of course, Zimbabwe dollars were worth essentially nothing. Since the 1970s inflation in Brazil went from relatively modest levels in the "double digits," to approximately 3,000% per year, and back to modest levels. During the same period inflation in Japan and the United States, while low by Brazilian standards, still varied significantly over time, having declined from over 10% in the 1970s to a couple of percent or less by the end of the first decade of the new millennium. Figure 4.1 which

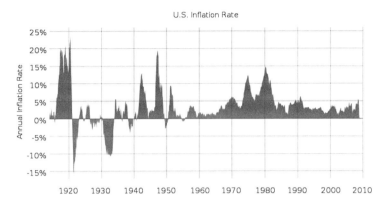

Fig. 4.1. Almost a century of U.S. inflation and deflation.

Source: United States Bureau of Labor http://en.wikipedia.org/wiki/File:US_Historical_Inflation.svg.

describes U.S. inflation history over almost a century — shows that inflation — a rising price level — is far more frequent than deflation — a declining price level — although there have been occasions, such as during the Great Depression, 1929–1933, when prices fell sharply.

Inflation rates can differ greatly between countries and within countries over time.

In this chapter we explain possible causes of inflation. We also consider the effects of inflation and the importance of how accurately inflation is forecasted by savers, workers and others. As we shall see in later chapters, unanticipated inflation is in many ways more important than the rate of inflation itself, having an important bearing on other macroeconomic phenomena, including unemployment, GDP and interest rates. This is why we set out to deal with as many aspects of inflation as we can, all in one chapter; later chapters can then build on these foundations. However, before dealing with the causes and effects of inflation it is useful to consider how it is measured, and the accuracy of the alternative measures that are used. We shall see that as with most important macroeconomic variables, published inflation statistics are only estimates, requiring some care in interpretation.[1]

---

[1]We recall that in Chapter 1 we spoke of *estimates* of GDP, national income and so on. Even money supply statistics are estimates, being based on sampling procedures, just as are unemployment estimates and so on.

MEASURING INFLATION

As we are all well aware, inflation reduces the buying power of any given dollar amount of income or savings. The rate of inflation is measured by the rate at which an index of prices goes up (or goes down in the case of deflation). The **price index** is designed to measure "prices in general" which requires that it provides a way of combining the prices of different items. Several price indexes are calculated of which two are particularly important. These are the Consumer Price Index (CPI), and the GDP Implicit Deflator.

> *The rate of inflation is the rate at which prices in general are increasing. It is computed from changes in an index which measures the level of prices in general.*

The Consumer Price Index, CPI

The **CPI** combines the prices of items purchased by an "average" or "representative" consumer. However, the representative consumer must be defined. This is not easy because each person has his or her own preferences which affect what they buy. For example, while some people like to precede their evening meal with such delights as caviar and expensive paté, others are content to forgo appetizers and settle for bologna and fried eggs. Similarly, while patrons of the arts might feel dissatisfied without tickets to the symphony and a visit to the opera, others get their pleasure from the cheaper activities of a hike in the country or an evening watching the TV.

To define the representative consumer, a survey is made of the spending of a sample of consumers during a base "year".[2] The survey focuses on urban households and records everything the sampled households purchase, and even the places where the households shop. An average is taken of what the households spend to determine the relative importance of different products. In this way the representative consumer's **market basket** is defined.

A highly simplified market basket is given in the first column of Table 4.1. The basket is computed from purchases during the base "year" 2005–2006. Table 4.1 also gives the prices of the items in the market basket.

---

[2]In fact, to reduce sampling error the survey is conducted over a couple of years, e.g., 2005–2006.

Table 4.1. The consumer price index values a base-year market basket in successive months or years.

Consumption item	Units purchased in base year, 2005–2006	Price per unit in 2005–2006	Price per unit in 2010
Beef	20 pounds	$1.80	$2.00
Bread	16 loaves	$1.50	$1.80
Potatoes	12 pounds	$0.50	$0.65
Rent	1 month	$800	$900
Electricity	2,000 kilowatt hours	$0.05	$0.075
Suits	1 suit	$149	$139

The Consumer Price Index values a base-year market basket at base-year prices and at later prices. The ratio of these two values gives the CPI for the later period. The rate of inflation is computed from the rate at which the cost of the basket changes over time. That is, the rate of inflation is the rate of change of the CPI.

The cost of the base year basket can therefore be calculated, and is:

Cost of 2005–2006 market basket in 2005–2006

$$= \$(20 \times 1.80) + \$(16 \times 1.50) + \$(12 \times 0.50) + \$(1 \times 800)$$
$$+ \$(2{,}000 \times 0.05) + \$(1 \times 149) = \$1{,}115.$$

Table 4.1 shows that by 2010 the price of most items has risen. The cost of the 2005–2006 market basket valued at 2010 prices is:

Cost of 2005–2006 market basket in 2010

$$= \$(20 \times 2.00) + \$(16 \times 1.8) + \$(12 \times 0.65) + \$(1 \times 900)$$
$$+ \$(2{,}000 \times 0.075) + \$(1 \times 139) = \$1{,}265.60.$$

The CPI index for 2010 compared with 2005–2006 is derived by taking the ratio of the two sums we have calculated, and multiplying by 100. Therefore, the CPI for 2010 compared with 2005–2006 is:

CPI (2010 versus 2005–2006)

$$= \frac{\text{Cost of 2005–2006 market basket in 2010}}{\text{Cost of 2005–2006 market basket in 2005–2006}} \times 100$$

$$= \frac{\$1{,}265.60}{\$1{,}115} \times 100 = 110.05.$$

More generally, the CPI for the current year is:

CPI (Current Year)

$$= \frac{\text{Cost of base-year market basket using current prices}}{\text{Cost of base-year market basket using base-year prices}} \times 100.$$

$$(4.1)$$

We see from the definition in Eq. (4.1) that the CPI compares the cost of the market basket in an earlier period with what it costs later. We find that in 2010 prices are 110% of what they were in 2005–2006 — a 10% increase over the five-year period.

The CPI measures the cost of a representative consumer's market basket vis-à-vis a base year.

The CPI is calculated each month enabling the monthly, quarterly or annual rate of inflation to be calculated. However, there can be quite a lot of "noise" in the index from one month to the next. To smooth out any errors from month to month, the inflation rate is often presented as the rate for the preceding 12 months. For example, in June 2014 inflation may be given as the percent increase from July 2013. Each month a new month is added and the last month in the calculation is removed. Further smoothing is frequently provided by leaving out the prices of volatile items such as food and energy, although some would argue that the resulting measure of inflation is not very meaningful given that such items are important influences on what is happening to the cost of living.

It is important to observe that:

(1) The CPI includes only consumption goods and services. It does not include products bought by businesses, government and foreigners that are part of a country's GDP.
(2) The CPI is based on purchases of a representative consumer, and therefore may not reflect the price level facing many actual consumers.
(3) The CPI is based on a relatively infrequently revised market basket. It is based on goods and services available in the base-year, and consequently omits newer products and includes products no longer consumed.
(4) The CPI is based on past, not present, consumption patterns. This causes more than random errors in inflation estimates. Generally, quantities

of items consumed for which prices have gone up relatively rapidly will generally have been reduced, and so the market basket based on the base-year quantities will overstate the relative importance of these items. At the same time, quantities of items consumed for which prices have gone up relatively slowly will generally have been increased, and so the market basket which is based on base-year quantities will understate the relative importance of these items. With more rapid inflation items overstated, and slower inflation items understated, the inflation rate is systematically biased upwards. This bias is the result of the so-called **substitution effect**.

(5) The CPI may be distorted by quality changes. It is generally argued that the quality of products such as TVs and automobiles increases over time. If adjustments for general product quality increases are not made the inflation rate will be overstated. For example, if a family car costs more over time but is also safer, more comfortable, more economical, easier to maintain, more rust resistant and so on, we would not want to measure inflation simply from the price paid. In some sense, if the car price is 10% higher but the car is 8% better, inflation in the car's price is closer to 2% than 10%. Efforts have to be made to adjust for product quality.

(6) Over time the outlets from which shoppers source the products they want to buy are changing. Factory outlets and large box wholesalers have become more important over time relative to small, high street retail stores. Online shopping has also grown as buyers seek lower prices of standard products. This "outlet effect" also contributes to an overstatement of the cost of a basket that does not take account of the savings from such changes in shopping patterns.

Each of the above observations implies that the CPI is an *estimate* of the price level, and that therefore inflation computed from the rate of change of the CPI is an *estimate* of inflation.

Inflation is estimated from the rate of change of the CPI.

There is an alternative price index that can be used to calculate the rate of inflation which avoids some of the approximations and limitations we have listed, although it has limitations of its own. This alternative price index is based on the national income and product accounts, and is called the GDP Deflator, or more fully, the GDP Implicit Deflator.

GDP (Implicit) Deflator

The **GDP Deflator** is implicit in the measures of nominal GDP and real GDP. Specifically, the GDP (Implicit) Deflator is the GDP in the current year at current prices — the nominal GDP — divided by the GDP in the current year assessed at base-year prices — the real GDP. That is:

$$\text{GDP Deflator for current year} = \frac{\text{GDP in current year at current prices}}{\text{GDP in current year at base-year prices}}. \qquad (4.2)$$

For example, the GDP Deflator for 2010 compared to 2005–2006 is defined by:

$$\text{GDP Deflator for 2010} = \frac{\text{2010 GDP valued at 2010 prices}}{\text{2010 GDP valued at 2005–2006 prices}}.$$

Symbolically, the GDP Deflator can be written as:

$$P = \frac{\text{Nominal GDP}}{\text{Real GDP}} = \frac{Y}{Q}, \qquad (4.3)$$

where P is the GDP Deflator, Y is nominal GDP, and Q is real GDP. For example, if the nominal GDP in 2010 is $15.6 trillion and the real GDP in 2010 at 2005–2006 prices is $14.4 trillion, the GDP Deflator for 2010 with a 2005–2006 base-year is:

$$P = \frac{\text{Nominal GDP}}{\text{Real GDP}} = \frac{\$15.6 \text{ trillion}}{\$14.4 \text{ trillion}} = 1.0833.$$

If the price level had not increased, the GDP Deflator would have had a value of 1.0; it is conventional to present the CPI with a base of 100, and the GDP Deflator with a base of one. Instead, we find from our example that inflation has occurred, and that prices in general have risen from 2005–2006 to 2010 by 8.33%.

The GDP (Implicit) Deflation is the GDP in the current year — the nominal GDP — divided by the GDP in a base year — the real GDP.

As with the CPI, the annual rate of inflation is calculated from the GDP Deflator by taking the change in the Deflator from one year to the next, and multiplying by 100. Specifically:

GDP Deflator inflation during year t

$$= \frac{\text{Deflator for year } t - \text{Deflator for year } (t-1)}{\text{Deflator for year } (t-1)} \times 100. \quad (4.4)$$

The price level and rate of inflation calculated from the GDP Deflator are generally different from those calculated from the CPI because:

(1) The GDP Deflator includes not only consumer goods and services prices, but also the prices of goods and services that are exported, invested in plant and equipment, and are produced by the government.
(2) Because all goods and services are included there is no need to define a representative consumer, and therefore no need to take surveys to determine the market basket. Rather, the weights of different items are based on relative outputs in the GDP.
(3) The GDP Deflator considers prices only of goods and services currently being produced, and therefore excludes prices of used cars, existing houses, and so on. Used good prices are included in the CPI.
(4) The GDP Deflator uses *current* period weights, those in the current GDP. The CPI, on the other hand, uses *previous* period weights, those in the base-year market basket.

While the first three of these differences between the CPI and GDP Deflator could cause either of the indexes to increase more, the fourth difference works towards a higher inflation measure via the CPI than via the GDP Deflator. We have already mentioned the upward bias in the inflation estimate from the CPI from the substitution effect, but it is worth repeating.

Within any overall rate of inflation some prices change at a rate different from other prices. For example, during the years for which the same base-period basket of consumption is used, heating oil prices might go up by 25% while natural gas prices increase only 10%. Beef prices might increase by 40% while chicken prices increase by only 5%. Consumers adjust to these changes in relative prices by substituting more of the items that have become relatively cheaper for the ones that have become relatively expensive. For example, there would be a shift towards greater use of natural gas vis-à-vis oil. More chicken and less beef would be eaten.

As we have explained, in the construction of the CPI we persist in using the base-year market basket for several years. If, as in our example, the relative prices of oil and beef increase and people economize on these items vis-à-vis natural gas and chicken, the substitutions are not reflected in the CPI until the next revision of the market basket of the representative consumer. This might take 10 years! While the older weights are still being used, a larger volume of oil and beef are included in the market basket than is currently being purchased. By using a larger volume than we really should for items whose prices have risen relatively quickly we attach too much importance to the higher-inflation items. As a result, inflation estimates based on the CPI index tend to overstate inflation: the index "over-includes" the faster increasing prices. Furthermore, the CPI "under-includes" the items with relatively slower moving prices since more of these will currently be bought than is shown in the market basket. With the faster increasing prices given too much weight in the consumer's basket, and the slower moving prices given too little weight, inflation given from the CPI will exceed the "true" rate of inflation.

Inflation calculated from the CPI tends to overstate the true rate of inflation.

The GDP (Implicit) Deflator suffers from the reverse problem to that of the CPI. As can be seen by looking at the definition of the GDP Deflator in Eq. (4.2), it is computed using *current* quantities, those in the current GDP. The use of current quantities means that goods and services that have risen rapidly in price and which are therefore used sparingly are given relatively little weight. In a similar manner, items which have faced relatively little inflation and are therefore purchased extensively, receive relatively heavy weight. With relatively rapidly advancing prices under-represented and slower moving prices over-represented, the GDP Deflator understates the true rate of inflation.

Inflation calculated from the GDP Deflator tends to understate the true rate of inflation.

Since the CPI overestimates inflation, if wages are revised according to the CPI they will overcompensate for increases in the cost of living.

However, compensation according to the GDP Deflator will do the reverse, and be insufficient compensation for inflation.

The Producer Price Index

Another frequently quoted index is the **Producer Price Index**, which used to be called the **Wholesale Price Index**. This index calculates the prices of materials at the wholesale level, items which are inputs into final goods and services. While not directly relevant for consumers, the Producer Price Index gives an idea of what might happen later to the CPI when the inputs have been converted to products and sold at the retail level. For this reason, inflation in the Producer Price Index is often taken as an indicator of future inflation in the CPI. The method of calculation of the Producer Price Index is like that for the CPI, except that the importance attached to different items is based on volumes sold at the wholesale level, rather than the basket bought by a consumer.

The Producer Price Index measures prices at the wholesale level.

THE CAUSES OF INFLATION

Having shown how to measure inflation from the rate of change of any of several price indexes, we can turn to the question of what causes inflation. This is easier said than done because different theories of inflation have been in vogue at different times, and there has never been consensus on the cause of the problem. We shall look at two theories that have been the most prominent and have vied with each other for general acceptance. These two theories are the Monetarists' Theory and the Keynesians' Theory, with the latter taking its name from British economist, Lord John Maynard Keynes. However, since the Keynesian theory was devised as a theory of the GDP and national income rather than as a theory of inflation, we shall leave the Keynesian explanation of inflation until we deal with the determination of GDP and the national income in Chapter 6.

Before beginning here with the Monetarist's inflation theory we can note that the division of opinion over the two competing hypotheses has been so sharp that it has split many of the leading economists into two distinct camps. It is the rare individual who can venture into either camp and embrace aspects of both schools of thought, despite the fact that the truth almost certainly involves judicious selection of parts of each of the two theories.

The two main theories of inflation are the Monetarists' Theory and the Keynesians' Theory.

The Quantity Theory of Money

The Monetarist's theory of inflation enjoys a long history and is known as the **quantity theory of money**. Initially developed and advanced in the 18th century by the **Classical School**, most particularly by David Hume and John Stuart Mill, and developed further in the early 20th century by U.S. economist Irving Fisher, the quantity theory fell out of favor during the revolution of macroeconomics that followed the publication of the *General Theory* by Lord John Maynard Keynes.[3]

Revised by Milton Friedman at the University of Chicago and his **Chicago School**, the quantity theory has gained support from numerous economists, politicians, central bankers and corporate executives. Briefly stated, the quantity theory of money says that inflation is caused by "too much money chasing too few goods."

Intuitive View of the Quantity Theory

Imagine a small island with a remarkable tree. Upon this tree, each and every year grow 1,000 highly unusual and useful fruits. These fruits constitute the entire national output of the island, and can be eaten, burned as fuel, made into clothes and paper products, and so on. Let us imagine that on this island with its annual crop of 1,000 fruits there are 1,000 bills saying "This is one dollar." This $1,000 is the money supply. Let us also assume that for some reason or other, the dollars are used, on average, once each year.

If 1,000 fruits are sold each year, and the 1,000 one dollar bills are used on average once each year for making payments, then by definition the fruits must cost an average of one dollar each: how else can $1,000 be handed to the fruit growers, and 1,000 fruits exchanged in return! If the number of fruits produced and sold each year were to remain at 1,000, while the

---

[3]The *General Theory* is an abbreviation of the title of Keynes' book. The full title is *The General Theory of Employment, Interest and Money* (Macmillan and Co. Ltd., London, 1936).

number of one dollar bills doubled to 2,000, with these still changing hands on average once a year, the average price of a fruit would rise to two dollars each. This must be so because $2,000 is changing hands in one direction while 1,000 fruits change hands in the other direction. (Alternatively, we can think in terms of the 1,000 one-dollar bills being withdrawn and replaced with 1,000 two-dollar bills that change hands once each year.) We find that in this case, when the money supply is doubled the price level also doubles. Of course, it is crucial in this example both that the number of fruits remains at 1,000 per year, and that the average turnover rate of the one-dollar bills remains once each year, whatever the money supply may be.

According to the quantity theory of money, inflation is caused by too much money chasing too few goods.

In our example, it seems reasonable to think of the national product being determined by the physical constraint of the number and fertility of trees, so that the most questionable part of our example involves not the constancy of output, but the assumption that money continues to be used once each year even when the supply of money is doubled. The number of times money is used each year is called the **velocity of circulation of money**, and the nature of this velocity has become a focal point in the study of the validity of the quantity theory of money.

The critics of the quantity theory say that when, e.g., the money supply is doubled so there are twice as many dollar bills, the velocity could halve. Then, e.g., our 1,000 fruits would still sell for one dollar each even if 2,000 one dollar bills exist because only half of the dollars are used each year. On the other hand, proponents of the quantity theory argue that the velocity of circulation of money is determined by the nature of the financial system in which payments are made, and that the nature of the financial system changes slowly. This, claim the advocates of the quantity theory, causes the velocity of circulation to be reasonably predictable rather than a will-o'-the-wisp, moving this way and that to offset changes in the money supply. For simplicity, just think as the velocity being constant.[4] With velocity of

---

[4]It can be argued that the velocity of circulation of money does not have to be constant for the quantity theory to be valid. As we will explain later in this chapter, all that is needed is a stable and predictable velocity, one that can be explained by economic forces such as interest rates that influence the demand for money.

circulation of money being constant, prices move in proportion to the money supply. (If we take the view that the 1,000 one-dollar bills are withdrawn and replaced with 1,000 two-dollar bills, the idea that the velocity stays at once per year may be easier to accept. The money supply doubles, and with the velocity of circulation of money still one time per year, so do fruit prices.)

> *The velocity of circulation of money is the average number of times money is used each year. Monetarists believe this velocity is reasonably predictable.*

The Quantity Theory Derived

The quantity theory can be derived from the **quantity equation of exchange**. The quantity equation of exchange relates the money supply to the value of transactions according to:

$$M \cdot V_T \equiv T, \qquad (4.5)$$

where M = money supply, T = value of transactions, V_T = transactions velocity of circulation of money.

The value of transactions includes all payments occurring in the economy, not just those made for final goods and services. For example, buying and selling of stocks and bonds, payments of wages and salaries, used cars, and taxes are all part of transactions. Equation (4.5) says that the amount of money multiplied by the number of times it is used during any period is the value of transactions occurring in that period. This is true as a matter of definition, which is why we use the identity sign, "$\equiv$" in Eq. (4.5); transactions velocity is defined as the value of transactions divided by the amount of money, i.e., $V_T \equiv T/M$, which is just a rearrangement of Eq. (4.5). For example, if there are \$1,000 of transactions during a year and only \$200 of money being used to facilitate these \$1,000 of transactions, on average each dollar must be used 5 times per year.

In reality, statistics on the value of transactions are difficult, if not nearly impossible to obtain. The measure that is available that corresponds most closely to total transactions is the GDP which records final output, or value added. If we replace the term T with the nominal GDP, Y, then we have from Eq. (4.5):

$$M \cdot V \equiv Y, \qquad (4.6)$$

where V is a different velocity than before, and is the *income* **velocity of circulation of money** rather than the *transactions* **velocity of circulation of money**. The income velocity is the average number of times money is used in the course of generating the nominal gross domestic product. For example, if the annual GDP is $500 and the money supply is $200, the income velocity is 2.5 per year.

Using the GDP in place of transactions does not make the quantity equation into a theory as long as we continue to define the velocity — in this case the income velocity — in terms of the other variables in the equation, i.e. Y/M. In order to move to a theory, we must determine V from outside the quantity equation of exchange, and the most straightforward way of doing this, among the many ways it can be done, is to assume V is constant.[5] We then have a theory, the quantity theory of money, which we can write as:

$$M \cdot V = Y. \qquad (4.7)$$

Equation (4.7), with V being assumed constant, is a theory that can be checked against the data: is $V = Y/M$ a constant?

If we refer back to the definition of the GDP Deflator in Eq. (4.3) we find:

$$P \equiv \frac{Y}{Q},$$

which can be rearranged into:

$$Y \equiv P \cdot Q.$$

This states that the nominal GDP is the price index, P, in the form of the GDP Deflator, multiplied by the real GDP, Q. If we use this in Eq. (4.7) we have another popular form of the quantity theory:

$$M \cdot V = P \cdot Q. \qquad (4.8)$$

In this form the quantity theory can be turned into a theory of inflation.

The quantity theory of money can be written as $M \cdot V = P \cdot Q$.

---

[5]An insightful view of velocity is described in Example 4.1. This indicates that even non-economic variables outside the quantity equation might affect velocity — such as the weather!

Since inflation is the rate at which the price level, P, is changing, to turn Eq. (4.8) into a theory of inflation we must examine how P is changing. Writing $\%\Delta M$, $\%\Delta Q$ and $\%\Delta P$ as the percentage changes respectively in M, Q, and P, and assuming V is constant so that $\%\Delta V = 0$, we can state Eq. (4.8) in percentage terms as:

$$\%\Delta M = \%\Delta P + \%\Delta Q,$$

or

$$\%\Delta P = \%\Delta M - \%\Delta Q. \qquad (4.9)$$

Equation (4.9) tells us that $\%\Delta P$, the rate of inflation, equals the rate of change of the money supply, $\%\Delta M$, minus the rate of change of real GDP, $\%\Delta Q$. According to Eq. (4.9), inflation occurs if the money supply is growing more rapidly than real output, and this explains why inflation has been attributed to "too much money chasing too few goods."

If we assume output growth is determined by the rate of change of technology and the supply of factors of production, we can take $\%\Delta Q$ as given.[6] We can then conclude from the quantity theory in Eq. (4.9) that variations in inflation, $\%\Delta P$, result from variations in the growth rate of the money supply, $\%\Delta M$. Since the amount of money in circulation can be influenced by the Federal Reserve System, according to the Monetarists, it is the Fed which determines the rate of inflation.

Example 4.1. A Fast Lesson in Velocity

The quantity equation makes it clear that a doubling of the money supply has the same effect on nominal GDP, which we have written as Y, as does a doubling of the velocity of circulation of money. This follows because it is the product of M and V that appears in the quantity equation, and so either has the same effect on the other side of the equation, i.e., Y. Sir Denis H. Robertson has offered a delightful demonstration of this symmetry between money supply and velocity. His story was adapted from an earlier and lengthier account by F.Y. Edgeworth (*Economic Journal*, 1919).

---

[6]Since neither technology nor factor supplies are affected by $\%\Delta M$, we can take $\%\Delta Q$ as given when considering the effects of variations in $\%\Delta M$.

"Here is a little story to illustrate this conception of the velocity of circulation of money. On Derby Day two men, Bob and Joe, invested in a barrel of beer, and set off to Epsom with the intention of selling it retail on the racecourse at sixpence a pint, the proceeds to be shared equally between them. On the way Bob, who had one threepenny-bit left in the world, began to feel a great thirst, and drank a pint of beer, paying Joe threepence as his share of the market price. A little later Joe yielded to the same desire, and drank a pint of beer, returning the threepence to Bob. The day was hot, and before long Bob was thirsty again, and so, a little later, was Joe. When they arrived at Epsom the threepence was back in Bob's pocket, and each had discharged in full his debts to the other: but the beer was all gone. One single threepenny-bit had performed a volume of transactions which would have required many shillings if the beer had been sold to the public in accordance with the original intention."

The threepence in this story is sufficient for all the transactions that occur in the mini-economy consisting of trade between Bob and Joe. It makes it clear that it is not just the quantity of money in existence that matters, but also the velocity at which it circulates. In turn, the velocity of circulation is affected by the willingness to demand money to hold versus the desire to spend it. The burning thirsts of Bob and Joe led to a burning desire to spend the threepence, therefore making the threepence a sufficient supply of liquidity for the trade between them. If just one of them had pocketed the money and not put it back into circulation the transactions would immediately have stopped — at least until they had reached their destination.

Source: Sir Denis H. Robertson, *Money* (University of Chicago Press, Chicago, 1959) p. 27.

According to the quantity theory of money, inflation is caused by the central bank allowing the money supply to grow more rapidly than real output, or GDP.

Before we leave the Monetarists' theory of inflation we should say a little more about how the quantity theory of money has been developed into a theory of the demand for money. This is important because it is in the form of a demand for money function that the quantity theory has most intensively been subjected to empirical examination.

The Quantity Theory as a Demand for Money

We can re-write the quantity theory in Eq. (4.8) as:

$$\frac{M}{P} = \frac{1}{V} \cdot Q \qquad (4.10)$$

The M in Eq. (4.10) can be interpreted as the amount of money people **want** to hold. That is, we can interpret M as the quantity of money **demanded** in an economy. Since P "deflates" M by the price of the basket of goods and services people buy, M/P can be interpreted as the **real** demand for money. (The conversion of nominal magnitudes to real magnitudes is always achieved by dividing nominal magnitudes by P. For example, since from Eq. (4.3), Q = Y/P, real GDP, Q, is found by dividing nominal GDP, Y, by the price level, P.) Therefore, Eq. (4.10) states that, assuming V is constant, the real buying power people want to hold as money is a constant proportion or multiple of real national income, or real GDP. (If V is constant, M/P varies only with the real GDP, Q.) An important implication of Eq. (4.10) is that if real GDP was to remain constant while the price level, P, doubled, people would demand twice the nominal money holdings, M. If we give this conclusion a moment of thought, we will see it makes good sense for the nominal demand for money to vary in proportion to the price level.

We hold money to make payments as needed. Money gives us the liquidity that allows us to avoid having to sell assets like bonds or stocks in order to make purchases. If the newspaper costs 50 cents, lunch costs $5, and so on, we might leave home in the morning with (say) $20 of money in our pocketbooks to meet both predictable and unpredictable needs. However, if suddenly newspapers increase in price to $1, lunches to $10 and so on, i.e., prices double, we would want to leave home in the morning with twice as much nominal money; it would take twice as much nominal money to have the same real buying power.

Ceteris paribus, the demand for nominal money holdings varies in proportion to the price level.

Equation (4.10) makes the extreme assumption that the real demand for money, M/P, is a constant proportion, 1/V, of real GNP, Q. The quantity theory as refined in the 20th century by Milton Friedman often takes a more moderate form in which velocity is not assumed constant. Rather, money demand is assumed to depend on interest rates and other factors that affect the opportunity cost of holding money (i.e., what is given up by holding money). As interest rates rise, the real demand for money is assumed to decline. If we can predict by how much interest rates affect money demand we can still use the quantity theory to explain inflation. Let us do this by considering the quantity theory in terms of money supply versus money demand.

Money Supply versus Money Demand

The quantity of money supplied and the quantity of money demanded must be equal for equilibrium to hold; as with everything else, equilibrium requires that quantity supplied equals quantity demanded. Let us consider how equilibrium is achieved, by assuming that the supply of and demand for money are initially equal — people are happy with the amount of money they are holding — and then there is a sudden 10% increase in the money supply. If the quantity of money supplied and demanded were equal before the supply of money was increased, the supply of money will exceed the demand for money after the increase: there is an excess supply of money. An excess supply of money means the public is holding money it does not want to hold; for the current rate of spending, the public would prefer to hold less than it is holding. (People can have too much money, not too much income. Too much money means they would rather hold less of their wealth as money and more of their wealth as earning assets such as bonds.) Two ways the public can attempt to get rid of the excess supply of money are on the one hand to buy more goods and services, and on the other hand to invest in bonds.[7] To the extent the money is used to buy more goods

---

[7]We say that the public will "attempt" to get rid of the unwanted money, because each individual can reduce money holdings only by transferring money to somebody else. In this sense, money is like the "hot potato" in the game of that name; somebody ends up holding it.

and services it will push up prices of goods and services via the increased demand. To the extent the money is used to buy bonds it will increase bond prices and lower **yields**.[8]

Let us consider first the buying of goods and services with the excess supply of money. *If* prices of goods and services were to increase 10% from the assumed 10% increase in the money supply, the quantity of money demanded would again equal the quantity supplied. This is because, as we have said, the demand of money varies in proportion to the price level. Therefore, *if* prices increase 10% from a 10% increase in the money supply, the quantity of money demanded would again equal the quantity supplied, and we have the quantity theory prediction of prices increasing by the rate of change in the money supply. Indeed, we have provided a mechanism for the quantity theory to work, namely via the actions of the public spending the excess supply of money on goods and services. But what is the effect of the excess supply of money working via buying more bonds and thereby reducing bond yields?

Lower bond yields following an increase in the money supply mean the opportunity cost of holding money is reduced; the opportunity cost of money is what could have been earned by holding bonds. This increases the quantity of money demanded towards the increased supply. The greater the influence of lower bond yields on the quantity of money demanded, the greater will be the extent to which restoration of money demand with the increased money supply will occur via lower bond yields rather than via higher prices of goods and services. Only if the demand for money does not increase at all as the opportunity cost of holding money declines do we need prices to increase by the full percent increase in the money supply.

Equilibrium between the quantity of money supplied and demanded can be restored by changes in the price level and by changes in bond yields.

---

[8]Yield is the percent return earned by holding a bond, and the reason increased bond prices reduce yields can be seen by example. Suppose an investor can buy a bond that offers $10 per year of interest on each $100 face value of bond, a yield of 10%, when suddenly bond prices increase from $100 to $110. Then the $10 of interest each year on the original investment is received on a bond with a market value of $110, a yield of only 9%.

Cost-Push versus Demand-Pull Inflation

Accommodation of Higher Wages: When we view the quantity theory from the perspective of money holders responding to changes in the money supply, we see inflation is the result of extra *demand* for goods and services. For this reason the quantity theory is a **demand-pull** explanation of inflation. But can the quantity theory also explain what is referred to as **cost-push inflation**? This is inflation caused by increases in wages and other costs of production which force up final product prices. Does the quantity theory's demand-pull flavor mean that Monetarists reject the view that inflation is sometimes caused by cost increases?

Cost-push inflation is often attributed to the effect of trade unions on wages. It is argued that increases in wages increase production costs and cause firms to increase prices. It is sometimes further argued that inflation can become self-perpetuating if the increase in prices causes trade unions to again demand higher wages to compensate for the increase in the cost of living. If wages again rise, so do prices, then wages, and so on, and we have the roots of inflation. How does a Monetarist respond to this reasoning that, at least on the surface, might appear to make sense?

> *The quantity theory of money is a demand-pull explanation of inflation. Cost-push inflation is caused by increases in production costs that are passed on in higher product prices.*

According to Monetarists, the problem with our foregoing description of cost-push inflation is that it does not tell us how continually rising wages and prices can be sustained. If the money supply is constant and the velocity of circulation of money is not continually expanding, it is not possible to pay continuously rising prices and wages, which is what we mean by inflation. Only if the cost-push inflation induces the central bank to repeatedly expand the money supply, or if the velocity of circulation is rising, can the cost-push explanation be valid for *sustained* inflation? So, might the central bank allow the money supply to continuously be expanded? It might if wage increases lead to rising unemployment. As we will explain in the next chapter, unemployment could occur if unions succeed in raising wages to above market-clearing levels; at higher wages but with the same prices of products, the quantity of labor demanded may decline relative to labor supply, which means higher unemployment. The increase in unemployment may induce the central bank to expand the money supply in an attempt to create jobs. If this happens the central bank has allowed itself to **accommodate** the original cause of inflation. Nevertheless, for *sustained* rising prices, this cycle of wage increases, followed by rising unemployment, followed by money supply increases, followed by rising prices, must continue *ad nauseam.*

Accommodation of Higher Energy Prices: When energy prices go up the immediate effect is inflationary since it means increased prices for gasoline, heating oil, and items requiring energy to produce, and these higher prices appear in indices used to measure inflation. However, if there is no more money in circulation and peoples' incomes remain unchanged, the need to pay more for energy reduces the ability to buy other products. For example, if gasoline and heating bills increase from $200 to $250 a month there is a reduction of $50 in income available for eating out, paying the rent, and so on. This will lower demand outside the energy sector and reduce prices there. This will offset the inflation in energy prices with no *long-term* effect on the overall price level. However, if the inability to buy other products causes job-losses in the non-energy sector, the central bank might increase the money supply to help maintain demand and prevent lay-offs. Unemployment from an energy price increase might in this way be avoided, but at the expense of accommodating the inflation triggered by higher energy prices.

Sustained cost-push inflation requires accommodation by the central bank.

How Bad Can Inflation Become?

The situation where inflation is completely out of hand is called **hyperinflation**, or sometimes, **galloping inflation**. Unlike the cause of small or moderate inflation about which there are at least two schools of thought (the Monetarists whose views we have given, and the Keynesians whose views await our account of the GDP and national income), when it comes to hyperinflation virtually all economists are Monetarists in that they agree that it is the result of printing more and more money.

Statistics on hyperinflation are stunning. For example, in Germany in November 1923, prices were 755,700 *million* times higher than in 1913. It cost many million Reichsbank marks merely to send a letter in the mail, and many postage stamp collectors have the evidence in their stamp albums. Inflation in Hungary reached the point where it took approximately 40 million paper pengos to buy a U.S. cent. Indeed, the 1931 Hungarian gold pengo, which was at that time worth one paper pengo, had by June 1946 become worth 13,000,000,000,000,000,000,000 paper pengos. Notes were circulated with a face value of 100,000,000,000,000,000,000 pengos. Larger and larger denominations merely required a different arrangement of ink. Unfortunately for those who suffered these hyperinflations, there was no shortage of ink for printing the many zeroes on the notes.

Extremely rapid inflation in the hundreds or thousands of percent per annum is called hyperinflation.

Hyperinflation was so bad at certain times in Hungary and Germany that people were paid at lunch time so they could shop before evening. Some people even joked that they would buy two beers each time they went to the bar because the beer deteriorated more slowly than did the money!

Hyperinflation has not been limited to short periods in certain European countries. For example, at the tail end of the 20th century inflation in Zimbabwe topped out at 5,000,000,000,000,000,000,000,000%. Yes, that is, 5 followed by 21 zeros. Bolivia, Brazil and other South American countries have experienced inflation of over a thousand percent per annum, with some very costly consequences. During hyperinflation the use of the country's paper money tends to be abandoned as people demand other items for settling financial obligations. The alternative media of exchange have included relatively stable external currencies such as the U.S. dollar in Latin America and in Israel, commodity monies such as gold and silver, and valued items such as cognac, wine and flour. Barter also becomes common. As we have seen in the previous chapter, barter is very inefficient. The beauty of paper money is that it is cheap to produce, and yet can serve to avoid the double coincidence of wants, serve as a unit of account, and so on — provided it is generally accepted. When we resort to barter we give up the gains from having a generally accepted medium of exchange. Resources are also wasted when there is hyperinflation with individuals and corporations devoting time to managing money so as to minimize the amount held and thereby minimize the damage done to buying power. In some hyperinflation countries people have held numerous credit card accounts and would use the one with the latest settlement date. Of course, shopkeepers would suspect this and hence charge a higher price for credit card purchases.

Hyperinflation can cause an abandonment of money, and a resort to barter, which is inefficient.

Hyperinflation cannot continue without vast quantities of money being added to the money supply; it cannot take more and more money to buy a loaf of bread without there being more and more money in circulation. It is therefore difficult not to agree with the Monetarists that hyperinflation is the result of an extremely rapid expansion of the money supply. Furthermore, the inflationary effects of a money supply expansion are augmented by an induced acceleration in the velocity of circulation of money. What happens is that when inflation from money supply expansion becomes widely recognized, people choose to spend the money they receive more quickly: the longer they hold onto it the more value it loses. The quicker people dispose of the money the more rapidly it circulates, i.e., the faster is its velocity of circulation. That is, money supply growth and velocity of circulation of money growth are positively connected.

INFLATION AS A HIDDEN TAX

Taxing by "Printing" Money

If hyperinflation means resort to the inefficiencies of commodity monies and barter, why has any country allowed it to occur? The answer is that inflation is a "tax" that can be applied when other taxes cannot be collected as, e.g., during or just after a war.

In order to see why inflation is a tax, we can consider two examples. While the examples do not involve governments, they immediately suggest why governments use the inflation tax.

An Englishman on Vacation: Here is the background: An honest and upright Englishman has for decades vacationed on the same Aegean island, paying for most of what he buys with checks. The islanders have become so confident in the soundness of the checks that they accept them from each other. Indeed, the checks circulate on the island alongside the island's own money, and are never returned to England for payment. Who pays for the Englishman's vacation?

Some people are tempted to answer that those who pay are the last ones accepting the Englishman's checks. This is incorrect because they too can spend the checks as long as the checks remain generally acceptable. The answer is that all the islanders pay. Clearly this is so because the Englishman does not pay, and the goods and services he consumes must come from somewhere.[9] The islanders pay by giving the Englishman the implicit power to "print" money. The "money" increases the island's price level, thereby reducing the buying power of the island's own money. (The higher prices can be rationalized via the quantity theory of money.) The holders of the island's own money therefore pay for the Englishman's vacation via a hidden "inflation tax." That is, the inflation applies a "tax" on the island's own money: it reduces how much the island's money will buy. For example, if the Englishman's checks allow him to consume 1% of the island's products, the island's own money buys 1% less. This is achieved by prices rising 1%. (Note that as well as assuming the production of goods and services in unaffected by the extra money in circulation — by employment being unchanged — we are also assuming the velocity of circulation of money is unaffected. If, on the other hand, the velocity of circulation of the island's money was to decline, offsetting the extra money supply, prices would not increase. In a sense he would be replacing the island's money rather than adding to it.)

Counterfeit Notes: Another revealing application of inflation as a tax concerns the effect of counterfeit bills. Suppose that someone has cleverly but deviously found a means to manufacture extremely realistic $20 bills. Suppose this person enjoys a fine time with the phony bills, eating great meals, enjoying an indefinite vacation, fine clothes, good wine, unlimited travel and expensive entertainment. Who is paying for the counterfeiter's pleasure? Furthermore, what is the economic mechanism that results in them paying?

It should be obvious that somebody pays for what the counterfeiter enjoys because if there is no change in employment and the economy's

---

[9]As explained later, if there is unemployment that is somehow reduced because of the Englishman's checks there would be a larger output. The Englishman would then consume the islanders' goods and services without correspondingly reducing the goods and services available for the islanders to consume.

output, more goods and services consumed by the counterfeiter means fewer goods and services for others to buy. The people who pay the tax from counterfeit money are those holding the genuine money. They pay because the addition to the supply of money from the counterfeit notes raises prices (e.g., as in the quantity theory of money) and thereby reduces the purchasing power of the genuine money.

The extent to which the legal money will buy fewer goods is the extent to which the inflation tax is paid. The amount of tax equals the amount of goods and services consumed by the counterfeiter because in real terms this is what is given up by others. We should note that those who pay the inflation tax are not only those who accept the phony money, because they in turn may use them in making purchases. It is everybody who hold genuine money that pays.

What is illegal for counterfeiters who collect "taxes" via printing money, is legal for central banks whose new money reduces the buying power of pre-existing money. By using the inflation tax governments can reduce the complaints that accompany income and sales taxes.

Those holding money are taxed by inflation, the proceeds going to those who provide the new money.

The Inflation Tax in Reverse

During the 19th century, many of America's industrial barons became outrageously wealthy and showed off their affluence by lighting cigars with $20 bills at extravagant, ostentatious events. Were these so-called robber barons destroying anything of value? The answer is clearly "no." All they burned were pieces of paper and nothing more; they were not destroying bread or clothes or anything of value in and of itself. In fact, when the robber barons set fire to money they were actually being generous. We should explain this rather surprising statement because it helps make clear the nature of money as having no value in and of itself.

When robber barons lit cigars with $20 bills they reduced the money supply. They also reduced their own ability to buy bread, clothes, more cigars, comfortable dinner parties, and so on. But what happened to the $20 of bread, clothes, and so on, that the robber barons denied themselves by their demonstration of affluence? To the extent these items were already produced they were made available for others to purchase, where these others were in general poorer. Prices were therefore reduced until the "liberated" items were sold. The lower prices follow from the quantity theory of money; the reduced money supply reduces the price level. In other words, by lighting cigars with $20 bills the robber barons were making $20 of goods available to poorer people via a reduced price level resulting from a reduced money supply: deflation rewards those holding money by increasing how much it will buy.[10] Money lost or destroyed by any means makes money holders richer, and those no longer with the money correspondingly poorer.

When people stuff dollar bills into their mattresses and leave them there, others make gains at the money hoarders' expense. Similarly, when foreigners use U.S. dollars for day-to-day purposes rather than use their own local monies, the American public gains by enjoying the products foreigners sold to acquire dollars, paying only with paper which does not return to the United States.

Inflation taxes holders of money, deflation rewards holders of money.

GAINERS AND LOSERS FROM INFLATION

People often talk as if everybody loses from inflation. A common view is that if prices did not increase, wages and salaries would nevertheless increase at their old rate, and incomes would buy more. This view is clearly false. If prices were not increasing, wages would not increase so rapidly. Wages might well go up because of increases in real incomes facilitated by advances in productivity and real GDP, but with stable prices, wage increases are limited to the real growth rate of national income and output.

A more accurate view of inflation suggests there are many who make substantial gains as well as many who lose. Indeed, the gains of some people are the losses of others. It is instructive to examine the major categories of gainers and losers. We begin by making an important distinction between anticipated and unanticipated inflation because the effects of inflation depend on the extent to which it was anticipated.

---

[10]When money is given away rather than burnt the gainers are the recipients, rather than all holders of money. Therefore, it is the distribution of gains rather than the size of gains that differs.

Anticipated versus Unanticipated Inflation

At any particular time, people hold a view about what the rate of inflation will be for the next year, or perhaps the next decade. While different people hold different anticipations, we can usefully assume there is some rate we can call the public's average anticipated rate of inflation.

The realized rate of inflation, i.e., the rate that actually occurs, could well be higher or lower than what the public had anticipated. The difference between the realized inflation and the anticipated inflation is **unanticipated inflation**, and this could equally be positive or negative as anticipations turn out to have been too low or too high.

> *Unanticipated inflation is the difference between expected and realized inflation. This difference can be positive or negative.*

Effects of Anticipated Inflation

In order to see the effects of anticipated inflation, let us suppose that by careful economic policies inflation has been zero, and that suddenly because of external factors, the public widely begins to expect inflation. Let us consider what this would do to wages and interest rates, and hence to those earning or paying wages, or earning or paying interest.

Wages and Anticipated Inflation: Wages are negotiated for future periods of time, perhaps for the upcoming year or next couple of years. When inflation is anticipated during the period of time for which wages are set, workers will bargain for higher wages to compensate for the anticipated higher prices. If they succeed they are not hurt by anticipated inflation. However, would we expect workers to obtain wages that increase at the anticipated rate of inflation?

An average employer should realize that paying wages that increase by the anticipated rate of inflation does not reduce expected profits if the prices of what they are producing are expected to increase at the same rate.[11] Therefore, we would expect employers to agree to pay wages that

---

[11] We refer to an "average employer" because individual employers care about the prices of the specific products that they sell versus the costs of producing these products. Workers, on the other hand, are concerned with the prices of a basket of goods.

reflect the anticipated rate of inflation; they would not be thrilled by this, but competition for labor will force it. Then, if the realized actual inflation is the same as was anticipated, wage earners do not gain or lose in real, buying-power terms. Similarly, employers on average do not gain or lose in real terms. There is, therefore, no real effect on wage earners or employers of anticipated inflation.

There should be no real effects on wage earners or employers if realized inflation is as anticipated.

Gains and losses from inflation occur when the actual, realized inflation is higher or lower than had been widely expected. Specifically, when inflation turns out to be higher than expected employers on average gain and workers lose. On the other hand, when inflation is lower than anticipated, workers gain and employers lose. The relevance of these effects depends on the size of the error in inflation predictions and on the length of contracts. If there were no wage contracts so that wages could be immediately revised as inflation is realized then there would be no gains or losses from unanticipated inflation. Also, many labor contracts contain a **cost-of-living adjustment (COLA)** clause which automatically results in higher wage rates when prices go up, whether the inflation was anticipated or not. In the presence of COLA clauses, workers do not lose and employers do not gain even from unanticipated inflation.

According to economists who believe people's expectations are "rational," unanticipated **disinflation** — inflation lower than was anticipated — is as likely as unanticipated inflation. As we shall see in the next chapter, by definition, "rational expectations" are those that consider all the relevant facts. People who consider all relevant facts are unlikely to consistently overestimate or to consistently underestimate inflation. This is not to say they make no mistakes. Rather, it says that the errors in forecasts by rational people are random, with an average forecasting error of zero.

Unanticipated inflation, where inflation is higher than expected, shifts buying power from those earning wages to those earning profits. Unanticipated disinflation, where inflation is lower than expected, causes the reverse shift in buying power.

Interest Rates and Anticipated Inflation: Anticipated inflation should not affect lenders or borrowers. In order to explain this, let us assume lenders have been earning 4% interest when anticipated inflation has been zero. A jump in anticipated inflation to say, 6% would reduce lending unless interest rates increased to 10%. This is because with 6% inflation, lenders need $106 after a year to buy what $100 would buy today, and only if they received back $110 on each $100 would they expect to earn 4% after adjusting for inflation. The 4% lenders expect to earn after inflation is called the **real interest rate**. If the **nominal** or **market interest rate** — the actual rate that lenders receive — does compensate them for anticipated inflation, then we can write:

$$\text{Nominal interest rate} = \text{Real interest rate} + \text{Anticipated inflation.}$$
$$(4.11)$$

That is, the nominal interest rate observed in the market is the real interest rate plus anticipated inflation. Alternatively, we can think of the real interest rate as the nominal interest rate minus anticipated inflation.

> *The nominal or market interest rate is the rate observed in the market. The real interest rate is the nominal interest rate minus anticipated inflation.*

The connection between nominal interest rates and anticipated inflation in Eq. (4.11) seems well-founded when we consider the interest rate that would be demanded by lenders in the face of anticipated inflation. However, in order to argue that nominal interest rates compensate for anticipated inflation, we must also ask if borrowers would be willing to pay higher interest rates.

What is purchased with borrowed funds, such as houses, new capital equipment and so on, should produce benefits in the form of increased expected future profits or market values that reflect anticipated inflation. In our example, if borrowers pay a 10% interest rate when houses or machines purchased with borrowed funds are expected to increase in market value by 6% per year, or to produce higher future profits worth 6% more per year, the *real* borrowing cost is only 4 (or $10 - 6$) %. This is the same real borrowing cost we assumed with 0% anticipated inflation. Therefore, borrowers should be prepared to pay nominal interest rates that reflect anticipated inflation. With borrowers willing to pay what lenders demand, nominal interest rates should reflect anticipated inflation. Consequently, there are no gains or losses if actual inflation is as anticipated.

Market interest rates compensate for anticipated inflation. Consequently, there should be no gains or losses of lenders versus borrowers from correctly anticipated inflation.

Unanticipated Inflation and Lenders versus Borrowers: When inflation is faster than anticipated, interest rates under-compensate lenders for the actual increase in prices that occurs. This is because, as seen from Eq. (4.11), only anticipated inflation is reflected in interest rates received by lenders and paid by borrowers. Consequently, unanticipated inflation makes lenders worse off than they expected, and makes borrowers better off than expected. The lenders lose because what they receive back buys fewer goods and services than they expected. The borrowers gain because they find themselves making interest payments which in terms of real buying power, are lower than they had expected. We find that unanticipated inflation rewards borrowers at the expense of lenders.

Since borrowers are **debtors** and lenders are **creditors**, the conclusion is sometimes alternatively stated that unanticipated inflation rewards debtors and penalizes creditors; see Example 4.2. Similarly, unanticipated disinflation, i.e., inflation that is smaller than expected and which means interest rates overcompensate lenders, rewards creditors and penalizes debtors.

Example 4.2. Inflation and the Balance Sheet

Inflation redistributes income and wealth. The following explains how this is related to the extent to which nominal interest rates reflect inflation.

"Inflation has many effects, but most discussed are its effects on the distribution of income and wealth. If inflation were fully and correctly anticipated, nominal interest rates on fixed claim assets would adjust to compensate for the declining purchasing power of the principal. Generally, however, interest rates have not completely compensated for inflation. As a result, periods of inflation have been accompanied by arbitrary transfers of real net worth from net monetary creditors to net monetary debtors when inflation is accelerating, or vice versa when it is decelerating.

The key factors in determining whether economic units will benefit from, or be harmed by, inflation are (1) whether the inflation is anticipated and (2) whether the economic units are net monetary creditors. Net monetary creditors are harmed by unanticipated inflation because the purchasing power of their monetary assets declines more than the real value of their monetary liabilities. Similarly, net monetary debtors benefit from unanticipated inflation. These effects take place without any action on the part of the economic unit and represent a passive redistribution of wealth.

Even if inflation is anticipated and reflected in nominal interest rates, added uncertainty about future prices can affect economic decisions. As a result, economic units will attempt to redistribute their assets for protection from inflation."

Source: Keith Carlson, "The U.S. Balance Sheet. What is it and What Does it Tell Us?" *Review*, Federal Reserve Bank of St. Louis, September–October 1991, p. 15.

Unanticipated inflation benefits debtors and penalizes creditors, while unanticipated disinflation benefits creditors and penalizes debtors.

The biggest debtor in most countries is the government which owes the national debt — the outstanding value of government borrowing from the public. It is therefore the government that gains most from inflation being faster than anticipated. The government gains because inflation reduces the real value of the debt. If the government gains so do taxpayers taken as a whole. This is because it is they who, in general, have to pay taxes to cover interest on outstanding debt. Therefore, we reach the conclusion that unanticipated inflation that hurts the holders of government debt, that is government bond holders, helps taxpayers. This fits the general conclusion reached above in that bondholders are creditors and taxpayers are indirectly debtors. That is, we again find unanticipated inflation redistributing wealth from creditors to debtors.

After the government the next most important group of debtors are the corporations. Corporations are debtors to the extent they have sold bonds or borrowed from banks. When corporations gain from unanticipated inflation the gains are really those of the shareholders, who are the owners of corporations. Therefore, with corporate debt the redistribution is between shareholders and bondholders, with unanticipated inflation favoring shareholders at the expense of bondholders and banks.

It is not only the big institutions, the government and corporations, which gain when inflation is faster than expected. Any debtor gains, including the many homeowners who have incurred mortgages. During the term of mortgages while interest rates are fixed, unanticipated inflation makes the value of houses increase more than what was expected, but leaves mortgage payments unchanged. Homeowners therefore gain from unanticipated inflation. The sizes of homeowners' gains are larger, the longer the period of mortgage over which interest rates are fixed. It is only with mortgages on which interest rates are continuously revised — called **flexible** or **adjustable rate mortgages** — that homeowners do not gain. Of course, what homeowners gain the providers of the mortgage funds lose, because the interest they receive does not compensate for the declining buying power of the mortgage principal. The creditors in the case of mortgages include banks, savings and loan associations, pension funds and insurance companies.

> *Unanticipated inflation hurts holders of government bonds and helps taxpayers. It also hurts holders of corporate bonds and helps shareholders, hurts issuers of mortgages and helps homeowners, and more generally redistributes wealth from creditors to debtors.*

Inflation Anticipations, Fixed Incomes and Uncertainty

The people most frequently identified in popular discussions as losing from inflation are those on fixed incomes, such as pensioners who depend on private savings and/or social security. It should be clear from what we have said that to the extent that anticipated inflation is compensated for in interest rates on retirement savings, it is only unanticipated inflation which reduces pensioners' real incomes. Furthermore, even unanticipated inflation should not lower the buying power of social security receipts which are **indexed** to inflation. (Inflation indexing means that social security checks are increased more-or-less in line with increases in the price level.) We therefore find that it is only unanticipated inflation that is likely to hurt those on fixed incomes, and their losses are likely to be made only on interest income on private savings, not on social security.

There is, however, a sense in which we are all hurt by inflation. This is because **uncertainty** about the rate of inflation can dampen confidence and thereby reduce investment and the rate of economic growth. Uncertainty results from not knowing whether inflation will be faster or slower than is currently expected. Some of the cost of uncertainty about inflation comes in the form of higher unemployment which we turn to next.

SUMMARY

(1) Inflation is the rate at which prices in general are increasing.

(2) The Consumer Price Index (CPI) measures prices in general from the cost of a market basket bought by a representative urban household. This basket is determined by surveys of consumers, and is periodically revised to reflect changing buying patterns.

(3) The GDP (Implicit) Deflator measures prices in general by including items according to their importance in the current gross domestic product. The GDP Deflator is derived by taking the ratio of the gross domestic product valued at current prices — the nominal GDP — to the gross domestic product valued at base-period prices — the real GDP.

(4) The CPI tends to overstate inflation because it does not allow for substitutions consumers make towards products that have become relatively cheaper than when the basket was being defined. Therefore, the CPI attaches too much weight to items that have increased relatively rapidly in price, and too little weight to items that have increased relatively slowly in price.

(5) The GDP Deflator tends to understate inflation.

(6) The quantity theory of money attributes inflation to "too much money chasing too few goods."

(7) The quantity theory of money can be cast as a theory of the demand for money. Increases in the money supply cause an excess supply of money that raises prices or lowers interest rates, thereby increasing the money demand to match the increase in the money supply.

(8) The quantity theory is a demand-pull explanation of inflation. Cost-push inflation, which is inflation due to increases in wages or in energy costs, can be sustained only if it is accommodated by monetary authorities.

(9) Hyperinflation can occur only from very rapid expansion of the money supply, and is likely to be observed when other means of collecting taxes have become infeasible. This is because inflation is a hidden tax, enabling those with the power to "print" money to enjoy goods and services at the expense of others.

(10) To the extent that anticipated inflation is built into interest rates and wages, it will cause little redistribution of buying power.

(11) Unanticipated inflation favors debtors at the expense of creditors, and employers at the expense of workers. Unanticipated disinflation favors creditors at the expense of debtors, and workers at the expense of employers.

(12) The major debtor gaining from unanticipated inflation is the government. Other debtors who gain from unanticipated inflation include corporations with debt, and homeowners who have fixed interest rate mortgages.

(13) People on fixed incomes are not hurt by inflation that was anticipated at the time they provided for their fixed incomes. When social security is indexed to the price level, recipients are not generally hurt, even by unanticipated inflation.

QUESTIONS

(1) What substitutions have consumers made since 2005 that would bias the CPI based on a typical 2005 market basket towards overstating inflation?

(2) Do you think that producer prices influence the CPI, or do you think the direction of influence is the reverse, with consumers' demands working back to influence prices of wholesale commodities?

(3) How would a Monetarist think about the effect of a government program which stimulates the economy by employing people to dig up boxes of money?

(4) Why, during wartime, have counterfeit monies been manufactured to drop on an enemy?

(5) Why should unanticipated inflation over a long time-period average zero?

(6) What type of information would enter into inflation forecasts?

(7) What happens to homeowners when there is an unanticipated disinflation, i.e., inflation that was slower than expected?

(8) What happens to mortgage lenders when there is unanticipated disinflation?

(9) Why do flexible interest rates overcome the redistribution otherwise resulting from unanticipated inflation?

(10) Assuming that:

Rate of growth of money supply = 6%

Rate of growth of real GDP = 4%

Anticipated inflation = 3%

Real interest rate = 2%

(i) What is the rate of inflation implied by the quantity theory of money assuming velocity is constant?

(ii) What would be the nominal interest rate?

(iii) If actual inflation turned out to be 4%, would creditors or debtors gain?

(iv) How might an anticipated change in velocity of circulation of money explain a higher anticipated rate of inflation than is implied by the quantity theory?

CONNECTIONS

ECONOMICS DOES NOT EXIST IN A VACUUM

Mention the word "inflation" to most people and they are likely to think about the matter we deal with in this book, namely rising prices. However, if the person hearing the word is a physicist it may bring something different to mind. To a physicist inflation is what occurs when, e.g., air is blown into a balloon or an automobile tire. More generally, in physics inflation refers to the phenomenon involving the expansion of volume, such as the volume of a contained gas. Surprisingly perhaps, while the physicist and economist have different phenomena in mind when considering inflation, the principles behind the phenomena are similar.

Contained gas atoms or molecules move in all directions at a variety of velocities. Let us consider a container in which there are N atoms or molecules each with mass of m, so their total mass is $M = N \cdot m$. Let us assume the average velocity of the atoms or molecules is v, and that in collisions of atoms or molecules with themselves or the walls of a container, **momentum** and **energy** are conserved. Using these terms and assumptions, the **kinetic theory of gases** can be stated as:[1]

$$M \cdot \frac{1}{3}\bar{v}^2 = P \cdot Q. \qquad (4A.1)$$

In Eq. (4A.1), M and $\bar{v}$ are as we have just defined them, respectively, the total mass of atoms or molecules, and their average velocity. In addition, P is the volume of the container and Q is the pressure on the container's surface. Alternatively, if we write $\overline{V} = \frac{1}{3}\bar{v}^2$, then we can write the kinetic

---

[1] The derivation of the kinetic theory can be found in most introductory physics textbooks. See, e.g., Joseph F. Mulligan, *Introductory College Physics* (McGraw-Hill, New York, 1985), *ibid.* pp. 228–31. For purposes of comparison of the kinetic theory and the quantity theory we use M instead of $N \cdot m$ in the kinetic theory. We also use P for "volume" and Q for "pressure," whereas in physics books volume is usually written as V and pressure as P. Of course, these changes are just matters of notation, and are made so the connection between the two theories is as clear as possible.

theory of gases as

$$M \cdot \overline{V} = P \cdot Q. \qquad (4A.2)$$

Let us compare the implications of Eq. (4A.2) with those of the quantity theory of money, which from Eq. (4.8) in this chapter can also be written:

$$M \cdot \overline{V} = P \cdot Q. \qquad (4.8)$$

As we have explained, the variable $M = N \cdot m$ is the number of atoms or molecules moving around a container, N, multiplied by their individual mass, m. We can think of N as being parallel to the number of dollar bills moving around an economy, and m as their average face-value, so that $M = N \cdot m$ is parallel to the money supply circulating in an economy. That is, we can draw a parallel between $M = N \cdot m$ in Eq. (4A.2) — the aggregate mass of atoms or molecules moving within a container of gas — and M in Eq. (4.8) — the aggregate money supply moving within a contained economy.

Let us consider a container like a balloon which expands such that the pressure, Q, on its surface is constant. In such a case the volume, P, inflates when there is an increase in the variables on the right-hand-side of Eq. (4A.2). Specifically, with Q constant, by increasing $M = N \cdot m$ we increase P in the same proportion as M. This is similar to what happens when we increase the money supply, M, in the quantity theory of money holding real GDP, Q, constant. In particular, the price level, P, inflates in the same proportion as M.

The parallel between the effect of $M = N \cdot m$ on P in the kinetic theory of gases, and of M on P in the quantity theory of money, should come as little surprise to those knowing both theories. As we have seen in this chapter, "pumping" more money into circulation with the same volume of goods and the same velocity of circulation, causes inflation in proportion to the money supply. Similarly, pumping more atoms or molecules of gas into a container with the same surface pressure and velocity of atoms or molecules causes inflation in proportion to the supply of atoms or molecules. This is because if the surface pressure is constant and velocity is constant, the number of atoms or molecules striking a given surface area in a given time must also be constant, and this requires expanding the volume of the container in proportion to the number of atoms or molecules. (Pressure is constant if collisions per unit area and time are constant, and the velocity and mass of atoms or molecules are also constant.)

The effect of changing the velocity of gas atoms or molecules on the volume of a contained gas is similar, although not precisely the same, to the effect of changing the velocity of circulation of money on prices. In particular, increasing the square of the velocity of gas atoms or molecules, $\bar{v}^2$, with their total mass and pressure constant, increases the volume of the gas proportionately; in Eq. (4A.1), if $M = N \cdot m$ and P are constant, P increases in proportion to $\bar{v}^2$. Similarly, increasing the velocity of circulation of money, $\bar{V}$ in Eq. (4.8), with money supply, M, and real output, Q, constant, increases the price level. Both the *ceteris paribus* effects of $\bar{v}^2$ on P in Eq. (4A.1) and of $\bar{V}$ on P in Eq. (4.8) are proportional effects.

The parallels between the kinetic theory of gases and the quantity theory of money follow because atoms and molecules impact when they collide with a container's surface, while money "impacts" when offered in exchange for goods and services. Atoms and molecules of gas charging around a container and applying pressure when brought into contact with its surface, behave very much like money moving around an economy and applying pressure when brought into contact with the economy's output.

We know that in a gas container such as a balloon, reducing pressure in one area increases the pressure somewhere else. The same is true in an economy. In particular, holding some prices down by, e.g., price controls, increases inflationary pressures on uncontrolled products. This is because money saved on controlled products is freed-up for buying the uncontrolled products.

Turning from the physics of inflation to other dimensions of the subject, we can note that inflation has been considered as a weapon for war, and as such is of interest to political scientists and historians. For example, both sides of the conflict in the Second World War considered dropping vast quantities of superb quality counterfeit notes on the enemy. Forged Bank of England notes found in Germany after the War were of such high quality they would have been virtually impossible to distinguish from genuine money. The idea was to cause economic chaos, and to deny the legitimate money-making authorities the power to use the inflation tax. Interestingly, despite going to the trouble of forging the monies, the counterfeit notes were not deployed by dropping them, *en masse*, from aircraft. Some historians have argued this was because the inflation weapon is so powerful neither side was willing to risk retaliation from the other.

While fear of retaliation has discouraged countries from using inflation as a weapon of war, inflation has nevertheless frequently resulted from war. This is because wars are extremely expensive and difficult to finance via explicit taxes. Governments have therefore resorted to "printing" money, i.e., using the inflation tax. The need to print money rather than use taxes on incomes, profits or sales is particularly strong in the aftermath of war when governments face huge expenditures shifting their economies from military to civilian activities, finding jobs for returning soldiers, restructuring factories and so on. As well as requirements for vast amounts of funds after war, the tax collection infrastructure may have been disrupted by war. Resort to the printing press is therefore common at such times, as in Continental Europe after the First World War.

Inflation has been often the cause of civil disorder. Historians trace the rise of Nazism in Germany in the 1920s and 1930s in part to the turmoil caused by the hyperinflation which ravaged the country. Recently, price increases of food in Poland in the mid-1980s and of staples in Brazil in the late-1980s led to street riots. Political scientists study both the overt consequences of very rapid inflation, and the more subtle consequences of moderate inflation that show up in opinion polls. For example, they have shown that increased uncertainty about inflation typically reduces political support for the U.S. President.

Countries that have experienced hyperinflation, such as interwar Germany and Hungary, appear to continue functioning more or less normally until a level of inflation is reached when money ceases to be used; people switch to using barter or commodity mediums of exchange such as brandy and cigarettes. At the point of abandoning money the economy grinds to a virtual standstill. The process is not unlike the **denaturing** of living cells that occurs at a high temperature. At low and moderate temperatures cells continue to function more or less normally, with little more than minor discomfort and some slowing of processes. However, there comes a point when the cell denatures, shuts down completely, and cannot be revived. This process is most familiar from what happens to an egg when the temperature reaches approximately 50°C; the egg cells change form and no subsequent cooling can make them return to their "pre-cooked" state. While there are a few examples of reversal of hyperinflation, usually the problem becomes so severe it is necessary to scrap the old money and to start again.

As well as being of interest to historians, political scientists, and physicists, inflation is studied by psychologists, cosmologists and other researchers. Psychologists are concerned with the formation of inflationary anticipations, which as we have shown, are important for the consequences of inflation. They are interested in the way inflationary anticipations are formed — whether expectations are rational, unbiased and so on — and people's attitudes to uncertainty about inflation. Cosmologists have a theory of expansion of the universe, **The Inflationary Theory of the Universe**, which describes transition from extremely dense matter at the Big Bang to the defuse lumpy matter currently occupying the universe. Economists have a parallel concern, the theory of the evolution of money: what is it that leads to general acceptability? Unfortunately, the theory of the evolution of money is no more easily resolved from the left-over evidence than the theory of expansion of the universe.

CHAPTER 5

UNEMPLOYMENT

"It's not what you pay a man, but what he costs you that counts."
Will Rogers

Key Concepts: Measuring unemployment; different causes of unemployment; the meaning of "full employment"; search theory of unemployment; aggregate supply of and demand for labor; unemployment and wage inflexibility; inflation versus unemployment; the natural rate of unemployment.

Each month, government officials, business analysts and others await the release of the unemployment statistics, hoping to obtain a picture of the general direction of the economy. Behind the cold, harsh facts of the unemployment figures lies the hardships and dejection of those unable to find suitable work. In this chapter, we examine a number of aspects of unemployment, including the way it is measured, what is meant by "full employment," whether full employment is necessarily accompanied by inflation, and why full employment rarely prevails. We shall see that to a large extent, unemployment is caused by inflexibility in the wage rate, and that contrary to popular opinion, there is no permanent solution to unemployment from adopting inflationary macroeconomic policies.

MEASURING AND CATEGORIZING UNEMPLOYMENT

Measuring Unemployment

Unemployment is not as clear-cut a concept as would appear from the confident way the term is used in everyday language. While many people know that it is the percent of the workforce without employment, what is not so well known is what exactly constitutes the workforce, and who in particular is counted as being unemployed.

In the United States, the size of the workforce and the number who are considered unemployed are determined via monthly household surveys by the Department of Labor of the U.S. Bureau of the Census. In these surveys and similar ones conducted in other countries, the relevant magnitudes are determined as follows:

(1) The number of people counted as "full-time unemployed" is the number who were not working full-time during the week prior to the survey interview, and who were actively looking for full-time work.

(2) The size of the workforce is the number of people who were fully employed during the week prior to the survey, plus the number who were not working, but who were actively looking for full-time work.

The monthly surveys are made representative of regional, racial, and other characteristics of the population so that although only a minute proportion of households are included each month, the estimates are reasonably accurate. Of course, the surveyors must be armed with definitions of "actively looking for full-time work" and "full-time," and whether job search was indeed active and employment was full-time are determined by asking further questions: did you have any job interviews; how many hours did you work?

The data from the surveys are used to calculate the full-time unemployment rate as the ratio of the number unemployed *vis-à-vis* the size of the full-time workforce. This is put on a percentage basis by multiplication by 100. Symbolically,

$$\text{Unemployment rate} = \frac{U}{E + U} \times 100, \qquad (5.1)$$

where U = number without full-time employment, but actively looking for full-time work, and E = number employed full-time.

The denominator in Eq. (5.1), $(E + U)$, is the workforce, which consists of those working, plus those not working but looking for work.

The full-time unemployment rate is the number of people without full-time work and actively seeking work divided by the workforce. The workforce consists of those with full-time work plus those not working but seeking full-time work.

In the U.S., in addition to calculating the full-time unemployment rate for the entire nation, the data are analyzed to compute rates of unemployment for different geographical locations, for blacks versus whites, for males versus females and for heads of families versus others. Data are also maintained for part-time workers, and for those not working who have given up trying to find a job, the so-called **discouraged workers**. As with the national income and product account statistics, further adjustments are made for the season, with these adjustments based on an examination of average month-to-month variations in unemployment over a number of earlier years.

Clearly, there are some difficulties with using the unemployment statistics as a precise measure of the unemployment problem. For example, people laid-off without any planned recall are not considered unemployed if they are waiting in hope of being taken back in their old job; they are not counted as unemployed because they are not actively looking for work. In a similar way, people who have been unemployed so long they have given up looking are not counted as being unemployed, although they are included separately in a discouraged worker category. Indeed, it is possible for the unemployment rate to decline when employment prospects are so bleak that there are more people who have given up looking. There are also difficulties introduced by part-time work that is being done because full-time jobs are not available; part-time workers are not counted in the full-time unemployment statistics, although statistics on part-time work are separately reported.

Structural and Frictional Unemployment

Even at the best of times, unemployment is not zero. This is because in a dynamic economy several forces are at work, including:

Changing Demands: People are constantly changing buying patterns. Consider, for example, how fashions change in footwear, from Oxfords to loafers to runners to lightweight walkers, the different styles generally being supplied by different companies. The wearing of hats rises and declines, with different styles from different suppliers having their day and then vanishing, along with their producers. Patterns of entertainment shift, from live theater to movies to home videos to cable, each requiring different skills to provide. Preferences change in the home, with different wall coverings, one year paper, then paint, then paper again; with different floors, from wood to linoleum to carpet to tile. In the face of these constantly changing buying patterns, workers are displaced in the companies facing declining demands. At the same time, new jobs are offered in the companies enjoying growing demand. However, even if displaced workers have the requisite skills, it takes time to locate the new openings. The new opportunities may be in different cities, and unemployed workers may want to look locally before digging up roots. While still looking the displaced workers are counted as unemployed.

Changing Technologies: While new technologies generally result in new jobs in producing the new products and capital equipment, they also make old skills obsolete. For example, the development of microcomputers for word-processing has created new jobs in hardware production, software development, manual preparation and computer literacy training. The skills needed in these new, expanding roles are different from those in the type-writer industry which was largely replaced by microprocessors, just as the skills needed for making typewriters were different from those for making the fountain pens that typewriters replaced. Old-fashioned watch and clock makers and repairers faced rapidly shrinking demands for their skillful hands as cell phones, smart phones, quartz clocks and watches created new jobs for technologists and microelectronics engineers. In the face of these changing technologies there may be many openings without the skilled workers to fill them, while at the same time there are many who are unemployed because their old skills are no longer in demand.

Changing Patterns of International Trade: Jobs are created and lost by **outsourcing**, free-trade agreements and other causes of changes in the patterns of international trade. For example, as Japan improved automobile design, quality and performance and attracted a growing share of the global auto market, U.S. and European workers have been displaced. At the same time, Japanese success in automobiles and other products has meant rising incomes and Japanese demand for American products, such as beef, fresh produce, wide-bodied jet aircraft, fast food, movies, and T.V. shows. The manufacturing muscle from the sustained growth of China, now the second largest economy and the world's biggest manufacturer, has had an even more dramatic and profound impact on jobs worldwide. Even if the number of jobs created by international trade were the same as the number lost, unemployment would temporarily rise; without training displaced workers cannot move to new opportunities demanding different skills. With the signing of the North American Free Trade Agreement (NAFTA) in 1992, which removed or reduced trade barriers on a substantial part of cross-border U.S., Canadian and Mexican trade, effects on jobs were substantial. An effort was made to smooth the transition by reducing tariffs gradually over 15 years. This lengthy phase-in, like that accompanying the U.S.-Canadian Free Trade Agreement of 1989, was motivated by the recognition that it takes time for employment to adjust following a shift in the pattern of trade. However, with the difficulty of retraining older workers and with the regional shifts in opportunities that occur, it can take a generation before the transition has fully occurred; old workers must retire and new workers must choose areas where job opportunities expand.

Job Shifting: In order to move ahead professionally it is not uncommon to have to change jobs. It is also not uncommon for people to leave one job for another to try something new. Frequently, the search for better job opportunities requires people to leave their old jobs; employers are often unwilling to let employees travel on company time for job interviews, especially when it is the employee's choice to leave. In the time between leaving an old job and locating a new one a person is counted as unemployed.

New Entrants to the Workforce: Not every high school or college graduate finds a job before graduation, and therefore the unemployment statistics include graduates who are looking for their first job.[1] Those actively looking for employment also include women returning to the labor market after an absence working at home raising their families.

Changing technologies, trade patterns and changing demands are often referred to as causes of **structural unemployment**; they contribute to unemployment as they change the industrial structure of an economy. Job shifting and new entrants to the workforce are causes of **frictional**

---

[1] To some extent, unemployment of new entrants to the workforce is a seasonal phenomenon. As such, it is taken care of in the seasonally adjusted unemployment statistics.

unemployment; both contribute to unemployment because it takes time for people to move from one endeavor to another.

Structural unemployment is caused by changing demands for different products, changing patterns of international trade and technologies of production. Frictional unemployment is caused by people shifting between jobs and new workers joining the workforce.

A Search Theory of Unemployment

For a given rate at which people are leaving one job in search for another — whether involuntarily (structural unemployment) or voluntarily (frictional unemployment) — the longer they are searching for new opportunities the higher is the unemployment rate. For example, suppose the workforce is 2 million, that 100,000 leave/lose jobs each month, and that it takes one month on average for workers to find new, satisfactory opportunities. Then at any time the unemployment rate will be 5%. If conditions change and it takes two-months to find a job — with 100,000 still leaving/losing jobs each month — the unemployment rate will increase to 10%. So what is it that determines the time between jobs while seeking alternative employment opportunities? We can tackle this question with a search theory of unemployment that is summarized in Fig. 5.1.

A search theory of unemployment can be developed in which a job seeker's decision on whether to spend another week not working but

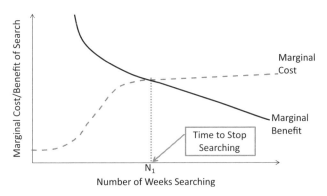

Fig. 5.1. A search theory of unemployment.
The marginal cost of job search is the value of foregone wages by continuing to search one more week. The marginal benefit of job search is the expected present value of higher wages enjoyed by spending another week trying to find a better paying opportunity than the best so far found.

actively seeking work — our definition of unemployment — depends on the expected marginal cost of spending another week looking for an acceptable job, versus the marginal expected benefit of looking for another week. Consider for simplicity an individual who has lost their job, possibly due to a structural change in the job market.

The marginal cost of spending the first week seeking a job is zero, where the zero marginal cost is the opportunity cost of spending one week trying to find a job: with no work offered, there is no lost income by actively looking for work.[2] Suppose that the job-seeker finds a job during the first week of looking for work, with this job starting the next week, that is, in week two. The marginal cost in week two of rejecting this job is the wage that would have been earned in that week. If the job-seeker continues looking and rejecting further job offers, the marginal cost is the highest wage they could have been earning by accepting a job.[3] Improvements in the best offer so far will become smaller the longer the job-seeker has looked. This is because the longer they look the more likely they will have found the best available jobs. This is shown in Fig. 5.1 by a flattening marginal cost curve that gives the marginal cost of rejecting offers and continuing to search as more and more weeks have been spent searching.

The marginal benefit of spending a further week job hunting after each period of search is the present value of the expected income improvement by looking a further week after that period of search. The benefit is a "present value" because if the job hunter is successful finding a higher paying job by further exploration, the higher wages might be enjoyed for many months or years.[4] The benefit is an expected value in a statistical

---

[2]In Fig. 5.1 we show a small marginal cost of job search even when there is no job offered. This could represent the value of work that could be done about the house, such as postponed chores if not out looking for a job. There might also be travel costs for interviews. If the job seeker has voluntarily left a job, the opportunity cost is what they would have earned.

[3]If the job opportunities persist we can think of this as "sampling with replacement." Then the marginal cost curve could never slope downwards. If job offers might be withdrawn the marginal cost could slope downwards. The job seeker can then be thought of sampling from jobs without replacement.

[4]The concept of present value is explained in the backgrounder in Chapter 2. See especially Table B2.1. The possible longevity of the benefit of search is reflected in the height of the marginal benefit of search curve for each amount of search.

sense: it is the most probable improvement. As the job hunter searches the available opportunities, the longer they have already looked the less is the expected benefit from further search. This explains the downward slope of the marginal benefit curve in Fig. 5.1. If all possibilities have been discovered and explored, the marginal benefit curve of continuing to look will approach the horizontal axis. It will remain above the horizontal axis only to the extent that new opportunities, not yet available, might arise.

The optimal number of weeks to search for work is where the marginal cost of search curve in Fig. 5.1 intersects the marginal benefit curve. We can use this figure to consider the effect of such influences as unemployment benefits and effective job-search technology on the unemployment rate. (Recall that for a given rate of workers leaving or losing jobs, the longer they look the higher is the rate of unemployment. For example, if they spend twice as long searching, the unemployment rate will be double.)

A search theory of unemployment can be based on the marginal cost of job search versus the marginal benefit.

The Effect of Unemployment Benefits: Figure 5.2 shows the effect of unemployment benefits on the length of time looking for work and hence on the unemployment rate. If the unemployed are able to collect unemployment benefits, this will lower the marginal cost of search curve. For

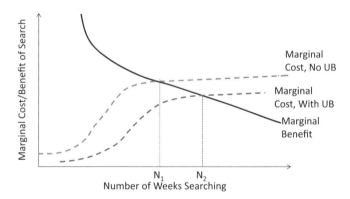

Fig. 5.2.   Effect of unemployment benefits, UB.
The marginal cost of job search is reduced by the ability to collect unemployment benefits. This will increase the number of weeks searching for a new job.

example, suppose a job seeker can collect $250 per week while actively seeking employment. Then the marginal cost of search curve will shift downwards by $250: the opportunity cost of remaining unemployed one more week is the wage that would have been earned, minus the $250 unemployment benefit. As Fig. 5.2 shows, this increases the time seeking employment that balances the marginal cost and marginal benefit. In the event that unemployment benefits expire after a particular number of weeks, then the marginal cost of search curve will shift down only for the number of weeks for which unemployment benefits are available.

Effect of Job/Worker Search Technology: In recent years, it has become easier for job seekers to identify the opportunities that exist, and for employers to inform the job market of their needs. Instead of having to pour over the classified ads for each city or town and call for more details about the job and employer, job seekers can browse the internet, receiving up-to-date information. Job openings are easy to advertise. In terms of Fig. 5.3, the marginal benefit of job search for the first week or even the first few days would be very high. The marginal benefit of search would then diminish rapidly: with all information available after a short investigation, there is not much marginal benefit from continued search. This means that the marginal benefit of search curve starts out high at the outset — top left — and then drops quickly. It will start out higher than the marginal benefit curve without

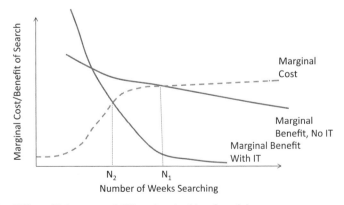

Fig. 5.3. Effect of job — search IT on time looking for a job.
The initial marginal benefit of spending time seeking out job opportunities is enhanced by job-search technologies such as the internet. This would reduce time in search.

the job-finding IT, and then quickly go below this curve. As Fig. 5.3 shows, this will shorten the optimal search period, thereby lowering the number actively engaged in job search.

> *The number of unemployed who are actively seeking employment will be higher the higher are unemployment benefits, and lower, the more effective is the job search information technology.*

Cyclical Unemployment

Figure 5.4 shows that the unemployment rate in the U.S. has varied substantially over the last half century. The pace of structural change does not vary sufficiently over time to explain the observed ups and downs in the proportion of people without jobs. Similarly, shifting between jobs and new entrants into the workforce, the causes of frictional unemployment, cannot explain such volatility. Rather, what the data on unemployment suggest is a cyclical element to unemployment. Indeed, it has been suggested that there are different cycles of different lengths overlaying the pattern of unemployment over time. Specifically, it has been argued that there may be cycles of a few years duration, of 8–10 years duration, and of about 50 years, all simultaneously driving the unemployment rate over time. Unfortunately,

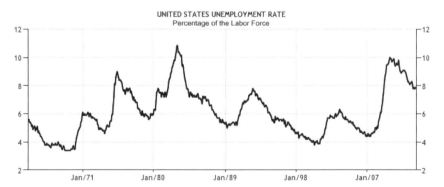

Fig. 5.4.   U.S. Unemployment rate last half century.
The U.S. unemployment rate for the last half century shows both small and large variations. It has been suggested that there are cycles of different lengths which are simultaneously occurring, one on top of the other. However, there is not sufficient regularity in the cyclical pattern of unemployment for consensus on the nature of the pattern or of its cause.

Source: http://www.tradingeconomics.com/united-states/unemployment-rate.

there is no consensus on the length of the unemployment cycle, or cycles, or on the theory behind cycles.

Full Employment

Since World War II, governments have striven for full employment, although different governments have held different views on how full employment should be defined. Because people remain without jobs even at the best of times, it is clearly inappropriate to define full employment as everybody who wants a job having one. A more useful and frequently adopted definition is where there are as many people looking for work as there are job openings. Specifically, full employment can be defined as the situation where there are as many people out of work and actively looking for employment, as there are openings. With this particular definition of full employment, everybody could in principle have a job. The problem is aligning those who are looking for work with the appropriate vacancies.

Full employment occurs when the number of job vacancies equals the number looking for work.

The definition of full employment in terms of equality of the number looking for work and the number of unfilled positions, is equivalent to defining full employment in terms of equality of the quantity of labor supplied and demanded. Specifically, if we think of the quantity of labor supplied as those already working plus those looking for work, and of the quantity of labor demanded as those already working plus the number of job vacancies, then the quantity supplied equals the quantity demanded if the number looking for jobs equals the number of vacancies; the quantity of labor supplied and demanded both contain the number already working, and therefore equality depends only on the number looking for jobs versus the number of vacancies. It follows that unemployment in excess of full employment occurs when the quantity of labor supplied exceeds the quantity of labor demanded. But why should such a disequilibrium between supply and demand occur, and why should the resulting unemployment have a cyclical element? As we shall show below, the answer has to do with the inflexibility of wages.

Full employment occurs when the quantity of labor supplied equals the quantity of labor demanded. Unemployment in excess of full employment occurs when the quantity of labor supplied exceeds the quantity of labor demanded.

UNEMPLOYMENT AND THE LABOR MARKET

If, as we have just argued, unemployment occurs when there is an excess of the quantity of labor supplied over the quantity demanded, then it follows that if the forces of supply and demand are free to work in labor markets, unemployment above the full employment level should be temporary. That is, if the price of labor, the wage, moves towards the equilibrium level, we will not observe unemployment rates above full employment other than during the time that wages are changing. However, the reality is that unemployment persists. This suggests that wages do not quickly adjust to equilibrium levels. Let us explain the role of slow wage adjustments within the framework of the labor market.

> *Unemployment is caused by wages adjusting too slowly for the labor market to remain in equilibrium.*

The Aggregate Demand for Labor

When deciding on the number of workers to employ, firms compare the amount each possible additional worker adds to the firm's total revenue versus what they add to total cost. Profit maximization means hiring more workers as long as they each add more to revenue than to cost. Each additional worker's cost is the wage paid for that worker.[5] What each additional worker adds to revenue is called the **value of the marginal product of labor (VMP)**. This is the **marginal physical product (MPP)** — the number of extra units of output produced by hiring that worker — times the price of output, that is:

$$\text{VMP} = \text{MPP} \times \text{Price.} \qquad (5.2)$$

The MPP of labor declines as more labor is employed. This is the consequence of the **law of diminishing marginal product of labor** which applies to the economy as a whole just as it does to any particular company; with a fixed amount of capital or land, after some level of employment the extra product of additional workers declines as more workers are hired. This

---

[5]The relevant wage is the full cost of hiring a worker that can include payroll taxes, vacation pay, pension contributions, health insurance, and so on. Increases in any of these can reduce employment just as an increase in wages can.

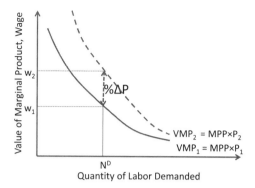

Fig. 5.5. The aggregate demand for labor.
The quantity of labor demanded is such that for the last worker employed, the value of the marginal product of that worker equals the wage paid. With VMP = MPP × Price, and with MPP diminishing as more labor is employed as a result of the law of diminishing marginal product, the demand curve for labor slopes downwards.

means that the aggregate demand for labor curve slopes downwards with respect to wages. That is, the lower is the wage, the greater is the quantity of labor demanded; the lower is the wage, the more workers can be employed before the VMP of the last worker equals the wage. Similarly, the demand curve for labor shifts upwards with increases in the MPP of labor and with the price of output, and in proportion to the MPP and price of output.

Figure 5.5 shows two downward-sloping aggregate demand curves for labor, one for each of two different prices of output, P_1 and P_2. The curves are labeled VMP_1 and VMP_2. The height of each curve at each quantity of labor is the VMP for that quantity of labor with output prices P_1 and P_2 respectively. For example, with the output price P_1 the quantity of labor demanded is N^D at the wage rate w_1. This is because to the left of N^D it would pay to hire more workers because they add more to total revenue, shown by the height of VMP_1, than the wage paid, w_1. To the right of N^D it would pay to hire fewer workers because the wage paid, w_1, exceeds what they add to revenue, VMP_1. N^D is the profit-maximizing quantity of labor to hire at wage w_1 with the output price P_1.

Figure 5.5 also shows what happens to the labor demand curve after an increase in the price level of what labor produces. The curve VMP_1 is the demand curve for labor before an increase in the price level while VMP_2 is the demand curve after the price level has increased. VMP_2 is above VMP_1

in proportion to the extent the price level has increased. For example, if the price level increases 25%, the demand curve VMP_2 is 25% higher than VMP_1 at every quantity of labor employed. Similarly, if the price level were to decrease, the demand curve for labor would shift downwards in proportion to the decline in prices.

> *The aggregate demand curve for labor is downward-sloping vis-à-vis the wage, and shifts up and down in proportion to changes in the price level of output.*

The Aggregate Supply of Labor

The supply of labor to an individual industry depends on the opportunity cost of labor in terms of what each successive worker could have earned in their next best alternative employment opportunity. The aggregate supply of labor also depends on the opportunity cost. In the case of the aggregate supply of labor the opportunity cost of working is what is given up by *not* working. The opportunity cost might therefore involve the chance to otherwise spend more time being educated, taking care of the family or house, going skiing, hiking, playing golf, and so on.

For a given price level, the higher are wages the more people will find the benefit of work to exceed the opportunity cost of work. For example, at higher wages there will be fewer stay-at-home parents, more people will delay retirement, more students will decide not to attend school or college, more members of the "leisure set" will decide work is not as terrible as was previously considered, and so on. In addition, at higher wages those already working might opt to work more hours. However, it is also possible that at very high wages some people will opt for more leisure, and therefore work fewer hours. This can occur when wages and incomes are so high that working for more income to buy yet more goods and services is not as desirable as enjoying more leisure.[6] Nevertheless, despite this possibility, it is usually assumed that the quantity of labor supplied increases with the wage as shown in Fig. 5.6.

> *Each individual balances the benefit of working with the opportunity cost of forgone leisure, education and so on. For a given price level, the higher is the*

---

[6]Higher wages can be considered as causing a "substitution effect" of work in place of leisure, offset by an "income effect" increasing the demand for leisure. When the latter exceeds the former, the supply curve of labor can be backward sloping.

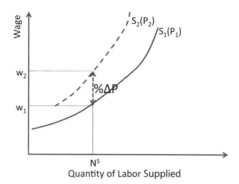

Fig. 5.6. The aggregate supply of labor.
The aggregate quantity of labor supplied depends on wages versus the opportunity cost of working in terms of leisure, further education and so on. For a given price level, the higher is the wage the more people will find it exceeds their opportunity cost and therefore will be willing to supply more labor.

wage the more people will consider the wage to exceed the opportunity cost, and the quantity of labor supplied will be higher.

The two upward-sloping labor supply curves in Fig. 5.6 are drawn for different price levels of what workers buy. The curve S_1 is the supply curve of labor before prices increase, and S_2 is the supply curve of labor after a 25% increase in prices. Taking any given quantity of labor supplied, for example, N^S, we find by drawing a vertical line at that quantity that it occurs with wages of w_1 per month at the original price level, P_1. After an increase in the price level of, e.g., 25%, the same quantity of labor is supplied at a wage of w_2 per month, where w_2 is 25% higher than w_1. This is because when prices increase by 25% it is necessary to have a 25% increase in the **nominal wage**, that is, the dollar amount received, for the **real wage** to remain unchanged; the real wage is the wage after allowance for the price level of what workers buy. Indeed, at each quantity of labor supplied it is necessary for the nominal wage to increase in proportion to the price level in order for the quantity of labor supplied to remain unchanged. This is because the quantity of labor supplied depends on the real wage, and the real wage is unchanged only if nominal wages and prices change by the same percentage.

The real wage is the wage after allowance for the price level of what workers buy. Because the quantity of labor supplied depends on the real wage, the supply of labor curve shifts up and down in proportion to the price level.

Unemployment and Equilibrium versus Actual Wages

In the preceding discussion we have explained that the demand curve for labor shifts up and down in proportion to the price level, and that the same is true for the supply curve of labor. Therefore, the equilibrium wage moves up and down in proportion to the price level. For example, if the supply and demand curves for labor both shift up 25% from a 25% increase in prices as in Fig. 5.7, the equilibrium nominal wage also increases 25%; S_2 and D_2 are respectively 25% above S_1 and D_1, and so w_2 is 25% above w_1. If the actual wage is always equal to the equilibrium wage the quantity of labor supplied remains equal to the quantity demanded, at N^F, and full employment is maintained. Then how can unemployment occur, where unemployment means an excess of the quantity of labor supplied over the quantity demanded? For unemployment the actual wage must exceed the equilibrium wage. For example, if the actual wage increases to w_3 when the labor supply and demand curves are S_2 and D_2, the quantity of labor supplied exceeds the quantity demanded by $(N^S - N^D)$.

If actual wages always equal equilibrium wages the quantity of labor demanded equals the quantity supplied, and there is full employment. Unemployment occurs when actual wages exceed equilibrium wages.

Let us illustrate how actual wages can differ from equilibrium wages by considering the supply and demand curves for labor more carefully, making a distinction between the *actual* curves and *anticipated* curves. We shall

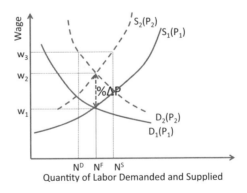

Fig. 5.7.   Actual vs. equilibrium wages and unemployment.
If the actual wage exceeds the equilibrium wage, and is, for example, w_3 when labor demand and supply curves are D_2 and S_2, there is a larger quantity of labor supplied than is demanded, and there is unemployment.

use this illustration not only to show how unemployment can occur, but also to show the relationship between inflation and unemployment.

Wage Rigidity, Inflation and Unemployment

Wages are not changed from day to day or even month to month as labor market conditions vary. Rather, wages are typically negotiated and set for an upcoming period of time, such as for the next one or two years. This is true whether wages are negotiated between employers and a trade union, or between workers and firms in personal wage contracts. For example, it might be agreed that the wage is to be $10.95 per hour for the next year, and $11.25 per hour for the following year in a two-year contract.

In reaching agreement on a wage that will apply for the next one or two years, it is necessary for employers and employees to judge what labor market conditions *will be* during that future time period. This means that in their wage negotiations both employers and employees have to anticipate what the price level is likely to be. Only by forming an expectation of what the price level will be, can employers and employees reach a view of what would be an appropriate wage to agree upon for the future. In effect, what workers and firms have to do is estimate what the future equilibrium wage will be, knowing that this depends on the future price level.[7]

Workers and firms must anticipate future equilibrium wages when setting wage contracts that will apply into the future. Anticipated future equilibrium wages depend on the anticipated price level.

While workers and firms will do their best to correctly anticipate the price level that will prevail during the wage contract period, the actual price level that materializes will not typically be exactly as expected. That is, actual inflation in general differs from anticipated inflation. To see the consequence of actual inflation differing from anticipated inflation, let us suppose in parts (a) and (b) of Fig. 5.8 that at the price level anticipated by both workers and firms, the demand and supply curves of labor are respectively D* and S*, where the asterisk signifies these curves are based

---

[7]The future equilibrium wage also depends on the future MPP of labor. We focus on the price level here because this enables us to also illustrate the relationship between unemployment and inflation.

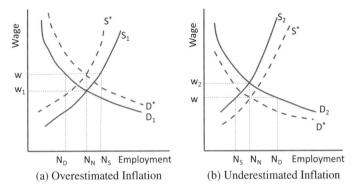

(a) Overestimated Inflation   (b) Underestimated Inflation

Fig. 5.8. Overestimation versus underestimation of inflation and unemployment. *When inflation is as was anticipated, the economy is at the natural (un)employment level, N_N. If inflation is overestimated as in part (a), unemployment will be above the natural unemployment level. If inflation is underestimated as in part (b), unemployment declines below the natural unemployment level.*

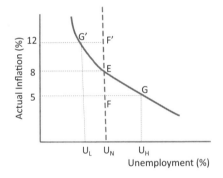

Fig. 5.9. Inflation and unemployment. *If inflation is lower than anticipated, unemployment increases if wages are inflexible downwards. However, when wages adjustments eventually occur unemployment returns to its "natural" level, U_N; we move from G to F. If inflation is greater than anticipated we have a temporary decline in unemployment, moving from E to G'. However, eventually we return to the natural unemployment rate at F'.*

on the anticipated price level. Let us also suppose that wages have been agreed upon and contracted at their anticipated market equilibrium level, w, given by the intersection of the curves D^* and S^*. Suppose, further for the sake of argument that the anticipated price level incorporated in D^* and S^* is based upon anticipation of 8% inflation.

If realized inflation is as anticipated the contracted wage rate, w, is the equilibrium wage, with $D^* = S^*$. This situation is described in Fig. 5.9, which relates actual inflation and the associated unemployment. With the wage at the equilibrium level that equates the demand for labor with the supply of labor we are at point E which is at the **natural rate of unemployment**, U_N. (By definition, the "natural rate of unemployment" is the hypothetical rate at which the demand for labor equals the supply of labor). With actual inflation equal to anticipated inflation we are at E in Fig. 5.9 with unemployment U_N and inflation of 8%.

The natural rate of unemployment is the hypothetical rate at which the demand for labor equals the supply of labor.

Let us next suppose that after wages have been contracted at w, based on inflationary anticipations of 8%, inflation turns out to be less than had been expected, being only 5%. With the lower inflation the future price level ends up below of what had been anticipated. After the lower than anticipated price level becomes recognized by workers and firms, the relevant, actual supply and demand for labor curves become S_1 and D_1 in part (a) of Fig. 5.8. If wages could fall to the new equilibrium, w_1, where $S_1 = D_1$, unemployment would remain at U_N. That is, if wages could be instantaneously revised to reflect actual inflation, unemployment would remain at the natural rate. However, in reality wages cannot easily be renegotiated to reflect actual inflation, especially when this means a wage reduction. Even though such a renegotiation of wages would mean jobs instead of unemployment for some workers, cuts in wages are usually resisted, not least in case this is seen as a sign of weakness in future wage negotiations. This is especially so when wages are negotiated by trade unions.[8] The difficulty of reducing wages to a new, lower equilibrium level than was anticipated is generally stated in terms of wages being "rigid" or "sticky" in a downward-direction.

When the equilibrium wage is lower than the actual contracted wage it is difficult to renegotiate lower wages. Wages are, therefore, said to be "rigid" or "sticky" in a downward-direction.

If wages are rigid downwards, unemployment occurs when actual inflation turns out to be lower than had been anticipated. This is shown in

---

[8]Despite the resistance to wage cuts there certainly are precedents. For example, U.S. auto workers accepted wage rollbacks in the early 1980s, and in Japan, numerous examples of rollbacks of previously negotiated wages have occurred.

Fig. 5.8(a). Specifically, with wages stuck at w when inflation is 5% instead of the expected 8%, and with the relevant supply and demand curves for labor becoming S_1 and D_1, unemployment is above the natural rate by the distance between S_1 and D_1 at wage, w. That is, unemployment is beyond the natural rate by ($N_S - N_D$) in Fig. 5.8(a).

If wages are rigid downwards, unemployment is above the natural rate when inflation is less than anticipated.

The unemployment beyond the natural rate in Fig. 5.8(a) occurs along with 5% actual inflation. We show this with point G in Fig. 5.9, which is drawn with unemployment of U_H and inflation of 5%.[9] That is, we move from E to G as a result of inflation being less than anticipated. It appears as if there is a trade-off between inflation and unemployment: in moving from point E to point G the higher unemployment is associated with lower inflation. However, this is only a temporary trade-off. This is because wages would eventually move towards equilibrium. That is, in subsequent wage agreements any previous overestimation of inflation would be allowed for, and wages would move towards the level where the quantity of labor supplied and demanded are equal. For example, if after unexpectedly dropping to 5%, inflation remained at 5%, unemployment would return to the natural level, U_N, along with the 5% inflation; with correctly anticipated inflation, wages would move to where the quantity of labor supplied and demanded are equal. In terms of Fig. 5.9, this would mean a movement from point G to point F, where point F shows 5% inflation and the natural unemployment rate, U_N. There is no trade-off between inflation and unemployment in the long run.

Let us next consider what would happen if, after an anticipated inflation of 8%, inflation turns out to be 12%. That is, in this case actual inflation exceeds expectations. The higher than anticipated inflation means a higher than anticipated future price level. The new supply and demand curves for labor are vertically above the original curves, and are shown in part (b) of Fig. 5.8 as S_2 and D_2. If wages are contracted and stuck at w because

---

[9]The distance ($N_S - N_D$) between S_1 and D_1 at wage, w, is a number of unemployed, not an unemployment rate. It must be converted into an unemployment rate before adding to U_N to reach a value such as U_H.

employers refuse to increase them, unemployment declines below U_N in Fig. 5.9: at the below-equilibrium wage there is more hiring of labor than is usual. With the 12% inflation and lower unemployment than U_N, we move from E to G′ in Fig. 5.9, where G′ denotes 12% inflation and reduced unemployment, U_L. (If it seems odd that unemployment can fall below the natural level, recall that even at the natural rate of unemployment there are unemployed workers). Again it seems that there is a trade-off between inflation and unemployment, with higher inflation associated with lower unemployment. However, if inflation remained at the higher rate of 12%, it would eventually be correctly anticipated by both workers and firms, and wages would consequently move towards their equilibrium level. Therefore, unemployment would eventually increase from the abnormally low rate, U_L, back to the natural rate, U_N, in Fig. 5.9. We would move from point G′ to point F′. Therefore there is no permanent decline in unemployment from higher than anticipated inflation.

Changes in unemployment from incorrectly anticipated inflation are temporary.

If we review what we have said we find that when inflation is lower than had been anticipated there is a temporary increase in unemployment. Similarly, when inflation is greater than had been anticipated there is a temporary decrease in unemployment. These outcomes occur because mistakes in forecasting inflation cause contracted wages to differ from their equilibrium level. If we plot the higher unemployment with the lower-than anticipated inflation, and the lower unemployment with the higher than anticipated inflation, as in Fig. 5.9, the points trace out a downward-sloping curve, G′EG. However, movements along the curve G′EG due to inflation forecasting errors are only short-run. In the long-run, i.e., after wages have been re-contracted, we return to the same rate of unemployment whatever is the rate of inflation. We have called this rate of unemployment the natural rate of unemployment because it is where the economy is naturally tending.

The natural rate of unemployment is the rate of unemployment which prevails in the long-run when inflation has become correctly anticipated. Underestimation of inflation causes unemployment to temporarily decline below the natural rate, while overestimation of inflation causes unemployment to temporarily increase above the natural rate.

The Phillip's Curve: A Short-run Phenomenon

An empirical relationship between inflation and unemployment looking like G'EG in Fig. 5.9 was found in a study by A.W. Phillips', and the curve with this shape has become known as the **Phillips' curve**.[10] Phillips examined data for Britain for the period 1861–1957, and found a general tendency towards higher inflation with lower unemployment, and vice versa.

The validity of the Phillips' curve has been challenged both empirically and theoretically. Empirically, it turns out that other than for some weak evidence for short periods of time, there is little or no support for a trade-off between inflation and unemployment. Indeed, the empirical evidence shows that higher inflation occurs as often with higher unemployment as with lower unemployment. Theoretically, the Phillips' curve has been challenged as being only a short run phenomenon, as we have explained. The theoretical challenge explains why it has been so difficult to empirically find Phillips' curves when examining data drawn from over a long period of time.

The Phillips' curve involves a trade-off between inflation and unemployment. However, any such trade-off is at most only a short-run phenomenon.

ALTERNATIVE THEORIES OF UNEMPLOYMENT

Rational Expectations and Macroeconomic Policy

The most important implication of the relation between inflation and unemployment that we have derived is that there is no sustained benefit in terms of reduced unemployment from increased inflation. There is a short-run decrease in unemployment from an unanticipated increase in inflation as the economy moves along a short-run Phillips' curve, but as the increased inflation becomes correctly anticipated so that wages return to equilibrium, unemployment returns to the natural rate. This has important consequences for the conduct of government policy. It suggests that trying to reduce unemployment by, e.g., increasing the rate of growth of the money supply, can achieve only temporary relief. Indeed, in the long run such a policy merely causes higher inflation.

---

[10]A.W. Phillips, "The Relation between Unemployment and the Rate of Change of Money Wages in the United Kingdom", *Econometrica*, (November 1958) pp. 283–99. As the title suggests, the vertical axis of Phillips' curve is wage inflation.

Some economists, led by Nobel prize-winning economist Robert Lucus Jr., have argued that it is not even possible to *temporarily* reduce unemployment by, e.g., increasing the rate of growth of the money supply. The reason for this agnostic view about the benefits of monetary policy is that these economists assume inflationary expectations are rational. By **rational expectations** they mean that all relevant information is reflected in peoples' anticipations of inflation, so that they are as likely to underestimate as to overestimate inflation; rational people do not ignore relevant information. This means that workers cannot be fooled by, e.g., an increase in the rate of inflation to accept a reduced real wage. Instead, workers will take account of, e.g., more rapid money supply growth, and build this into wage agreements. Indeed, if expectations are rational, errors in forecasting inflation during one period of time are unlikely to be repeated in the next period of time, so that unemployment is likely to vary randomly around the natural rate.[11]

> *Rational expectations are based on all relevant information. If peoples' expectations are rational, there is not even a temporary trade-off between unemployment and inflation.*

Those who believe inflationary expectations are rational have argued that governments should avoid **discretionary stabilization policy** — policy consciously used to stabilize unemployment and real economic growth. Instead, they believe governments should just try to reduce uncertainties by not changing policies too often. Policy changes, they argue, increase uncertainty, and in this way reduce the amount of investment in new capital. In turn, this causes slower economic growth. We consider this possibility in the next chapter.

Efficiency Wages and Persistent Unemployment

Those basing their views on the rationality of expectations have difficulty explaining persistent unemployment above the natural level, and yet at times such unemployment persists. This has given rise to a search for an alternative theory of unemployment which can explain why high unemployment

---

[11] By "random" variation in the unemployment rate, we mean that the rate of unemployment is not predictable from one wage contract period to the next. Nevertheless, unemployment could stay high or low for a long period of time if the length of wage contracts is long.

sometimes lasts many years.[12] One alternative theory is based on the gains employers derive from paying employees more than necessary. This alternative theory is known as the **efficiency wage theory** because it associates the efficiency or productivity of workers with the wages they are paid. Specifically, according to the efficiency wage theory, MPPs at each level of employment are larger at higher wages. The efficiency wage theory uses a variety of arguments to reach a positive association between wages and worker productivity. The essential idea of these arguments is that firms pay above-equilibrium wages to induce workers to be more productive, but at the above-equilibrium wages, the quantity of labor supplied exceeds the quantity demanded, that is, there is unemployment above the natural level. Furthermore, there is no force to reduce this unemployment because firms *want* to keep wages high.

According to the efficiency wage theory, wages might exceed the equilibrium level as a result of firms paying workers higher wages to increase productivity.

Example 5.1. Economists Fully Employed Explaining Unemployment

Unemployment extracts a high price. Of course, the highest price is borne by those desperately trying to find a job, but others pay too in taxes to provide assistance, and more generally, in lost potential output in the economy as a whole. Therefore, it is little surprise that the unemployment problem has attracted some of the best economic minds of all time, tempted by the challenge of reducing this social ill. The following article from *The Wall Street Journal* takes a long view of the path that economists have travelled in their search for *the* ultimate answer. The article takes us through the theories discussed in this chapter, and touches on insights dealt with in Chapter 6.

"When George Akerlof was 11 years old, he worried about this: If his father lost his job, he would stop spending, causing someone else to

---

[12]As Example 5.1 explains, the search for a theory of persistent unemployment has captured the interest of a large number of America's leading economists.

lose a job, who would also stop spending, and so on until the economy crashed to a halt.

Fortunately, young Georges' theory was flawed. His father periodically did lose his job, but the economy survived.

That early intellectual misfire did not discourage Mr. Akerlof, now an economist at the University of California at Berkeley, from continuing to think about unemployment. He and his wife, Janet Yellen, are members of a small band of maverick economists exploring new theories of joblessness. The group, which includes Joseph Stiglitz at Princeton and Lawrence Summers at Harvard, is pursuing ideas that eventually could help explain why unemployment stays high despite relatively healthy economic growth.

"It is one of the first theories to offer an intellectually coherent explanation of normal unemployment," says Kenneth Arrow, a Nobellaureate economist at Stanford. "I think that is a very important development."

Unemployment has always puzzled economists. Classical theorists assumed that if the demand for goods fell, wages and prices would fall as well, restoring the balance in the economy and keeping everyone employed. Confronted with high unemployment during the depression, British economist John Maynard Keynes tried to modify classical theory. He and his followers argued in part that wages are "sticky" and slow to fall, causing at times a market imbalance that results in joblessness. But even the Keynesians could not explain adequately why joblessness would persist for long periods.

The new theories expand on Keynesian ideas. They say businesses may find it in their long-term interest to pay workers more than the market requires. By paying higher wages, they can increase worker productivity and their profits, these economists contend. As a result, wages stay too high, and the workings of the market cannot assure everyone a job. Businesses stay competitive, but unemployment persists.

The path from abstract theory to practical economic policy is long and rugged. For example, many dismissed out of hand Mr. Keynes's unemployment theories when they were first published in 1936; a couple of decades later, his theories set the assumptions underlying government policies around the globe. As Mr. Keynes himself wrote, practical men may disdain academic theory but nonetheless "are usually the slaves of some defunct economist."

Whether the new theories will guide future policy makers is far from clear. The theories are young, and skeptics abound. "It is hard to say what their ultimate significance will be," says Robert Solow, a professor of economics at the Massachusetts Institute of Technology.

But the ideas are attracting some bright minds and seem to signal an important change in the direction of macroeconomics, the study of the economy's overall performance. After a decade of disillusionment, macroeconomists are focusing with renewed vigor on unemployment and other important problems. "I think we are in a very exciting period for macroeconomics," says MIT's Paul Samuelson, another Nobel laureate.

In the late 1970s and early 1980s, some academic macroeconomists began to doubt whether they had a role to play in public policy. Inflation and its effects seemed to shoot down many traditional Keynesian theories, and "supply-side" politicians and journalists dominated economic debates with their proposals to spur growth by cutting taxes. Many economists thought that "supply-side economics was silly from an academic point of view," contends John Taylor, a Stanford professor, and "serious macroeconomists felt blown out of the water."

Many academics turned away from policy problems and concentrated on sharpening their technical skills. "Rational expectations" theory became the rage. The theory emerges from the idea that individuals and businesses act rationally based on their expectations of the economy's future course. Based on this notion, young academics constructed complex mathematical models of economic activity.

However, these models rarely bore much resemblance to reality. Among other things, they reverted to the classical idea that Adam Smith's "invisible hand" would guarantee all willing workers a job. Unemployment was assumed to be "voluntary." The government's jobless figures, many of these economists say, measure only "the demand for leisure." ...

Classical economists, trained in free-market theory, have always found it difficult to understand why, in the words of economist Robert Hall at the Hoover Institution, "the labor market does not behave like the onion market." When the supply of onions exceeds the demand for onions, prices fall. But when the supply of labor exceeds the demand for labor — that is, when there is unemployment — wages do not always fall.

In a free market, classical economists argue, a company should not be able to pay workers more than the going wage for a prolonged period. If Ace Widget Co. offers workers $5 an hour when workers who seem equally qualified are willing to work for $3 an hour, another widget entrepreneur will seize the bargain and drive Ace out of business.

But the new theory — known as "efficiency wage theory" — provides a possible answer as to why a company may pay more than the market requires. If Ace Widget employees work harder because they are paid more, then low-wage companies may not be able to compete with Ace. Wages remain higher than necessary, and the result is persistent unemployment. The traditional free-market story breaks down. "Adam Smith's invisible hand turns out to be a little bit palsied," Mr. Stiglitz says.

Harvard's Prof. Summers is one of the newer converts to the efficiency-wage theory. Though only 30 years old, he is already considered one of the bright new lights in economics. He introduces the theory to a group of New York University graduate students with this story:

In 1914, in the midst of a recession, Ford Motor Co. made a startling decision to raise its wage for industrial workers to $5 a day. At the time, prevailing daily wages at other companies ranged from $2 to $3. Ford's announcement lured to its gates thousands of people hoping for a job.

Conventional economic theory suggested that the move would prove disastrous. But Henry Ford insisted that it was good business. In a history of Ford Motor, Alan Nevins writes that the dramatic move had "improved the discipline of the workers, given them more loyal interest in the institution and raised their personal efficiency."

Scribbling a mathematical model on the blackboard to explain this change in attitude, Mr. Summers says companies pay above-market wages to keep employees from neglecting their work. Unable to monitor workers closely, a company can catch only a fraction of those who shirk. If the company pays the "market-clearing" wage that traditional theory suggests, a worker risks little by shirking: if caught, he faces only temporary discomfort before finding another job at the going wage.

But if the company pays higher wages, the shirker's risks rise; if caught, he may face a long bout of unemployment while seeking an equivalent job or he may end up in a lower-paying job.

At Berkeley, Mr. Akerlof and Ms. Yellen have developed a somewhat different brand of the efficiency-wage theory based in part on insights that Mr. Akerlof gathered from sociological studies.

For an economist to use sociology in his work, Ms. Yellen says, is a bit like "wearing a loud shirt." Economists view people as motivated by rational, economic concerns; sociologists are more likely to delve into the irrational. Hoover's Mr. Hall reflects the attitude of most of his colleagues in saying he stops reading whenever he sees the work "sociological" in an economics paper.

Mr. Akerlof defends his efficiency-wage work. "With a little sociology, it is very easy to show how unemployment occurs," he says. In recent years, he has been reading sociological studies of "gift exchange," and he believes that in them he has found a convincing explanation of why companies pay higher wages than the market requires.

Mr. Akerlof argues that an employee's effort depends partially on the "norms" of the group in which he works. By paying workers a "gift" wage in excess of the minimum required, a company can raise group norms and get back a "gift" of extra effort. The theory also helps to explain why companies may not fire or pay lower wages to less productive workers. Such moves would undermine the morale of all of a company's workers and reduce productivity.

In many ways, Princeton's Prof. Stiglitz is the father of efficiency-wage theories. A classmate of Mr. Akerlof's at MIT, Mr. Stiglitz began thinking about such theories during a visit to Kenya in 1969. Economists studying underdeveloped countries had for sometime realized that higher wages could make workers more productive by improving their nutrition. But Mr. Stiglitz suspected that a related phenomenon might explain unemployment in the developed world.

By paying above-market wages, he reasons, a company might be able to reduce turnover and cut training costs. And he has studied the possibility that companies may pay higher wages to improve the quality of their employees. Unable to assess fully the skills of each potential employee, a company may improve the odds that it will get and retain good workers by paying more money.

"Any of these explanations by themselves may seem a little shaky," he says. "But I think the truth may be a complicated interaction of all of them. . . ."

Source: Alan Murray, "Jobless Puzzle: Why Unemployment Lingers on Stirs Renewed Interest," *The Wall Street Journal*, December 26, 1985, pp. 1, 4.

One line of argument that has been advanced is that higher wages prevent workers slacking or shirking on the job. According to this argument, it may be cheaper for firms to pay higher wages rather than try to identify slackers by hiring inspectors, which add to costs and may also reduce morale.

An alternative explanation for paying above-equilibrium wages is based on the sociological role of gifts, which tend to be reciprocal and create a bond. If we think of extra wages as a gift from firms to workers, it makes sense to think firms can expect a gift in return in terms of increased worker loyalty. Other factors which might induce firms to pay above-equilibrium wages are efforts to reduce costly turnover and retraining, and to increase the quality of the workforce. Another factor, which works during downturns, is the reluctance to cut wages and then let workers make their own decisions about who leaves; those leaving are likely to be the best workers because these have the best opportunities. Firms may prefer to maintain wages at above the equilibrium level, and then decide themselves who to lay off. Whatever is the explanation of above-equilibrium wages, the result is a persistent excess supply of labor. What the efficiency wage theory suggests is that this can result from profit-maximizing behavior of firms.

THE COST OF INFLATION VERSUS UNEMPLOYMENT

There is a high social cost to unemployment. The most obvious cost is borne by the unemployed themselves who suffer the hardship of financial deprivation, and the psychological impact of not feeling they have a place in society. If the psychological suffering is particularly severe it can be felt within families where children may experience damage in terms of their own motivation and chance to receive further education, and where wives and children may even suffer physical abuse. These severe costs contrast with those of inflation which, as we saw in the previous chapter, are faced primarily in terms of wealth redistribution, and result more from errors in inflationary anticipations than from the inflation itself. Most of the costs of inflation therefore cancel with the gains, while the lost incomes of the unemployed and the lost output of the nation are truly lost and can never be recovered.

Because of the relatively large social costs of unemployment, various groups have urged economic policy makers to lower unemployment, even if this means a chance of higher inflation. However, as we have seen, any gain in reduced unemployment via government policy which increases inflation is only temporary. For this reason, those supporting government restraint, often referred to as **austerity**, have argued that attempts to reduce unemployment give short-term gain, but long-term pain, and a rising debt burden. On the other hand, people supporting a more active role of government argue that there are other ways of getting people back to work, including as we shall see in the next chapter, government-funded projects and general increases in government spending, as well as **quantitative easing** — essentially increasing the money supply. Furthermore, they argue that because there is no opportunity cost when an unemployed person finds work — there is no forgone, alternative output — it is worthwhile taking steps to help maintain full employment. For example, when the government pays unemployed people to plant trees, clean up inner-city streets and parks, repair roads, or provide assistance to the elderly, if these jobs would not otherwise have been done and those employed would have been idle, the benefits of the government projects come at zero opportunity cost.

Without attaching values to the costs of inflation and unemployment we cannot make proper trade-offs between them. It is unlikely that we will ever be able to attach such costs. Not least of the problems in attaching costs is that the same rate of inflation carries a different cost according to how predictable it is, and the same rate of unemployment carries a different cost according to whether it is due to the same people remaining unemployed for lengthy periods, or due to a large number suffering short-term unemployment.[13] The latter type of unemployment can be argued to involve a lower cost than the former since short absences from the job market may be more affordable by using savings, and may offer an opportunity to paint the house or finish a chore. There is a further difficulty of giving a social value to what the unemployed would have produced — nuclear weapons versus bread, for example — but this is a general problem in valuing national income as we saw in Chapter 1.

SUMMARY

(1) The workforce is determined by a monthly household survey, and consists of the number working full-time the week before the survey, plus the number not working but actively looking for full-time work. The number without a full-time job and seeking employment is written as a fraction of the workforce to compute the rate of full-time unemployment.

(2) Full employment can be defined as the situation where as many people are looking for jobs as there are jobs available. There are always people looking for jobs and employers seeking workers because of changes in demands and methods of production, shifting patterns of international trade, new people joining the workforce, and people leaving jobs to search for better opportunities.

---

[13]We could have one million unemployed via, for example one million out of work all year, or via one million losing jobs and one million finding jobs each month. For this reason, the unemployment surveys ask about the duration of unemployment.

(3) Full employment can also be defined in terms of equality between the supply of and demand for labor. The latter view lends itself to an explanation of unemployment in terms of supply and demand analysis, and suggests unemployment above the full employment level is due to actual wages being higher than equilibrium wages.

(4) According to the search theory of unemployment the unemployed who are actively seeking work can be considered as comparing the marginal cost of search with the marginal benefit of search.

(5) The search theory suggests unemployment will decrease with improvements in information technology for finding jobs, and increase with improvements in unemployment benefits.

(6) The equilibrium wage is where the quantity of labor supplied is equal to the quantity of labor demanded. The actual wage can differ from the equilibrium wage if wages are inflexible.

(7) If wages are flexible an economy always has full employment. Wages then move in proportion to the price level.

(8) Actual inflation may differ from the anticipated rate built into contracted wages, making contracted wages differ from equilibrium wages. If wages are rigid downwards, unemployment increases when inflation is lower than was anticipated. However, eventually an economy returns to the natural rate of unemployment as anticipations become correct and wages move to equilibrium levels. Therefore, there is no long-term benefit in reduced unemployment from higher inflation.

(9) The Phillips' curve is a downward-sloping relation between inflation and unemployment, suggesting a trade-off between the two problems. However, since Phillips' original study, there has been little empirical support and no theoretical support for a long-run trade-off between inflation and unemployment.

(10) If workers' and employers' expectations are rational, being based on all relevant factors that could affect future equilibrium wages, there is not even a short run inflation-unemployment trade-off.

(11) Unemployment may persist if wages are kept high in order to increase productivity of workers. Above-equilibrium wages may increase productivity if they reduce slacking-on-the-job, or result in worker loyalty.

(12) The cost of unemployment is higher than that of inflation. However, it is difficult to quantify either of these costs, so a social choice between them cannot easily be made.

QUESTIONS

(1) In some European countries, unemployment is measured from the number registering as being unemployed at government offices, with registration often being necessary for the unemployed to collect benefits. How do you think this method of estimating unemployment compares to the survey method used in the United States, and which do you think on average produces the higher unemployment estimates from the same "true" unemployment rate?

(2) It has been said that free trade with a low wage country such as Mexico causes the permanent loss of American jobs. Do you think this claim is valid?

(3) How might retraining programs reduce unemployment?

(4) How might a lengthening of the period during which unemployment benefits can be collected affect the unemployment rate?

(5) What determines how quickly equilibrium wages are reached?

(6) How can an unexpected decline in the MPP of labor cause unemployment by making negotiated wages too high?

(7) Might longer-term wage contracts make the Phillips' curve valid for longer periods?

(8) How is it that firms who pay above the going market wage are able to survive in a competitive industry?

.

PHYSICAL AND HUMAN DIMENSIONS
OF REDUNDANCY

Not everybody thinks of work as being synonymous with employment, or of redundancy as being synonymous with unemployment. For example, to physicists, **work** is not what people do for wages, or what students do when studying. Rather, physicists define work as "the force applied to an object, multiplied by the distance the object moves in the direction of the force." This means that while some of what is done in the course of employment is work, specifically that of a physical kind such as pushing a plough or pulling a load, most of what people do on the job or while studying is not "work" as understood in physics. However, despite the different meanings of "work", when it comes to the amount of work that is done versus the amount of work that might have been done, physicists and economists think in similar ways.

In judging different kinds of machines, physicists and engineers use a concept to which economists can easily relate, namely efficiency. A standard physics textbook definition of efficiency, e, is:[1]

$$e = \frac{\text{work output}}{\text{work input}} \times 100\%.$$

The purpose of this measure is to describe numerically how well a machine is operating relative to other machines and relative to the "perfect" machine, which cannot exist in practice, but for which e = 100%.

To measure how well the economy operates relative to other economies and to the "perfect" economy, which also cannot exist in practice, economists use measures like the physicists' efficiency. An economy may not function "perfectly" because not all of each factor of production is working. The percentage of labor not working is measured by the unemployment rate, which can easily be converted into an employment rate;

---

[1] Joseph F. Mulligan, *Introductory College Physics*, (McGraw Hill, New York, 1985), *ibid.*, p. 156.

the employment rate is simply 100 minus the unemployment rate. While based on only one input, labor, the employment rate, like the physicists' e, describes how well the economy is doing relative to an ideal state. Similarly, economists employ a measure, the **capital utilization rate**, to describe how close the economy is to using all of its capital stock. Again, like e, this describes how well the economy is doing relative to an ideal state.[2]

Machines have efficiencies below 100% because of such factors as **friction** which, as we have seen, is also a reason for unemployment, frictional unemployment. Both machines and economies can also suffer from structural problems.

Engineers have learned that in designing a machine for a task it is generally desirable to build in slack. This can reduce down-time and provide room for handling heavier loadings when absolutely necessary. The human body also has some built-in slack. For example, the heart can handle heavier loads than normal for short periods of time, and this has helped in survival. The economy is very similar to machines and living organisms in benefitting from having some slack in employment of capital and labor. The slack reduces wear-and-tear on machines and people, and is a necessary part of a dynamic, evolving economy.

Biologists have found an interesting example of "unemployment" in the case of the DNA molecule in living cells. It would appear that more than 95% of the information in the molecule is redundant, going unused.[3] While slack or flexibility is of value when conditions are changing, this amount of redundancy is difficult to explain. It can be argued that it is the low cost of carrying the redundant information that allows it to be carried

---

[2]Economists also employ a measure of **potential GDP**, which is what the gross domestic product would be if *all* factors of production were fully employed, and then compute:

$$\frac{\text{Actual GDP}}{\text{Potential GDP}} \times 100\%.$$

Because potential GDP is based on there being some unemployment, that occurring at "full employment," the ratio of actual to potential GDP can be 100% when the employment rate and capacity utilization rate are below 100%. The ratio of actual to potential GDP is similar to what physicists call Carnot Efficiency. This is the efficiency of a machine relative to the best *technically possible* machine.

[3]Richard Dawkins, *The Blind Watchmaker*, (Longman; Harlow, England, 1986), *ibid.*, p. 116.

from generation to generation. Furthermore, the "redundant" information could have value later when the environment has changed, making retained, previously unfavored mutations useful in the new environment. It is also possible that the "redundant" DNA is working in a capacity comparable to middle management, directing which genes should be at work and which genes should be taking a break.

Unemployment can have devastating psychological and social consequences, adding noticeably to case loads of social and public health workers. The unemployed suffer from increased anxiety, decreased life satisfaction, difficulty concentrating, and listlessness.[4] The consequences can spill over to those keeping their jobs, but fearing the fate of their redundant colleagues. With the unemployed also suffering from boredom and anger, family members may be affected, especially when distress leads to alcoholism and depression.

The depth of despair that can fall upon those who are displaced is often the result of being cut-off from the social contact that goes with working. Moreover, there is a commonly-felt duty to work, to maintain dependents and to be "doing something". The first question asked when meeting someone is often "And what do you do?" The work ethic runs deep, leaving a gaping hole for the unemployed and the underemployed.

The duty to work and the indignity associated with not working is made especially clear in W.R. Greg's summary of what the philosopher Thomas Carlyle had done for his age: "He has preached ... the duty and the dignity of work, with an eloquence which has often made the idle shake off their idleness, and the frivolous feel ashamed of their frivolity."[5]

The sociological aspects of unemployment go beyond the human consequences suffered by those taken away from their work and work-related social contact. Statistics show decisively that those likely to suffer unemployment are in the same sociological categories as those suffering from other forms of discrimination. In particular, unemployment is more likely to affect blacks than whites, women than men, blue-collar than white-collar

---

[4] See Stephen E.G. Lea, Roger M. Tarpy and Paul Webley, *The Individual in the Economy: A Survey of Economic Psychology* (Cambridge University Press, Cambridge, 1987), especially p. 157 and the references contained therein.
[5] W.R. Greg, "Kingsley and Carlyle" in *Literary and Social Judgements* (London, 1877), vol. 1, p. 171.

workers, lower-class than upper-class people, and the young versus the middle-aged.

The perceived imperative to work, and its human consequence for the unemployed, has prompted religious leaders to question fighting inflation with high unemployment, a fight which we have shown in the text to offer no more than a temporary victory. For example, in their Pastoral Letter, *Catholic Social Teaching and the American Economy*, the Bishops of the U.S. Roman Catholic church have made it clear that their sympathies are with those suffering from unemployment, not those affected by inflation.

When it has been particularly severe, unemployment has become part of history. Grim images of soup lines of despondent people during the Great Depression, and of men and women fighting for the occasional job offered at the factory gate, fill history book accounts of the "Dirty Thirties". The statistics of up to 25% without jobs hide the human tragedies behind the statistics, the men and women desperately fighting to keep themselves and their families from starvation. Also earlier, in Victorian times, the squalid conditions of the Poor Houses, full of diseased and downtrodden orphans and hopeless individuals, are part of the history of unemployment. Urbanization and unemployment together meant that for many, the gutter or the Poor House was their home, and the Soup Kitchen their only hope of staving off starvation and disease.

The tragedies of the unemployed inspired novelists like Charles Dickens and John Steinbeck. In novels from *Oliver Twist* to *Hard Times* Dickens depicts with passionate concern for their unrelieved misery, the depravity that fell on the unemployed of Victorian England. In depression-era America, the tragic experiences of Dust Bowl Okies inspired John Steinbeck in his masterpiece *The Grapes of Wrath*. Steinbeck employs tropes such as "tractored out" and speaks of "The tractors which threw men out of work, the belt lines which carry loads, the machines which produce...", linking the plight of the heroic Joad family with the mechanization he believed to be the cause of unemployment.[6] Nevertheless, Steinbeck grapples with the tension between the unemployment due to mechanization, and the higher standard of living he recognized as flowing from mechanization.[7]

---

[6] John Steinbeck, *The Grapes of Wrath* (Viking Press, New York, 1939), p. 325.
[7] Steinbeck, *op. cit.,* Chapter 25.

Today, the safety net has been lifted to prevent some of the worst physical consequences of unemployment, but the matter remains one of public concern. This concern can translate into the opinion polls and government job-creation programs, just as in the past the New Deal, which gave Americans the Tennessee Valley Authority, the Bonneville and Hoover Dams, and rural electrification, came about as a result of public concern over the unemployment of the Great Depression.

Geographers, too, have found it necessary to consider the consequences of chronic unemployment. For example, the immigration to the Americas sprang from a lack of jobs in Ireland, Russia, Italy, Greece, and China, among other countries. The search for jobs sparked the migration of Americans within the United States from the Appalachians to the North-East and Mid-West, and more recently from the Rust Belt to the Sun Belt.

The ways different cultures deal with shifts in labor supplies and demands vary; for example, Japanese workers accept wage cuts to avoid unemployment more readily than Americans or Europeans. The social and historical factors behind these cultural differences, as well as behind the "gift exchange" mentioned in this chapter in the context of efficiency wage theory, interest sociologists and anthropologists. They are, of course, also of interest to researchers in the business/economics areas of labor relations and organizational behavior.

Thomas Malthus, the philosopher and member of the English clergy mentioned in Chapter 2, had a particularly pessimistic view about the labor market which determines unemployment. Malthus argued that in the long-run, the supply of labor would expand until it had driven the wage rate to the subsistence level — the real wage at which people could just survive. Malthus based his dismal view of the labor market on his observation of Nature, where populations of species expand until the limits of available resources, and where large numbers perish at the maximum feasible populations; high birth rates just balance the death rates. Experience in the richer countries has shown that economic prosperity invalidates Malthus' dismal predictions. However, with so many dying from hunger and disease, the parallels between Nature and the labor market remain disturbingly evident in many parts of the Third World.

CHAPTER 6

ECONOMIC FLUCTUATIONS AND GROWTH

"I do not think the President understands why there is high inflation and high unemployment at the same time. But then neither does anybody else."
United States Treasury Official

Key Concepts: Long-term growth versus short-run output fluctuations; macroeconomic equilibrium; multiplier effects of changes in spending; price versus output responses to changes in aggregate demand; supply shocks; the paradox of thrift; role of fiscal policy; the circular flow of income; business cycles; influences on long-term growth; forecasting short-term output fluctuations and long-term growth.

TRENDS VERSUS FLUCTUATIONS IN REAL GDP

This chapter considers the reasons for fluctuations in real Gross Domestic Product (GDP), and also explains the principal factors affecting the rate of economic progress reflected in the trend of the real GDP. We shall see that different factors affect fluctuations than affect trends, and also that economists differ in the emphasis they place on different factors. Let us begin by considering the case of fluctuations in real GDP, and examine first the perspective taken by the Keynesians who, as we mentioned in Chapter 2, are those adhering to the ideas of the influential British economist, Lord John Maynard Keynes, whose book, *The General Theory of Employment Interest and Money*, sparked a revolution in macroeconomic thinking.

Different factors cause short-run fluctuations in real GDP than influence the long-run growth in real GDP.

KEYNESIAN THEORY OF FLUCTUATIONS IN GDP

The Keynesian theory of fluctuations in the GDP is based on the relation-ship between desired purchases, often referred to as **desired expenditures**, versus the actual output of goods and services. In particular, Keynesians argue that the GDP grows more rapidly than usual when people collectively want to buy more goods and services than are being produced. In the case of storable goods this is temporarily possible by running down inventory stocks, while in the case of services it is likely to result in queuing. If there is unused productive capacity when desired purchases/expenditures exceed output, the increase in GDP is in the real GDP, which we have denoted as Q, and if the economy is fully employed the increase is in prices, P. The traditional Keynesian arguments were invoked at a time of depression when the world's economies had substantial unused pro-ductive capacity. Therefore, it was the real GDP, or Q, that was assumed to increase, and not prices, P.[1] However, since an increase in Q with P constant still means an increase in nominal GDP, Y, we can think of the increase as being in nominal GDP, Y. (Recall from Chapter 1 that $Y = P \cdot Q$, so that a higher Q or a higher P means a higher Y). Similarly, Keynesians argue that when desired purchases/expenditures are less than output so that some output is unsold, firms react by reducing output, thereby lowering real GDP, or by reducing prices. In either case nominal GDP declines. Only when desired purchases are equal to output is there no tendency for the GDP to change relative to long-term trend. Therefore, the Key-nesian theory of fluctuations in GDP around the trend rate of economic growth involves an examination of the factors which determine desired expenditures.

Nominal GDP increases when desired expenditure exceeds output, and declines when desired expenditure is less than output.

We can think of desired expenditure, E, as being made up of the same components itemized in our discussion of the national income and product

---

[1]Later we deal in more detail with the circumstances under which real GDP or prices respond to differences between desired purchases and output.

accounts in Chapter 2. In particular, we can write:

$$E = C + I + G + (Ex - Im), \qquad (6.1)$$

where C = desired consumption, I = desired investment, G = desired expenditure by government, Ex = desired expenditure by foreigners, i.e., exports, and Im = desired imports.

Equation (6.1) categorizes desired expenditure, E, in the same way we categorized the GDP, Y, in Eq. (1.5). However, we should note that although we use the same symbols here as before, the C, I, G, Ex, and Im in Eq. (6.1) are all *desired amounts that people want to purchase*, whereas in Eq. (1.5) they refer to *actual amounts produced*.

Desired consumption, C, is the value of goods and services households want to purchase. Desired investment, I, is the amount firms would like to spend on new plant, equipment and increased inventory holdings to help provide for future production and sales. Desired government expenditure, G, are those on education, health, defense, infrastructure, administration and so on. Desired expenditure by foreigners on a nation's goods and services are, of course, exports, while desired imports are what households, firms, and the government would like to purchase from abroad. Equation (6.1) therefore breaks up desired total spending into that of households, firms, the government, and the foreign sector.

Desired expenditures change when there is a change in desired consumption, investment, government spending, exports or imports.

We can find out what causes variations in E, and thereby causes fluctuations in GDP, by considering the factors behind each of the components of desired expenditure. We can then show why it is that the GDP varies until desired expenditure equals the GDP.

Desired Consumption: Common sense and a vast accumulation of empirical evidence suggest that the amount people want to spend on consumption depends primarily on their after-tax income: the higher is a person's income after taxes, the higher is that person's consumption. Because a higher income after taxes, for given tax rates, means a higher before-tax income, we can also say that desired consumption varies with before-tax

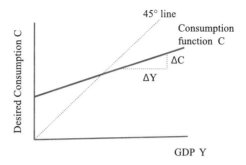

Fig. 6.1.   Consumption function.
The consumption function shows the extent to which desired consumption changes as national income or GDP changes.

income. For example, if before-tax income increases by $1, after-tax income might increase by 75 cents, and desired consumption might in turn increase by 60 cents. We could then say that desired consumption increases by 60% of the increase in before-tax income.

Since each individual is likely to want to increase consumption as their before-tax income increases, it is also the case that aggregate desired consumption in an economy is higher, the higher is aggregate before-tax income. The income for the economy as a whole is the national income, which is approximately the same as the GDP, or Y. Therefore, aggregate consumption varies in the same direction as the GDP, as shown geometrically by the line labeled C in Fig. 6.1. This line is called the **consumption function**. The slope of the consumption function shows the change in C that results from a change in Y.[2] The slope of the consumption function is less than 1, e.g., 0.6, because the change in desired consumption is smaller than the change in GDP. This is both because after-tax income does not increase as much as before-tax income, and because some after-tax income is saved. For example, if the slope of the consumption function is 0.6, then for every $1 increase in Y there is a 60 cents increase in desired consumption, with the remaining 40 cents consisting of taxes and savings.

> *The consumption function shows the change in desired consumption associated with a change in national income, or GDP.*

---

[2]The slope of a line is the change in height divided by the change along the horizontal axis. For example, the 45° line from the origin in Fig. 6.1 has a slope of 1.0.

The extent to which desired consumption changes with income is very important in Keynesian economics. It is called the **marginal propensity to consume (MPC)**. Specifically, the MPC is the value of the change in desired consumption per dollar change in nominal GDP. That is, MPC, can be written as:

$$MPC = \frac{\Delta C}{\Delta Y} \tag{6.2}$$

where

ΔC = change in desired consumption,
ΔY = change in nominal GDP.

In our example of each extra dollar of Y resulting in extra desired consumption of 60 cents, the MPC is:

$$MPC = \frac{0.60}{1.00} = 0.6$$

The MPC is the value of the change in desired consumption per dollar of change in the nominal GDP.

When consumption changes because GDP is changing, the change in consumption is called **induced consumption**; it is induced by the change in GDP and national income. This means a movement *along* the consumption function in Fig. 6.1. The consumption functions itself *shifts* up and down as a result of changes in such factors as consumer confidence, and interest rates for financing purchases of new automobiles, houses and major appliances. These shifts affect the level of the intercept of the consumption function, i.e., where the consumption function touches the vertical axis. Numerous studies of the relationship between consumption and income have shown that the slope of the consumption function, the MPC, is relatively constant, while the level of the function, as given by the intercept, fluctuates. As we shall see, it is these fluctuations in the intercept that cause fluctuations in the GDP. The value of the intercept of the consumption function, i.e., what consumption would be at a zero GDP, is called **autonomous consumption**. This part of consumption does not depend on the GDP.

Induced consumption is the part that depends on the GDP. Autonomous consumption is the part that does not depend on the GDP.

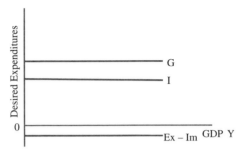

Fig. 6.2. Desired investment, government spending and exports minus imports. *For simplicity we assume desired investment, I, government spending, G, and exports minus imports, Ex − Im, are the same for all levels of GDP, Y.*

Desired Investment: As drawn in Fig. 6.2, investment is assumed to be unrelated to the GDP, Y.[3] This is reflected in the drawing of the **investment function** as a horizontal line.

The lower are interest rates, the more investment will occur at all values of Y, and the higher up the vertical axis in Fig. 6.2 will be the investment function.[4] Similarly, the higher are interest rates, the lower is the investment function. Others relevant factors determining the height of the investment function are expectations for sales of extra output produced with the help of newly acquired capital, prospects for economic and political stability, corporate taxes, and even what Keynes referred to as "animal spirits" — the result of psychological factors. As we shall see, by affecting the height of the investment function, I, all these factors can cause fluctuations in GDP.

> *The investment function shows desired investment at different values of the GDP. The height of the investment function depends on interest rates, business confidence, and corporate taxes.*

Desired Expenditure by Government: In Fig. 6.2 we treat desired government spending, G, as being unrelated to the GDP. We could alternatively

---

[3]This assumption is for simplicity. At the cost of complexity, we might want to make desired investment depend not on the level of GDP, but on the rate of growth of GDP: as we will mention later, when the economy is growing rapidly businesses want to expand their capacity.

[4]The effect of interest rates on investment is covered in the next chapter. For the time being the reader is requested to accept this.

have drawn a downward slope on G if we felt that higher income and output reduces the amount the government wants to spend; the government might feel less obligated to spend in a stronger economy. However, the effect of the GDP on government spending is likely to be small, and allowing for such an effect would have little impact on the overall picture. Therefore, we show G as horizontal, and argue that shifts of this line up and down the vertical axis are the result of political decisions. It is the effect of these political decisions on the volatility of GDP that interests us.

Government spending depends largely on political decisions.

Desired Expenditure by Foreigners, Exports: Desired spending by foreigners, i.e., exports, Ex, depends on foreign incomes, not domestic incomes. Therefore, if we were to draw Ex on its own against Y, we would draw a horizontal line. However, we do not show Ex on its own. Rather, we show desired exports minus desired imports. The difference between exports and imports, (Ex − Im) is called the **balance of trade surplus** when positive, and the **balance of trade deficit** when negative.

Desired Imports: The amount of goods and services people buy from abroad increases with national income. That is, Im increases with Y. With Im being subtracted from Ex in constructing the line (Ex − Im) in Fig. 6.2, (Ex − Im) slopes downwards as we move towards higher Y. However, for simplicity we assume imports depends so little on Y that (Ex − Im) is horizontal. But what is it that makes (Ex − Im) shift up and down?

Ceteris paribus, the higher are domestic prices versus foreign prices, the smaller are exports and the larger are imports. Therefore, *ceteris paribus* the higher are domestic versus foreign prices, the smaller is (Ex − Im). Similarly, the lower are foreign incomes the smaller are exports and the lower is (Ex − Im). The height of (Ex − Im) is also affected by exchange rates, and import tariffs and quotas. We draw (Ex − Im) below the horizontal axis, which is the situation if imports exceed exports. As with I and G, variations in the height of (Ex − Im) can cause fluctuations in GDP.

The balance of trade depends on domestic versus foreign prices, exchange rates, tariffs and quotas.

Finding the Equilibrium GDP

We have noted that when desired expenditure, E, is not equal to the GDP, Y, GDP tends to be changing, and only when E equals Y does GDP remain steady. Using the categorization of E in Eq. (6.2) this means GDP is steady only when

$$E = Y,$$

i.e.,

$$C + I + G + (Ex - Im) = Y, \qquad (6.3)$$

where C, I, G, Ex, and Im are components of desired expenditure, and Y is actual GDP.

To find out what Eq. (6.3) implies for the level of the GDP, and for the factors which can change this level, let us consider Fig. 6.3. The figure shows each of the components of desired expenditure. These components can be added to obtain total desired expenditure. This requires the "vertical addition" of C, I, G, and (Ex − Im). Vertical addition means adding the value of C to the value of each of I, G, and (Ex − Im) at each value of Y. The result of adding all these lines is the line E in Fig. 6.3. [Since (Ex − Im) is assumed to be negative — a balance of trade deficit — this reduces the height of the line E in Fig. 6.3, but all the other components of desired expenditures put the resulting line E above the line C.]

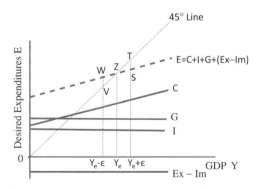

Fig. 6.3.   Equilibrium GDP where desired spending equals GDP.
The 45° line shows potential equilibria where desired expenditures, E, on the vertical axis equals GDP on the horizontal axis. The actual equilibrium is at Y_e. Above Y_e, GDP exceeds E and the economy shrinks. Below Y_e, E exceeds Y and the economy expands.

The slope of the line E is the same as the slope of the consumption function, C, because consumption is assumed to be the only element of total desired expenditure which depends on Y. Therefore, the change in total desired expenditure induced by a change in Y is the result of the induced change in C. However, the intercept of line E on the vertical axis is the result of all the components of desired expenditures. *Ceteris paribus*, the larger is the intercept of any component of expenditure, the higher up the vertical axis is the intercept of the total expenditure line, E.

The 45° line in Fig. 6.3 gives those points in the diagram where the value on the vertical axis equals the value on the horizontal axis. Therefore, points on the 45° line are points where desired expenditure, measured along the vertical axis, equals GDP, measured along the horizontal axis. This enables us to locate the level of GDP where $E = Y$. This is found by determining where the desired expenditure line, $E = C + I + G + (Ex - Im)$, intersects the 45° line.

The GDP where the desired expenditure line, E, cuts the 45° line is Y_e. At a GDP below Y_e, such as at the GDP, $(Y_e - \varepsilon)$, the height of the desired expenditure line E is above the 45° line, so E exceeds Y. [The height of the 45° line equals Y because along the line $E = Y$.] At a level of GDP above Y_e, such as at the GDP, $(Y_e + \varepsilon)$, we have the reverse situation. Here line E is below the 45° line, and hence E is less than Y. Only at Y_e is $E = Y$.

The level of income where $E = Y$, i.e., Y_e, is called the **equilibrium GDP**. It is called the equilibrium GDP because only at Y_e does the amount of goods and services people *want* to buy, E, equal the amount of goods and services *actually* produced, Y, so there is no reason for GDP to change.

The equilibrium GDP is that level at which desired expenditure is equal to actual output.

The GDP, Y_e, is a **stable equilibrium** in that if GDP is disturbed from this level while the E line remains unchanged, forces will return GDP to this level. To see this, suppose that after initially being Y_e in Fig. 6.3, there is a sudden increase in GDP to $(Y_e + \varepsilon)$. We can see by drawing a line from the horizontal axis up to line E at the GDP of $(Y_e + \varepsilon)$, that E is less than Y by the distance between T and S. That is, the public wants to buy $T - S$ less than is being produced. This would result in lower production or lower prices, either of which would cause a declining Y. Keynesians argue that if prices are "sticky" in a downward direction, then it is a decline in real GDP, Q, that is, the basis of the decline in Y.

If instead of increasing, GDP declined to $(Y_e - \varepsilon)$, E would be greater than Y by the distance between V and W. That is, people would want to buy V – W more than is being produced, causing firms to increase production or prices. Either would cause an increase in GDP, Y. However, Keynesians traditionally argue that if there is a lot of underutilized capacity in the economy it is real GDP, Q, and not prices, P, that increases.

When desired expenditure exceeds actual output GDP expands, and when desired expenditure is smaller than actual output GDP contracts.

The actual signal as to whether desired expenditure, E, is larger or smaller than production, Y, comes in the form of an unplanned change in inventory stocks. This is because when people want to buy more than is currently being produced, firms meet the extra demand by running down their inventories. This signals firms to increase production. Similarly, when people want to buy less than is being produced, the unsold goods are added to inventories. This signals firms to reduce production.

The changes in inventories that signal firms whether to increase or decrease production are counted as part of *actual* investment. For example, when production exceeds desired expenditure causing inventories to increase, the increase in inventory is included in actual investment, and is hence part of the actual expenditure of firms. Therefore, by definition, the actual value of expenditure, including changes in inventory stocks, must equal the value of output. However, while the national income accounts always show *actual* expenditure equal to actual output, only at the equilibrium GDP is *desired* expenditure equal to actual expenditure, with both equal to GDP.

Keynesian Factors Causing Fluctuations in the GDP

Suppose we begin with desired consumption, investment, government spending and exports minus imports such that the total desired expenditure line is E_1 in Fig. 6.4, and equilibrium GDP is therefore Y_1. Then, suppose there is an increase in desired investment at all levels of GDP from I_1 to I_2. Since the total desired expenditure line is obtained by adding C, I, G and (Ex – Im), the effect of an increase in investment from I_1 to I_2 is to

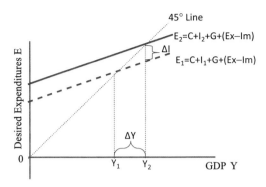

Fig. 6.4. The multiplier from trickle-down spending.
After an exogenous increase in I *the equilibrium GDP at which* E $=$ Y *increases by a multiple of the increase in* I. *There are also multiplier effects from increases in autonomous consumption,* G *and* Ex, *and from autonomous reductions in* Im.

shift the aggregate desired expenditure line upwards from E_1 to E_2, where E_2 contains the higher desired investment, I_2. The new E_2 differs from E_1 at each GDP only because E_2 contains the higher desired investment, I_2. With the new desired expenditure line we obtain a new equilibrium GDP, Y_2, which is higher than the original equilibrium GDP, Y_1. The new equilibrium GDP would be achieved via desired expenditures exceeding output at the original equilibrium, Y_1, causing an unplanned reduction in inventories, and a consequent increase in output or prices.

An increase in government spending, G, net exports, (Ex − Im), or in the autonomous component of consumption C — that part reflected in the intercept of the consumption function — will all have the same effect as an increase in investment; all shift the expenditure line upwards, causing an increase in the equilibrium GDP. Similarly, decreases in government spending, net exports or autonomous consumption reduce the equilibrium GDP.

Some of the factors which could cause an increase in desired expenditure, and hence in equilibrium GDP, are listed in Table 6.1, along with the components of desired expenditure they affect. These are the factors which a Keynesian would list if asked for the causes of fluctuations in the GDP.

The fact that increases in desired investment, government spending, and so on, cause increases in the GDP should come as little or no surprise. What might come as a surprise is the *extent* to which income is increased

Table 6.1. Keynesian factors which could cause an increased in the GDP.

Increased I	Increased G	Increased (Ex − Im)	Increased C
Lower interest rates	Politically determined	Lower domestic prices relative to foreign prices	Lower taxes
Higher expected sales or future profitability		Depreciation in country's exchange rate	Improved confidence
Wearing out of existing capital		Higher incomes in foreign countries	Lower interest rates on consumer debt
Reduced corporate income taxes		Higher tariffs on imports	
"Animal spirits"			

by an increase in desired investment, government spending, and so on. As an examination of Fig. 6.4 indicates, the change in income shown by $\Delta Y = (Y_2 - Y_1)$ is larger than the change in investment, $\Delta I = (I_2 - I_1)$, that brought it about. That is, the change in investment from I_1 to I_2, which equals the vertical distance between E_1 and E_2, is smaller than ΔY, the change in the GDP. Let us consider why GDP can increase by a multiple of the increase in investment or any other component of expenditures, E.

> *Equilibrium GDP is changed by a change in investment, government spending, net exports, or autonomous consumption. Equilibrium GDP changes by a multiple of the change in desired expenditure.*

The Multiplier

The relationship between the original change in desired expenditure and the change in the GDP is called the **multiplier**. The multiplier is defined as

$$\text{Multiplier} = \frac{\text{Change in equilibrium GDP}}{\text{Change in autonomous expenditure}} \qquad (6.4)$$

and where by **autonomous expenditure** we mean expenditure that is not induced by the GDP itself.

> *The multiplier is equal to the multiple by which the change in equilibrium GDP exceeds the change in autonomous expenditure that caused the change in GDP.*

Table 6.2. The multiplier is higher if the MPC is higher.

	MPC = 0.8		MPC = 0.9	
	Recipient's income	Accumulated income	Recipient's income	Accumulated income
Original injection	$1.00 bln	$1.00 bln	$1.00 bln	$1.00 bln
Second stage	0.80	1.80	0.90	1.90
Third stage	0.64	2.44	0.81	2.71
Fourth stage	0.51	2.95	0.73	3.44
Fifth stage	0.41	3.36	0.66	4.10
Sixth stage	0.33	3.69	0.59	4.69
Seventh stage	0.26	3.95	0.53	5.22
Eighth stage	0.21	4.15	0.48	5.70
Ninth stage	0.17	4.32	0.43	6.13
Tenth stage	0.13	4.45	0.39	6.52
⋮		⋮		⋮
Total		$5.00 bln		$10.00 bln

The denominator of the multiplier, which we have called the "change in autonomous expenditure," is the original change in desired expenditure that brings about the change in equilibrium GDP, and which is not itself caused by the change in GDP. The GDP can change by more than the change in desired expenditure because of what is popularly referred to as "trickle-down". For example, suppose the government spends $1 billion to hire labor during a time of heavy unemployment. Table 6.2 shows this as the "original injection" of spending. Table 6.2 shows that when the MPC is 0.8, the recipients of the initial $1 billion of wages spend an extra $0.8 billion on food, housing, travel, and so on. This is shown as the "second stage". The recipients of the extra $0.8 billion, for whom this is income, spend 0.8 of what they receive, which is $0.8 \times \$0.8$ billion $= \$0.64$ billion. This is shown as the "third stage." At each successive stage, 0.8 of receipts from the previous stage are spent. By adding up the extra incomes from all stages we find that from an initial $1 billion increase in spending when MPC = 0.8, the GDP is increased by $5 billion.

With the multiplier defined as in Eq. (6.4), we find for an MPC = 0.8:

$$\text{Multiplier} = \frac{\$\,5\text{ billion}}{\$\,1\text{ billion}} = 5.$$

If we calculate the multiplier when MPC = 0.9 in Table 6.2, we discover it has doubled to

$$\text{Multiplier} = \frac{\$10 \text{ billion}}{\$1 \text{ billion}} = 10.$$

We can calculate the multiplier without having to calculate the extra spending at each stage by noting that:

$$\text{Multiplier} = \frac{1}{1 - \text{MPC}}. \tag{6.5}$$

In particular, we see that when MPC = 0.8 the multiplier is $1/(1-0.8) = 5$, and when MPC = 0.9, the multiplier is $1/(1 - 0.9) = 10$.

The multiplier is larger the larger is the MPC.

Real GDP versus Price Fluctuations

With slack such as with unemployment in excess of 20% in many countries during the Great Depression of 1929–1933, Keynesians believed extra expenditures would translate into more being produced, not higher prices. In the case of desired expenditure being less than output, Keynesians would expect a decline in real GDP rather than prices due to prices being "sticky" in a downward direction. So far we have not explained what we mean by "slack" and "sticky prices". Let us rectify this situation, and do so by considering Fig. 6.5.

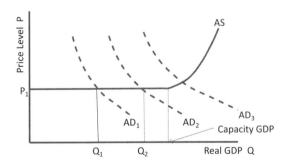

Fig. 6.5.   Aggregate demand and real GDP versus prices.
The AD curves slope down because a lower price level raises the real value of fixed face value assets including money, plus exports. If prices rise only after GDP reaches capacity, variations in AD are associated with variations in real GDP below capacity and with nominal GDP above capacity.

Figure 6.5 shows **aggregate demand curves** and an **aggregate supply curve** for an economy. These curves should not be confused with those used in the microeconomic theory of supply and demand because here we are referring to total or aggregate demand and supply in an economy, not supply and demand in individual markets.

The aggregate demand curve shows how much demand there is for an economy's total output at different price levels. It does not slope downwards because lower prices make one good cheaper than another good, which is the reason for downward-sloping demand in microeconomics. Rather, the aggregate demand curve slopes downwards because:

(1) A lower price level makes peoples' assets with a given face value, such as currency, worth more. This is called a **wealth effect**, and leads to increased consumption, C.

(2) A lower price level reduces the demand for money. (If things cost less you need less money to pay for them. This was explained in Chapter 3). For a given money supply, the lower demand for money means an excess supply of money. This causes extra expenditure on goods and bonds as people try to reduce their money holdings. The buying of goods directly affects total expenditure, E, via affecting C. The buying of bonds causes higher bond prices. This means lower interest rates, and more investment, I.[5]

(3) A lower price level makes a country's exports cheaper vis-à-vis those in other countries, thereby increasing exports, Ex.

We see that a lower price level can cause an increase in the aggregate quantity of goods and services demanded. Therefore, the aggregate demand curve slopes downwards in Fig. 6.5.

The aggregate demand curve slopes downwards with respect to the price level because lower prices increase real wealth, cause an excess supply of money and make exports cheaper.

The reason the aggregate supply curve slopes upwards, as in Fig. 6.5, depends on whether we are considering the short-run or long-run. In the

---

[5]The connection between bond prices and interest rates is discussed more fully in the next chapter.

short-run, as the economy expands the quality of inputs drawn into production diminishes; the best inputs are used first, then the next-best and so
on. Therefore, as the economy expands costs increase, and these costs are
eventually passed on in higher prices. That is, in the short-run P increases
as real GDP expands because of diminishing input quality. In the long-run,
expansion of the real GDP increases input prices. These eventually translate
into higher product prices.

> *The aggregate supply curve slopes upwards with respect to the price level in the
> short-run because lower quality inputs are drawn into production as real GDP
> expands, and this increases costs and prices. The aggregate supply curve slopes
> upwards in the long-run because input prices increase as real GDP expands, and
> higher input prices eventually cause higher output prices.*

We have drawn the aggregate supply curve, AS, in Fig. 6.5 as horizontal
until the economy reaches its **capacity GDP**, which is the output that can
be produced with all factors fully employed. After this level of GDP the
AS curve slopes upwards.[6] The short run aggregate supply curve takes this
shape if input quality remains constant until the economy reaches capacity,
and then input quality suddenly diminishes. The long-run aggregate supply
curve takes this shape if input prices are constant when factors are not fully
employed, and then factor prices increase when the economy reaches its
capacity GDP. Of course, in reality there is likely to be a smoother path of
the AS curve around capacity GDP.

> *Capacity real GDP is the economy's output when all factors of production are
> fully employed.*

Figure 6.5 shows that fluctuations in aggregate demand result in fluctuations in real GDP but not in prices if aggregate demand is below the
capacity GDP. For example, if aggregate demand shifts from AD_1 to AD_2,
real GDP increases from Q_1 to Q_2, in line with the horizontal shift in the
aggregate demand curve. The price level remains unchanged at P_1. This happens because there is slack in the economy, with production below capacity.

---

[6]As we explained in Chapter 5, even at full employment not all factors of production are
working. Therefore, it is possible for output to increase above the full-employment level, at
least temporarily.

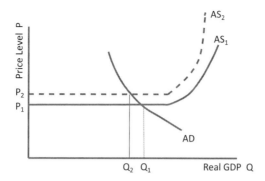

Fig. 6.6. Supply shocks and stagflation.
If the entire AS curve shifts up from an increase in production costs at all outputs this can result in stagflation with rising prices and declining GDP.

However, if aggregate demand increases as high as AD_3, increases in aggregate demand translate into higher prices rather than higher real GDP.

We can use an aggregate supply — aggregate demand figure to consider not only shifts in demand, like those from AD_1 to AD_2 to AD_3 in Fig. 6.5, but also to consider **supply shocks**; supply shocks are sudden upward shifts in the aggregate supply curve. This is done in Fig. 6.6.

A supply shock is a sudden upward shift in the aggregate supply curve.

An example of a supply shock is a jump in the price of oil. Such a jump means higher production costs at all outputs of the economy. That is, the aggregate supply curve, AS, suddenly shifts upwards. The height of the aggregate supply curve gives the price level at which each level of real GDP is supplied, and this price level increases with increase in the cost of production. Figure 6.6 shows that an upward-shift in the aggregate supply curve results in a *higher* price level and a *lower* real GDP. That is, unlike demand fluctuations such as those in Fig. 6.5, where the price level and real GDP can move in the same direction, at least beyond capacity GDP, in the case of supply shocks the price level and real GDP move in opposite directions.

Changes in aggregate demand can change real GDP and the price level in the same direction. Changes in aggregate supply change real GDP and the price level in opposite directions.

Supply Shocks and Stagflation

The shape of the short-run Phillips' curve discussed in the previous chapter suggests that higher inflation, or at least, unanticipated inflation, is associated with lower unemployment. Since the real GDP is higher when unemployment is lower — more people working means more output — it follows from a short-run Phillips' curve that higher (unanticipated) inflation would be associated with higher real GDP. This was the view of most economists until the economic experience of the period of late 1960s to the early 1980s, during which time inflation was rapid even when the real GDP was growing slowly or even declining. Economists coined a new term for this condition, **stagflation**, a hybrid of **stagnation**, meaning a slowly growing or shrinking real GDP, and inflation.

Stagflation is the combination of a stagnating real GDP and high inflation.

Examination of Fig. 6.6 shows that stagflation is what we would expect after supply shocks, such as after a jump in the price of oil. Consideration of the implications of Fig. 6.6 shows that any presumption high inflation would be associated with a rapidly increasing real GDP is based on an assumption that demand shifts and not supply shifts are the cause of fluctuations in real GDP. Keynesian economists tended to think in such demand-shift terms until the stagflation following the oil price shocks of 1973 and 1979. Today, it is recognized that either aggregate demand or supply can shift, although demand is more likely to fluctuate than supply.

The Paradox of Thrift

The traditional Keynesian view that fluctuations in real GDP are due to fluctuations in aggregate demand led naturally to a view that governments should intervene to keep aggregate demand steady, thereby reducing the fluctuations in real GDP, unemployment and so on. The belief that such intervention is necessary was reinforced not only by the chronic unemployment that existed just prior to the publication of Keynes' *General Theory*, but also by Keynes' recognition of how aggregate spending responds to increasing unemployment.

When an economy becomes weaker and people lose their jobs it is natural for those still working to prepare for tougher times ahead by increasing their savings. After all, if others are losing their jobs, it could also happen to them, and it is better to be prepared. Therefore, as unemployment grows, those with jobs tend to increase savings, which in turn means spending less of their incomes. That is, as unemployment grows, consumption declines. Keynes dubbed this phenomenon the **paradox of thrift**. It is a paradox because at the very time that increased expenditure is needed to put people back to work, what individuals naturally do to protect themselves is reduce expenditure. This makes matters worse. Keynes and those who have adhered to his ideas were led to advocate steps by the government to counteract what would happen quite naturally to the other private components of aggregate demand as conditions in an economy worsened.

The paradox of thrift is that as the economy slows, people reduce expenditure even through the economy needs increased expenditure.

The idea of intervening in the economy revolves around the role of fiscal policy. Keynesians see this not only as a way of overcoming the paradox of thrift, but also as a way of keeping real GDP from fluctuating.

The Role of Fiscal Policy

We have seen that when an economy is operating at below capacity, an increase in desired expenditure and hence in aggregate demand causes an increase in real GDP, and a reduction in desired expenditure causes a decline in real GDP. However, if a decline in, e.g., investment I, is matched by an equal increase in government spending, G, total desired expenditure can be prevented from changing. This is clear from Fig. 6.3, where the value of G can be varied in the opposite direction to variations in I to keep the height of the E line, and hence the equilibrium GDP, unchanged. We can also see this from the definition of desired expenditure as:

$$E = C + I + G + (Ex - Im), \qquad (6.1)$$

where G can be varied to offset variations in I to keep E constant. According to traditional Keynesians, the task of government is to keep track of C, I and (Ex − Im), and to change its expenditure (or taxes which can affect the height of C) to maintain a constant aggregate demand and maintain full employment.

A difficulty that the government has in implementing **discretionary fiscal policy** — the conscious manipulation of government spending and taxes — is taking action sufficiently early. The ability to act early is affected by the need to:

(1) Recognise the problem.
(2) Select the solution.
(3) Implement the solution.
(4) Allow for delay before the policy works.

That is, there are a number of lags in recognizing the problem, taking action and so on. The recognition lag is reduced by maintaining the regular collection of data on the factors influencing the GDP, and on behavior of the GDP itself. However, data tend to reveal a problem only after it has begun, and even if the problem were recognized early on, there is still the policy selection lag, the implementation lag, and the lag in the policy working.

Discretionary fiscal policy is the conscious variation of government spending and taxes to maintain a steady GDP and full employment.

It has been argued by some Monetarists that the lags in recognition, policy selection, implementation, and response are so long that by the time the policy is working, the economy is likely to be rebounding on its own steam. Fiscal policy might then make fluctuations in GDP even larger than they would have been without fiscal interference.

Whether or not active discretionary fiscal policy can keep an economy on an even keel is, of course, at the center of debate over the role of government in the economy. Not surprisingly, the data have been scrutinized for evidence on lags and policy effectiveness, but the very fact that both supporters and opponents of active government intervention can still be found is evidence no conclusive answer has been reached.

AN ALTERNATIVE VIEW OF EQUILIBRIUM: LEAKAGES VERSUS INJECTIONS

Finding the equilibrium GDP by looking for the GDP at which desired expenditure equals actual output, as we have in Fig. 6.3, is not the only way

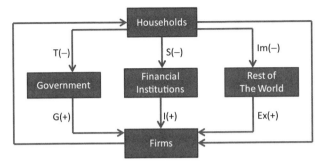

Fig. 6.7. Principal components of the circular flow of income.
Only when the sum of withdrawals from the circular flow of income, T, S, and Im, *equals the sum of injections, G, I and* Ex, *is the GDP under no pressure to change.*

of locating the equilibrium GDP. An alternative and equivalent method is based on the flows between different sectors of an economy.

Figure 6.7 shows the **circular flow of income** between firms and households. If households receive all the incomes paid by firms, and then households spend all these incomes on products made by the firms, the flow of income can circulate indefinitely without changing. For example, if firms produce $1 trillion of final goods and services and pay $1 trillion to households in wages, rents, interest and profits, and then households spend this $1 trillion on the products sold by firms, the firms can then produce another $1 trillion of final goods and services, pay the households, who then buy the firms' products, and so on. This circular flow is characterized by the arrows on the outside of Fig. 6.7 going from firms to households and from households to firms.

However, in reality the flow of funds between households and firms is subject to leakages. There are also some injections into the flow from outside. The leakages from the circular flow of income result from funds received by households that are not subsequently spent on firms within the economy because of imports, savings and taxes. The injections into the circular flow of income result from exports, business investment and government spending. Let us begin by considering the effects on the circular flow of income of imports and exports.

If households spend all they receive from firms, and then firms pay all they receive to households, the circular flow of income can continue unabated.

Imports constitute a leakage from the circular flow because they mean that some of what households receive as income from firms is not spent on goods and services produced by domestic firms. Instead, it leaks abroad, being spent on imported products. This is shown in Fig. 6.7 by Im(−), i.e. imports of households from the rest of the world.[7] The negative sign next to Im(−) shows this is a leakage from the circular flow of income between domestic firms and domestic households.

Another reason households do not spend all they earn on firms is because some income is paid to the government as taxes. This is shown in Fig. 6.7 by T(−), households' taxes. An additional leakage between households and firms occurs because some household after-tax income is saved and placed in financial institutions. This is shown by S(−).

Offsetting the leakages from the circular flow of income are a number of injections. These are shown by (+) signs in Fig. 6.7. Injections result from exports, Ex(+), which are part of spending on the output of domestic firms, but are not due to the spending of domestic households. Injections also result from business investment, I(+), which is financed through financial intermediation involving commercial banks, stock and bond markets and so on. Finally, injections come from government expenditure, G(+). We assume government buys only from firms.

The circular flow of income cannot remain stable if more flows out than flows in, or if more flows in than flows out. If injections exceed withdrawals, the circular flow of income will expand. A useful analogy to the circular flow of income with its leakages versus injections, is a bathtub or sink. If more flows into a bathtub (the injections) than goes down the drain (the leakages), the bathtub will overflow. This is like the situation of expansion of an economy. If, on the other hand, more flows down the drain than flows in from the tap, the bathtub or sink will empty. In an economy, withdrawals exceeding injections means a decline in the GDP. The only way that the level of water or the level of GDP is maintained is for injections to equal withdrawals. That is, for GDP to be in equilibrium, injections must equal withdrawals.

---

[7]For simplicity we assume only households, and not government or firms, buy imports. Similarly, for simplicity we assume only households pay taxes and save. We also ignore transfer payments such as welfare from the government to households.

If injections equal withdrawals then the items with (+) signs in Fig. 6.7 have a total value equal to the combined value of the items with (−) signs. (To extend our analogue of a sink, this is like a sink with three faucets and three drain holes where the sum of flows in equals the sum of flows out.) This means that for a stable circular flow of income we need:

$$I + G + Ex = S + T + Im. \tag{6.6}$$

The left-hand side is the sum of injections, and the right-hand side is the sum of withdrawals.

A stable circular flow of income requires that total injections into the circular flow of income — investment plus government spending plus exports — equals total withdrawals from the circular flow of income — savings plus taxes plus imports.

The condition for a stable income in Eq. (6.6) is equivalent to the condition we described earlier, namely, $E = Y$. This can be seen by adding C to both sides of Eq. (6.6) and moving Im to the left-hand side, giving:

$$C + I + G + (Ex - Im) = C + S + T. \tag{6.7}$$

The left-hand side is E, as it was defined and used in Eq. (6.1). The right-hand side of Eq. (6.7) is Y, because by definition, before-tax household income, Y, is either taken as taxes, consumed, or saved, i.e.

$$Y \equiv C + S + T.$$

Hence, Eq. (6.7) equates E on the left-hand side with Y on the right-hand side, and Eq. (6.6) is equivalent to $E = Y$.

Equation (6.6) and Fig. 6.7, which consider injections versus withdrawals, while equivalent to the equality of E and Y, put different emphasis on the factors affecting the equilibrium GDP. In particular, Eq. (6.6) and Fig. 6.7 make it clear that achievement of the equilibrium GDP depends on:

1. Savings, S, versus investment, I: *Ceteris paribus*, the higher are savings, which are a withdrawal from the circular flow of income, relative to investment, which is an injection, the more pressure there is for the economy to shrink. Similarly, the higher is investment relative to savings the more pressure there is for the economy to expand. The tendency for any imbalance between savings and investment to occur depends on commercial banks and financial markets in which stocks and bonds are traded. In well-functioning financial markets savings and investment are brought into line by changes in interest rates, and more generally in the **cost of capital**. (The cost of capital is the cost of raising funds for business expansion. If businesses use debt financing — borrowing from commercial banks or selling corporate bonds — the cost of funds is the interest rate. If businesses use **equity financing** — selling stocks which are claims to the ownership of companies — the cost of capital is the **expected return** that must be offered to shareholders. The expected return is a cost of financing because the higher it is, the more the profitability of existing shareholders must be shared with new shareholders who are providing financing.) So, how could it be that savings could be different from investment?

John Maynard Keynes in his *General Theory* identified a situation where savings could exceed investment, and where they would not be brought back in line by a decline in the cost of capital. (Normally, if savings exceed investment the cost of capital declines, which reduces the amount saved and increases the amount borrowed until they are equal.) The situation Keynes identified is known as the **liquidity trap**. Keynes argued that a negative cost of capital cannot occur when savers have the option of holding money: why accept a negative return when you can hold cash with a zero return? Therefore, as the cost of capital approaches zero, if savings still exceed investment there is no force to bring them in line. There have been times when such conditions have occurred, such as the Great Depression when interest rates were less that one-quarter of a percent and in Japan in the last decade of the 20th century and first decade of the 21st century.

2. Exports, Ex, versus Imports, Im: Equation (6.6) and Fig. 6.7 show that the state of a nation's balance of trade — its exports, Ex, versus imports, Im — can also be important for a steady national product. *Ceteris paribus*, if a country is buying more from abroad than it sells, this can cause a declining GDP. On the other hand, when exports exceed imports the trade surplus would contribute to an expanding economy. Just as the cost of capital provides a potential mechanism to bring about a balance of savings and investment, so, in the case of imports and exports, there is a potential mechanism for balance via the exchange rate. And just as there are circumstances in which the cost of capital may not restore balance between savings and investment, so it can be that the exchange rate may not align exports and imports.

Exports give rise to a demand for a country's currency, and imports give rise to a supply of a country's currency.[8] It follows that if exchange rates are allowed to vary freely according to supply and demand, and if there are no other forces on exchange rates other than exports and imports, then eventually Ex would equal Im. However, in reality many currencies are not free to vary in price: the exchange rate is fixed by the government. Furthermore, there are other factors giving rise to currency demands and supplies, most obviously those associated with international borrowing and investment. When a country's residents invest abroad they supply their currency to the foreign exchange market: they need to buy the foreign currency to pay for the foreign assets. When foreign currency borrowing occurs there is a demand for the borrower's currency: the foreign currency is sold in exchange for the currency of the borrowing country.

If the exchange rate is determined by *overall* supply of and demand for a county's currency, when foreign investment and borrowing are not equal, overall balance between currency demand and supply will occur with imports not equal to exports. For example, if foreign investment exceeds foreign currency borrowing so there is a net supply of the country's currency, there will be a net demand for the currency from exports versus imports. Similarly, if foreign currency borrowing exceeds foreign currency investment so there is a net demand for the country's currency, with overall balance of supply and demand there must be a net supply of the currency from the country's imports versus exports. We find that Im versus Ex in Fig. 6.7 and Eq. (6.6) depend on a country's international borrowing and investment. *Ceteris paribus*, the larger is a country's net foreign investment, which contributes to currency supply, the larger will be Ex versus Im which contributes to the offsetting currency demand.

3. Government Spending, G, versus Taxes, T: Government spending and taxes in Fig. 6.7 and Eq. (6.6), and the associated fiscal deficits or surpluses, are determined largely in the political arena. The injections versus withdrawals view of the equilibrium circular flow of income makes it clear that stabilization of the GDP would involve setting G versus T at a value that offsets the situation created by the combined effect of S versus I and

---

[8]The factors influencing exchange rates are discussed more in detail in Chapter 8.

Ex versus Im. With political pressure to reduce taxes, provide help for the needy, invest in critical infrastructure, health, education and so on, achieving balance in the circular flow of national income is extremely difficult.

INFLATIONARY EXPECTATIONS AND GDP FLUCTUATIONS

The arguments in the previous chapter about how differences between realized inflation and anticipated inflation cause variations in unemployment, can also be used to explain fluctuations in real GDP. In order to extend the arguments of the previous chapter to fluctuations in the real GDP, we must first describe the connection between employment and output. This connection is provided by the **production function**, which is a relationship showing how much output is obtained from various quantities of inputs of factors of production. There are production functions for individual products, and also a production function for the nation as a whole. The production function of the nation is called the **aggregate production function**.

An aggregate production function describes how much output a nation gets from various levels of inputs.

The Aggregate Production Function: Real GDP versus Employment

The aggregate production function tells us what size of real GDP will result from different inputs of capital, labor, and other inputs. The volume of real GDP clearly depends on the quality as well as the quantity of capital and labor, and on the efficiency with which the inputs are used, with efficiency of input-use determined in part by the quality of management.

The quality of labor depends on the level of education, and the quality of capital depends on the state of knowledge and available technology. These can be assumed to be fixed in the short-run. Furthermore, the effectiveness of management can also be assumed fixed in the short-run. These assumptions are based on the view that the level of education of workers, available technology, and the ability of management are the result of the accumulation of knowledge, which while constantly improving, advances relatively little in a short period; even when rapid learning is taking place the flow of new knowledge during any given year is small relative to the

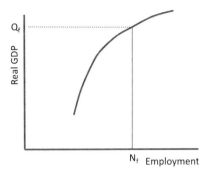

Fig. 6.8. The aggregate production function.
Variations in real GDP around the full employment level are caused by variations in employment and hence in unemployment.

stock of knowledge inherited from all of previous history. The *quantity* of capital can also be assumed fixed in the short-run for a similar reason that the *quality* of labor, capital, and management are assumed to be fixed; it takes many years to build up the stock of factories, production equipment, roads, bridges, and so on.

The assumptions of a fixed quality of capital, labor and managerial ability, and a fixed quantity of capital, allow us to concentrate on the only remaining variable, the quantity of labor. That is, given our assumptions we can explain short-run changes in real GDP in terms of the quantity of labor employed. The connection between real GDP and employment is described diagrammatically in Fig. 6.8. The figure shows that the higher is employment, the higher is the real GDP. Because factors of production other than labor are fixed, the added real GDP for given increases in employment become smaller as employment expands. This is the result of the law of diminishing marginal product which, as we saw in Chapter 5, states that when constrained by a fixed amount of a factor of production, adding more of a variable factor of production eventually adds less and less to output. We have marked the level of employment at which full employment occurs as N_f, and the level of real GDP associated with this level of employment, the full employment GDP, as Q_f.

With the quality of labor, capital and management, and the quantity of capital all fixed in the short-run, variations in real GDP result from variations in the quantity of labor employed.

Unanticipated Inflation and Real GDP

When explaining unemployment we argued that because of inflexible wages, employment increases when inflation exceeds what had been anticipated; this is when contracted wages are too low. Consequently, increases in real GDP occur when there is unanticipated inflation. Similarly, reductions in employment and real GDP occur when inflation is smaller than had been anticipated; this is when contracted wages are too high. This is summarized in Fig. 6.9, which shows unanticipated inflation and unanticipated disinflation on the vertical axis, and changes in real GDP on the horizontal axis. When inflation is correctly anticipated we show real GDP growing at the trend rate which is due to the normal advance of productivity and so on. Faster growth in real GDP than the trend rate occurs when realized inflation exceeds expectations, i.e., when there is unanticipated inflation. Slower growth than the trend rate occurs when realized inflation is below expectations, i.e., when there is unanticipated disinflation. A substantial amount of unanticipated disinflation can even cause the growth in real GDP to be negative. In Fig. 6.9, this occurs if unanticipated disinflation exceeds OA.

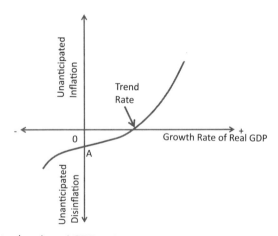

Fig. 6.9. Fluctuations in real GDP and unanticipated inflation.
At 0 on the vertical axis inflation is correctly anticipated and GDP growth is at its trend rate. When inflation is faster than anticipated, GDP growth is above trend, and when inflation is slower than anticipated GDP growth is below trend.

Rational Expectations and Real GDP Fluctuations

In Chapter 5 we explained that if inflationary expectations are rational, then inflation is just as likely to be overestimated as underestimated. This is because by rational expectations we mean that all relevant information about what could affect future inflation is taken into account in inflation forecasts. Under such conditions inflation is as likely to be over-estimated as under-estimated. If inflation expectations are indeed rational, then in terms of Fig. 6.9 the economy is just as likely to have unanticipated inflation — i.e., be above zero on the vertical axis — as have unanticipated disinflation — i.e., be below zero on the vertical axis. The growth rate of the real GDP would then fluctuate around its trend, being as often above the trend as below.

Ceteris paribus, real GDP will grow at above its trend when there is unanticipated inflation, and below its trend when there is unanticipated disinflation.

The length of time the growth rate of real GDP is above or below the trend depends on the length of wage contracts. This is because if, e.g., there is unanticipated disinflation and wages are therefore too high, the longer are wage contracts the longer wages will remain above equilibrium.[9] This means that even though expectations may be rational, unemployment could be high or low for months or even years on end. For example, if inflation unexpectedly declines, but many wage contracts have two or even three years before they expire, unemployment could persist for two or three years. Therefore, instead of having just short-term, random fluctuations of unemployment and hence of real GDP growth around the trend, the economy could exhibit variations that take the longer up and down sweeps characteristic of a business cycle.

PHASES OF THE BUSINESS CYCLE

The **business cycle**, or **trade cycle** as it used to be called, refers to a recurring pattern of variations of GDP growth rates around the trend, and the

---

[9]At any time there are newly agreed wage contracts, expiring contracts, and contracts with various lengths of continuing validity. Our comments therefore relate to the *average* length of wage contracts in the economy.

associated variations of unemployment around the natural rate of unemployment. There are four phases to a business cycle; the **trough**, which is when unemployment is highest and real GDP is lowest; the **recovery**, when unemployment declines and real GDP growth is increasing; the **peak**, when unemployment is lowest and real GDP is highest; and the **contraction**, when unemployment is increasing and real GDP growth is decreasing. Other terms used in the context of the business cycle are **boom**, when the economy is at a peak, and **recession**, when the economy is at a trough. The term recession is usually used to describe the situation of two successive calendar quarters of a declining real GDP, although there is an official declaration of recessions made by the National Bureau of Economic Research (NBER), according to its **reference cycle**.

In all our discussion about rational expectations and the business cycle, we have spoken in terms of fluctuations of the GDP growth rate about its trend, rather than of fluctuations around zero. This is because an economy typically grows, with recessions being only temporary and relatively short pauses in that growth. Let us consider the factors affecting the trend rate of growth in real GDP. As we shall see, the trend rate itself can take on different values at different times and in different countries.

DETERMINANTS OF THE TREND GROWTH IN REAL GDP

Labor, Capital and Managerial Inputs

Growth rates of real GDPs have exceeded population growth rates by several percent in most countries, meaning improved living standards. Some economies have grown at or near to 10% per year for sustained periods, such as China — now the world's second largest economy and largest manufacturer — and India. Other countries, such as Japan, have barely made any progress at all.[10] Not surprisingly, since economic growth is the result of developments in the overall economy, many factors are responsible for

---

[10]On a per capita basis, Japan has not done as badly as might appear from the GDP statistics. This is the result of Japan having a declining population, and because Japan's GNP — which includes foreign factor income — has grown faster than Japan's GDP: many Japanese corporations are earning from overseas operations.

the trend in the real GDP. In particular, the real GDP has expanded over time as a result of:

(1) Growth in the quantity of capital.
(2) Growth in the quantity of labor.
(3) Growth in the quality of capital.
(4) Growth in the quality of labor.
(5) Growth in the efficiency of production due to technological advance and improvements in management.

Our account of fluctuations in real GDP concentrated on the second factor, the quantity of labor, and assumed everything else to be constant. While this is a reasonable assumption when considering fluctuations in real GDP from quarter to quarter, or even from year to year, it could not explain the trend rate of growth of real GDP over a number of years. For this we must study all the influences on growth of real GDP listed above. Let us consider each in turn.

Growth in the Quantity of Capital: Growth in the quantity of capital is the immediate consequence of **net investment**. Net investment is defined as **gross investment**, which is the total value of investment, minus depreciation. Depreciation is the value of capital which wears out during an interval of time. As we said in Chapter 1, depreciation is also referred to as capital consumption.

> *The capital stock grows when there is net investment. Net investment is the total investment called gross investment, minus depreciation.*

As we shall see in the next chapter, net investment depends on the profitability and risk associated with new plant and equipment. When investors have the funds to invest, profitability is judged relative to the opportunity cost of investment in terms of returns available on bonds and other alternatives. When investors do not have the funds, profitability depends on the cost of raising them. The cost of raising capital in the form of debt and opportunity cost of investor-owned debt capital both increase with increases in interest rates. The cost of capital in the form of equity increases with the required expected return that must be offered to new shareholders. Investment is also affected by the tax rate on income from investment — higher taxes reduce investment — and uncertainty about the business environment — increased uncertainty reduces investment.

Ceteris paribus, net investment is higher the lower are the cost of capital, taxes and uncertainty.

Growth in the Quantity of Labor: While the trend growth rate in the number of people is largely determined by demographic factors such as birth rates, migration rates and death rates, the size of the workforce is also related to economic factors. We have already seen while discussing the labor market in Chapter 5 that the quantity of labor supplied, in terms of hours worked or the number of people working, depends on real wages. This is because real wages affect the choice between working and alternative activities, such as additional education, retirement, leisure, and work at home. However, there are also other relevant factors, some of which are economic, and others which are legal or sociological.

There has been a substantial increase in the percentage of the workforce made up of women. This has significantly contributed to the growth of real GDP in the aggregate and, of course, the incomes of those families with the extra source of income. The basis of the increase in the female workforce participation rate is related in part to the sociological and political liberation women have experienced, but may also be due to labor saving technological changes in the home such as microwaves, dishwashers and so on. Whatever the cause, the increase in the number of women in the workforce has been an important source of growth in real GDP. The size of the workforce is also affected by legal factors such as the minimum age at which people can enter the workforce, and the presence or absence of mandatory retirement laws.

A further factor that can influence the supply of labor is the income tax rate. The reward for selecting work rather than an alternative activity, such as retirement or school, is the *after-tax* real wage rate.

The quantity of labor depends on demographic, economic, sociological and legal factors.

Growth in Quality of Capital: While it is difficult in practice to distinguish between the quantity and quality of capital there is strong evidence that real

GDP has grown as a result of improvements in the technology incorporated into machines as a result of research and development (R&D). This is especially true in manufacturing, but is also true in other domains. Today, communications and information technology (IT) is causing a revolution in the service sector that could overshadow the industrial revolution of the 18th century. Several of the fastest growing corporations and companies with the highest market capitalization are IT companies.

Technological advance does not just result from major scientific break-throughs by researchers in government institutes, huge corporations, and large research-oriented universities. Rather, many of the improvements in production methods that have been incorporated in capital equipment have occurred in small or medium-sized firms, and have resulted from inno-vative solutions to very specific isolated problems. Ingenuity is not the sole domain of scientists with years of expensive, formal education, but a quality that surfaces in small workshops, offices and similar places of employment. However, the chance that ingenious solutions will be found, whether in large or small settings, depends on there being a well-educated workforce.

Growth in Quality of Labor: Education represents an investment in human capital that, as with investment in physical capital, has allowed increased output to come from the same number of hours of labor input. The benefit has been enjoyed both directly from a better-educated workforce, and indi-rectly via the contribution that educated people have made to the quality of physical capital.

Growth in Effectiveness of Management: Not all the increases in real GDP can be attributed to growth in the quantity and quality of capital and labor. Production requires that labor and capital are used effectively, and this requires effective business management.

Improvements in management have taken a variety of forms, some of which have had pervasive effects on the economy. Perhaps one of the most important of these managerial improvements is the widespread application of **just-in-time inventory control systems**. Aided by parallel developments in IT and communication systems, companies have installed mechanisms for ordering just what they need as it is needed, and for suppliers to deliver according to precise schedules. This cuts down on losses from waiting for crucial parts to arrive, and on storage costs from the need to hold inventory in case of unexpected delays. Other managerial improvements have occurred in quality control, financial management, cost accounting methods and organizational efficiencies. These improvements in management have been a result of better education in general, and perhaps by business education in particular; courses are now common in production control, financial management, organizational design, cost accounting and the other managerial areas in which advances have been made.

Other Influences on the Trend Growth Rate of Real GDP

Factor Supplies: The availability of factors of production can affect the trend rate of growth of real GDP as well as fluctuations of real GDP around the trend. In our discussion of fluctuations of real GDP, we called a sudden disruption in the availability of an input such as oil, a supply shock. If the availability of an input diminishes gradually over the long-run, this can affect the trend rate of growth. For example, if Canada was to run out of untapped sources of hydroelectric power, the ability to continue to grow by producing and selling electrical power would diminish, reducing the growth rate of Canada's real GDP.

Better Allocation of Resources and Economies of Scale: With a vast pool of talented people distributed over all sociological and ethnic groups, as work-related barriers have been removed, more women, blacks, and so on, have been better able to develop their potential. This is an improvement in the allocation and utilization of resources, and has benefited society in general as well as those with expanded opportunities. The allocation of resources has also been improved between nations by international trade. This has allowed nations to exploit their advantages to everybody's benefit, as well as to exploit economies of scale. All these allocational gains translate into long-term gains in the real GDP.

The Importance of Different Factors

Table 6.3 shows the estimates of the contribution of different factors responsible for economic growth according to the work of Edward Denison. We can see that all of the factors we have listed are part of the explanation

Table 6.3. Contributions to growth in real GDP.

Percent of U.S. annual growth, 1929–1982, attributable to:

Quantity of capital	0.56%
Quantity of labor	0.77%
Quality of capital	0.66%
Quality of labor	0.57%
Better allocation of resources and economies of scale	0.36%
Total	2.92%

Source: Edward F. Denison, *Trends in American Economic Growth, 1929–1982*, Brooking Institution, Washington DC, 1985.
No individual cause of economic growth is dominant. This in turn suggests that no individual policy that the government might impose could have a dominant impact.

of growing real GDP. No individual factor appears to dominate the others. Therefore, it is unlikely that any individual policy that the government might adopt could have a dominant effect. Indeed, it is remarkable how evenly divided are the different contributing factors to overall economic growth. While there is the potential for errors in the estimates, and for the potential importance of the different factors to change over time, it would appear that we must look to every factor we have listed in order to fully explain economic growth.

No individual factor influencing long-term, or trend, economic growth has a dominant effect.

Taxes and Long-term Economic Growth

Net investment, and hence growth in the quantity of capital, depends on tax rates on income earned on investment. This is because the tax on income from investment affects the after-tax profitability of investment. The quantity of labor supplied also depends on tax rates because the decision to work and hours of work depend on after-tax real wages. If higher tax rates do indeed reduce growth in the quantity of capital and quantity of labor, then higher tax rates can reduce the growth rate of the economy. The view that increasing tax rates reduce the rate of growth of real GDP is a major

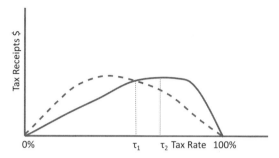

Fig. 6.10.   Laffer curve.
An increase in the tax rate from τ₁ to τ₂ might increase tax receipts, as with the solid line, or decrease tax receipts, as with the broken line, depending on the disincentive effects of higher tax rates.

component of **supply-side economics**. Supply-side economics emphasizes the supply of inputs in the determination of economic growth, and relates input supply to the incentives to work and invest. It was an economic philosophy that shaped economic policy in the 1980s, and was used to argue for general reductions in tax rates.

A leading advocate of tax reductions to stimulate investment and hard work is Arthur Laffer, who argues that the effect of taxes on labor supply, capital investment, and the willingness to report income to the tax authorities, is so substantial that lower tax *rates* could actually result in higher tax *revenues*; the lower rates on their own would mean less taxes collected, but the extra employment, investment and willingness to report income could more than offset this.[11] Laffer's claim is illustrated by the **Laffer curve** in Fig. 6.10. We draw two curves, and note that both curves show total tax revenues of zero at a 0% tax rate and at a 100% tax rate. The zero tax revenue at a zero tax rate is simply because no taxes are collected at such a rate. The zero tax revenue at a 100% tax rate is because there would be no incentive to work, invest or report any income if all income was taken in taxes. The important question is how the Laffer curve is shaped. If the Laffer curve is shaped like the solid line in Fig. 6.10, then increasing the tax rate from τ_1 to τ_2 increases tax receipts. However, if the correct curve

---

[11]The avoidance of reporting income to tax authorities is the principal motivation for the underground economy.

is really the broken line, raising the tax rate from τ_1 to τ_2 reduces total tax revenue.[12]

The Laffer curve relates tax revenues to tax rates.

Example 6.1: The Laffer or Khaldûn Curve?

Not much is new, as the following extract clearly shows.

"It should be shown that at the beginning of a dynasty, taxation yields a large revenue from small assessments. At the end of the dynasty, taxation yields a small revenue from large assessments.

The reason for this is that when the dynasty follows the ways of Islam, it imposes only such taxes as are stipulated by the religious law, such as charity taxes, the land tax, and the poll tax. These have fixed limits that cannot be exceeded . . . .

Therefore, the individual imposts and assessments, which together constitute the tax revenue, are low. When tax assessments and imposts upon the subjects are low, the latter have the energy and desire to do things. Cultural enterprises grow and increase, because the low taxes bring satisfaction. When cultural enterprises grow, the number of individual imposts and assessments mounts. In consequence, the tax revenue, which is the sum total of (the individual assessments), increases.

When the dynasty continues in power and their rulers follow each other in succession, they become sophisticated. The Bedouin attitude and simplicity lose their significance, and the Bedouin qualities of moderation and restraint disappear . . . . As a result, the individual imposts and assessments upon the subjects, agricultural laborers, farmers, and all the other taxpayers, increase. Every individual impost and assessment is greatly increased, in order to obtain a higher tax revenue . . . . Eventually, the taxes will weigh heavily upon the subjects and overburden them . . . .

. . . The result is that the interest of subjects in cultural enterprises disappears, when they compare expenditures and taxes with their income and gain and see the little profit they make, they lose all hope.

---

[12]As Example 6.1 shows, the Laffer Curve might have been discovered in the 14th century.

Therefore, many of them refrain from all cultural activity. The result is that the total tax revenue goes down, as individual assessments go down. Often, when the decrease is noticed, the amounts of individual imposts are increased. This is considered a means of compensating for the decrease. Finally, individual imposts and assessments reach their limit. It would be of no avail to increase them further. The costs of all cultural enterprise are now too high, the taxes are too heavy, and the profits anticipated fail to materialize. Finally, civilization is destroyed, because the incentive for cultural activity is gone."

Source: Ibn Khaldûn, *The Muqaddimah*, 1377. Translated by Franz Rosenthal, edited and abridged by N.J. Dawood. (Princeton, N.J.: Princeton Univ. Press, 1967) pp. 230–31.

FORECASTING GDP

Short-Term Forecasts

Different factors are responsible for short-term fluctuations in real GDP than long-term trends. In the case of short-term forecasts, say, for up to a year, real GDP should grow relatively rapidly, when realized inflation exceeds anticipated inflation. Similarly, real GDP should decline, at least below its trend, when realized inflation is less than anticipated inflation. However, we have seen that these effects on real GDP are short-term. This is because if workers' expectations are rational, the same errors in anticipations are not repeated indefinitely. That is, people should not underestimate or overestimate inflation for long periods.

Actual inflation is likely to exceed what had been anticipated when inflation is increasing, and so we expect increasing real GDP to occur, albeit temporarily, with increasing inflation. But how can we predict when inflation is likely to increase? Monetarists look at statistics on the money supply. However, the weekly or monthly data which are available are very volatile, fluctuating a great deal from week to week or month to month. Therefore, it is difficult to clearly identify lasting changes in the growth rate of the money supply which, according to the quantity theory, should precede increases or decreases of inflation.

Keynesians recognize, as do Monetarists, that employment is determined in the labor market, and that therefore it is the actual wage versus the equilibrium wage that matters. They are therefore also concerned with errors in inflationary anticipations which can cause wages to differ from their equilibrium level, but they also consider other factors. In particular, Keynesians believe that declines in autonomous consumption, investment, government spending, or exports could cause a decline in the demand for labor, making contracted wages too high, thereby causing unemployment and a slowdown or decline in real GDP. They also believe this can happen as a result of increased savings, taxes, or imports. These are the same factors they believe can reduce aggregate demand. Therefore, when trying to forecast short-run changes in GDP, Keynesians consider the factors listed in Table 6.1, which are the factors affecting the components of desired expenditure.

Long-Term Forecasts

As we have seen, economists from both major schools of thought recognize that long-term growth in real GDP occurs as a result of changes in the quantity and quality of factors of production. They both look at net investment, which determines the future quantity of capital, current spending on R&D, which determines the future quality of capital, the growth rate and age composition of the population, which determine the future quantity of labor, and current spending on education, which determines the future quality of labor, capital, and management.

Monetarists and Keynesians disagree about the policies which will best achieve a rapid growth of the quantity and quality of capital, and hence of future GDP. As we shall see in the next chapter, Monetarists think fiscal deficits, where government spending exceeds taxes, **crowd-out** private spending on investment via the effect of fiscal deficits on interest rates. In particular, they believe interest rates ration the available supply of funds for borrowing, so that if more funds are being siphoned-off to cover fiscal deficits, interest rates increase to limit investment to the value of remaining funds. In this way, Monetarists believe fiscal deficits reduce growth of real GDP. Keynesians argue that to the extent fiscal deficits are used only to make up for deficient demand in the private sector, they help keep resources active which would otherwise have been idle: there is no opportunity cost of foregone production. Furthermore, if these resources are used to build roads, airports, communication satellites, knowledge, and so on, they add to the stock of capital, in particular, **public capital**, and therefore to future real GDP.

In deciding whether a fiscal deficit is merely compensating for deficient demand in the private sector, or the cause of too much total demand, we can examine the **full-employment deficit**, which is sometimes also referred to as the **high-employment fiscal deficit** or the **cyclically adjusted fiscal deficit**. By definition, the full-employment deficit is what the fiscal deficit would be if the economy were fully employed.

> *The full-employment deficit is the fiscal deficit that would occur if the economy was operating at full-employment.*

During recessions government tax revenues are low because peoples' and firms' incomes on which taxes are collected are low. The low tax revenues contribute towards a larger fiscal deficit. Cutting the deficit would mean higher taxes or lower government spending at a time of heavy unemployment, making matters worse. Indeed, it is fortunate that the structure of taxes brings about a larger fiscal deficit during a recession. The automatically caused fiscal deficit serves as a **built-in stabilizer**, helping to keep the economy on a relatively even keel. To judge whether an actual fiscal deficit is the result of a built-in stabilizer or the result of a **structural deficit** — a deficit that would occur even if there had been full employment — it is necessary to compute what the fiscal deficit would have been if there had been full employment. In turn, this means calculating what taxes and government spending would have been at full employment.

Leading Indicators

There are numerous statistical measures that indicate whether economic conditions are likely to improve or worsen. These measures are referred to as **leading indicators**, and include:

(1) Average workweek.
(2) Average weekly initial claims for unemployment.
(3) New orders for consumer goods and materials, adjusted for inflation.
(4) Net business formation.

(5) Stock prices.
(6) Contracts and orders for plant and equipment, adjusted for inflation.
(7) New building permits for private housing.
(8) Retail sales.
(9) Change in inventories, adjusted for inflation.
(10) Change in sensitive materials prices.
(11) Money supply (M2), adjusted for inflation.
(12) Change in credit outstanding.

These measures are combined into a monthly **index of leading economic indicators** which is closely watched by government and business economists. The use of an index rather than any individual factor tends to smooth out erroneous signals that might be given from individual component measures. The reason for the inclusion of many of the series in the index of leading economic indicators is self-evident, but it is still illustrative to look at the rationale going into their selection.

The index of leading economic indicators combines various factors each of which relates to the direction of the economy.

Before employers begin to hire extra labor they frequently expand the amount of overtime available to their existing employees. This offers more flexibility if an increase in demand turns out to be temporary, and is also a useful stopgap while the selection of new workers is being made. The average number of hours worked is hence a measure that increases before the number of people employed increases. The same is true for the number of initial claims for unemployment compensation. However, because claims for unemployment tend to decline only as the economy expands and increase as the economy contracts; statistics on initial claims for unemployment compensation have a short **lead time**.

New orders for consumer goods, measured in real terms to reflect the quantity of goods being ordered, not only precede production and hence employment — orders being placed before the goods are produced — but is also related to consumer confidence. While not itself an index of consumer confidence, orders for large appliances and so on, tend to be related to confidence about the future.

Net business formation, which measures the difference between the number of new incorporations and the number of failures, reflects both the employment opportunities of the future, and the confidence business people have about future earning potential. The inclusion of stock prices is also based on confidence about the future, since stock prices are a barometer of investors' expectations about expected earnings of companies.

Contracts and orders for plant and equipment are the initial step in business investment, and we have already seen how investment can impact on the GDP. The value of contracts and orders for plant and equipment is an indicator of future job opportunities in making plant and equipment, including the multiplier effects this has on the economy, and of the confidence of business decision-makers about future demand.

Increases in building permits serve as a measure of confidence of those deciding to build. In addition, peak employment in house-construction occurs sometime after building has begun, which itself occurs after permits have been granted. For example, trades-people doing plumbing, wiring, carpeting, roofing, and so on, are active several months after foundations are put in place. Furthermore, people with new houses tend to buy new furniture, appliances and so on. This makes statistics on housing permits an important signal of future economic activity.

The level of retail sales is both a measure of confidence and a signal about how much to produce. The change in inventory stocks is also a measure of confidence. However, inventory changes could work in either direction as a forecasting tool. Firms build up inventories of finished goods in anticipation of strong sales. A *planned* increase in inventories can therefore be viewed as a sign business people are confident that sales will increase. On the other hand, when sales are unexpectedly low there is an *unplanned* increase in inventory. Therefore, rising *actual* inventory stocks could signal strong business confidence or unexpectedly poor economic conditions. Generally, it is believed that in the initial stages of recovery the planned inventory build-up in anticipation of sales is the dominant effect. Consequently, inventory accumulation is viewed as a positive sign.

The prices of basic materials like those of metals and lumber move up and down more than the prices of most consumer goods, and indeed, prices move in anticipation of final demand since basic materials must be bought before final goods are manufactured. Therefore, materials prices serve as an indicator of future demand.

It might be thought that the money supply is included in the index of leading indicators because of the arguments we have given about the possible effects of money on future real GDP, but the inclusion of money can also be rationalized differently. Some economists argue that as businesses borrow for plant equipment, and consumers take on loans to buy consumer durables, there is an expansion of both sides of banks' balance sheets — larger assets in the form of loans, and larger liabilities as customer deposits expand. In this way, the confidence and actions of businesses and consumers translate into an increase in the money supply. The same rationale is behind the inclusion of credit outstanding in the index of leading indication; more credit is granted when both lenders and borrowers have confidence in the future.

SUMMARY

(1) Different factors cause short-run fluctuations in real GDP than affect the trend rate of growth of real GDP.

(2) Traditional Keynesian arguments apply to an economy with substantial unused capacity, so expansions take the form of increasing real GDP rather than increasing prices. Similarly, by assuming downwardly sticky prices, contractions take the form of decreasing real GDP rather than declining prices.

(3) The equilibrium real GDP is where desired expenditure equals actual output. When desired expenditure exceeds output there is an increase in the equilibrium GDP, and when desired expenditure is smaller than output there is a reduction in the equilibrium GDP.

(4) The marginal propensity to consume (MPC) is the fraction of an increase in GDP spent on consumption. The MPC is smaller than unity because some GDP is collected in taxes, and because some of increased income is saved.

(5) Keynesians believe that the factors which cause fluctuations in GDP are those that affect desired investment, consumption, government spending, and the balance of trade.

(6) Increased spending causes increases in the equilibrium GDP by a multiple of the original spending increase. The multiple by which the equilibrium GDP increases vis-à-vis spending is called the multiplier.

(7) The multiplier is the result of trickling-down, as successive people spend extra income, and is larger the more that trickles down. Therefore, the multiplier is larger, the larger is the MPC.

(8) The Keynesian view that expansions and contractions in desired expenditure result in fluctuating real GDP rather than prices can be explained in terms of an aggregate supply curve that is horizontal below capacity output. In such a circumstance, variations in aggregate demand translate into variations in real GDP.

(9) Aggregate supply shocks, such as those caused by rapidly increasing imported-oil prices, cause an increase in the price level at the same time as the real GDP is decreasing. Such a situation is called stagflation.

(10) When real GDP is declining and unemployment is increasing, individuals who still have jobs reduce consumption in case they lose their jobs. This behavior makes matters worse, and is called the paradox of thrift.

(11) Equilibrium income is where desired expenditure equals GDP, or where withdrawals from the circular flow of income equal injections. The withdrawals are taxes, savings and imports, and the injections are investment, government spending, and exports.

(12) Real GDP increases when there is unanticipated inflation, and decreases when there is unanticipated disinflation.

(13) A recurring pattern of variations in the real GDP is called a business or trade cycle. A business cycle involves moving from peak, to contraction, to trough, to expansion, and back to a peak again.

(14) The long-run trend in real GDP can be forecast by looking at growth in the quantity and quality of factors of production.

(15) Growth in the capital stock requires net investment. Net investment is gross investment minus depreciation.

(16) The number of hours of labor supplied depends on income tax rates. Therefore, lower tax rates can increase the quantity of labor supplied, and thereby increase real GDP.

(17) The quality of capital is improved by improvements in technology which themselves come from research and development (R&D).

(18) Education improves the quality of labor, and also helps improve the quality of capital because it trains people who do research and development.

(19) Growth in the quantity and quality of all factors of production have contributed to economic growth.

(20) In making short-term forecasts of the real GDP, Monetarists examine money supply statistics, while Keynesians look at the factors influencing desired consumption, investment, government spending and net exports. In making longer-term forecasts of the real GDP, all economists look at the size of net investment, R&D expenditure, demographic trends, education and so on.

(21) Because income and sales tax receipts decline as the GDP declines, there is an automatic built-in stabilizer in an economy; deficit spending occurs during recessions. The full employment fiscal deficit or surplus is what it would be at full employment.

(22) The index of leading economic indicators is formed from several measures reflecting future economic activity.

QUESTIONS

(1) Assume the following values of desired expenditure:

$$\text{Autonomous consumption} = \$100 \text{ billion}$$
$$\text{Marginal propensity to consume (MPC)} = 0.6$$
$$\text{Investment} = \$20 \text{ billion}$$
$$\text{Government spending} = \$30 \text{ billion}$$
$$\text{Net-exports} = -\$10 \text{ billion}$$

What is the value of the equilibrium GDP?

(2) What would happen to unplanned changes in inventories in the above question if actual GDP was $340 billion? What would happen if the actual GDP was $360 billion?

(3) Assume investment increases to $25 billion. What is the new equilibrium GDP, and what is the size of the multiplier?

(4) How do you think the multiplier is affected by the income tax rate?

(5) In what ways is the downward slope on the aggregate demand curve different from the downward slope on demand curves for individual goods and services?

(6) Add arrows to Fig. 6.7 representing firms' taxes, firms' savings, government transfers to households, household borrowing, firms' imports,

and government imports. Use the extended figure to show that Eq. (6.6) holds in equilibrium, where S is all savings, T is all taxes, and so on.

(7) How might an increase in the growth rate of the money supply increase real GDP?

(8) How might education improve economic growth both directly and indirectly? Why don't very poor nations devote more resources to education to improve their future standards of living?

(9) Why is the full-employment fiscal deficit or surplus a more meaningful way of comparing the intended fiscal stimulus than the actual fiscal deficit or surplus?

(10) Do you think a policy of making people retire early would help unemployment and living standards in the long-run?

(11) Why is productivity so important for economic progress?

(12) In what ways can the government help or hinder long-term economic performance?

CONNECTIONS

BALANCING ACTS AND PERPETUAL MOTION

The process of production can be thought of as the creation of "order" from "disorderly" natural resources. That is, we can think of appetizing food on supermarket shelves and shining automobiles in their showrooms, as being the result of creating the desired order of matter from the "chaotic" distribution of resources from which the products are made. In other words, the process of converting nutrients into food, or iron ore into automobiles, can be considered as a process of adding value by giving resources a higher, desired form of organization. Viewed in this way, the gross domestic product (GDP) appears in sharp contrast to that essential principle of physics, the inviable **second law of thermodynamics**. According to this law, the universe exhibits increasing disorder, or increasing **entropy**. For example, if different parts of a body of matter have varying amounts of heat, the warmer parts lose heat to the cooler parts until the heat is evenly distributed. The heat is then at a greater level of disorder, or alternatively, at a higher entropy. Everything from the motion of heavenly bodies to the behavior of atoms is subject to the second law of thermodynamics, making it clear there must be a level at which order is sacrificed in the productive activity of an economy; in economics as in physics "there can be no such thing as a free lunch".[1]

If the domain of measurement is expanded from the calculation of the GDP to one that includes the exploitation of order held inside natural resources going into the GDP, such as the breaking-down of long hydrocarbon chains in fuel used as energy, or of molecules that make up the nutrients and other resources of nature, we find that we are still subject to the second law of thermodynamics. Any appearance of a violation of this law is only because we employ partial measurement when computing the sum of values added in the economy that constitutes the real GDP. But how much disorder, or entropy, is caused by our efforts to satisfy our desires

---

[1]This expression simply means that everything has an opportunity cost.

for material satisfaction? We can cast the tension between the environment and economy in such terms. The side one takes depends essentially on the view of how long the planet's finite stock of ordered matter can last at the existing rate of depletion; we empty Nature's bank account when we use energy at a faster rate than it is created by the Sun.

The circular flow of income between firms and households resembles recycling principles known as the carbon and nitrogen cycles. As we saw in this chapter, if injections balance leakages in the circular flow of income between households and firms, the circular flow is in equilibrium, without tendency to run down or expand. If leakages from the flow of income in the form of taxes, savings and imports, are exactly balanced by the injections from government spending, investment and exports, the circular flow can continue indefinitely. Similar principles apply to the balancing acts of the carbon and nitrogen cycles. For example, the carbon cycle involves a balance between carbon dioxide emissions from the respiration of animals and decay of plants, and the absorption of carbon dioxide by green plants, with the energy driving all this coming from the Sun. The nitrogen cycle involves similar balancing of flows between plants, animals and bacteria, with the ability of the soil to support living matter being dependent on the circular flow of nitrogen being maintained; any difference between leakages and injections would rapidly destroy the balance on which life depends.

As well as distinct parallels involving the application of thermodynamic and recycling principles that unite the natural sciences with economics in the context of the GDP, there are additional connections through the application of **simple non-linear dynamic systems** which are processes which result in **chaos**. A growing list of scientific phenomena, from the weather, to the flow of a stream, to smoke from a cigarette, to evolution of a species, to the stock market have been found to follow potentially simple, non-linear dynamic processes, where the tiniest change in specification completely changes behavior. The characteristic of such chaotic processes is that while motion from one point to the next or even over a small number of points is reasonably predictable, it is not possible to tell what will happen over longer horizons. For example, weather predictions for the next day are generally quite accurate, for the next few days weather predictions are useful, but beyond that, weather forecasts have little validity; the tiniest change in starting conditions can mean a totally different outcome in the long-run.[2] The same is true for the smoke rising from a cigarette. The motion at the source is predictable, but there is little that can be said of where any particular particle of smoke will be a couple of yards from the source; the most minuscule draft could cause the smoke to follow an eventually, totally different path. Just as with the weather, smoke, and so many other physical phenomena, so it is with the national income and product. From quarter to quarter it is possible to predict, e.g., the growth rate of the real GDP with a reasonable degree of accuracy. It is also possible to make forecasts with some limited validity for growth rates in about one year. However, beyond this, forecasts of the growth rate of the GDP are no more accurate than the long range weather forecasts that so often miss the mark.

Turning from the physical to the social sciences, we can note that just as inflation and unemployment have impacts on the political stage, so does the behavior of the real GDP. The expectation of advances in the standard of living is so built into the psyche of voters that they vent their frustrations at the polls when dissatisfied with the pace of progress. This pace of progress is most clearly visible to elected officials from the GDP statistics. That is, even though each voter is likely to consider her or his own economic achievements vis-à-vis what they had anticipated, it is in the aggregate statistics showing the real GDP that the typical voter's progress is most evident. Secret ballots may ensure that politicians no longer buy votes, but it is still pocketbook issues that matter at election time.

Progress, as it is reflected in the real GDP, and **consumerism**, which has become the driving force even of formerly socialistic economies, are intimately related. Dreams are based on progress, on having more, on doing better, on being transformed by a higher income and a greater buying-power. Human wants appear insatiable, and advances in the real GDP are the route to the greater luxury and comfort that people demand and expect. This appetite for perpetual progress has been so built into societal norms that it is a basic axiom, rarely questioned except by the odd philosopher who reevaluates the dominant currents that have been set in motion by

---

[2]As it has been put, a butterfly flapping its wings could set off a violent hurricane in a distant place. This and other remarkable claims for the ubiquitous principle of chaos are contained in James Gleick's very readable book, *Chaos* (Viking Press, New York, 1987).

homo-economicus, i.e., by modern economic man. However, it would be an injustice not to mention the detractors who have noted that economic progress does not necessarily go hand in hand with spiritual values, with a deeper human condition, and today more than anything else, with preservation of the environment. Such a critic of the "controlling ideology" of progress is modern American philosopher, Christopher Lasch.[3] While a great deal can be said in favor of targeting for an ever-growing real GDP, the critics of progress such as Lasch and the philosophers he cites, makes it clear that there is more to human achievement than is reflected in the national income and product accounts.

---

[3] See Christopher Lasch, *The True and Only Heaven: Progress and Its Critics* (New York, Norton, 1991).

CHAPTER 7

INTEREST RATES

"Gentlemen prefer bonds"
Andrew Mellon

Key Concepts: Interest rates and the supply of loanable funds; interest rates and the demand for loanable funds; the equilibrium interest rate; the market versus equilibrium interest rate; monetary policy and interest rates; real growth and interest rates; anticipated inflation and interest rates; real versus nominal interest rates; fiscal deficits, crowding-out and interest rates; international capital flows and interest rates.

THE INTEREST IN INTEREST RATES

Interest rates have a substantial effect on borrowing and spending decisions of businesses and consumers, and thereby on employment, GDP, and other measures of macroeconomic activity. For example, as we shall see, interest rates influence the willingness of businesses to invest in new plant and equipment, and in turn, the current and future size of the GDP.

At the same time that interest rates affect the economy, the economy affects interest rates. This occurs as a result of the effects that national income, inflation and confidence about the future have on the willingness of consumers and businesses to borrow and invest, and hence on the price of borrowing, which is the interest rate. With the direction of flow being in both directions, from interest rates to the economy and from the economy to interest rates, in order to explain interest rates we need a theory that captures this two-way flow of influence. Such a theory is the **loanable funds theory**. While there are numerous other theories of interest rates, the loanable funds theory embraces many aspects of these other theories, and therefore serves as an ideal window onto the world of interest rates.

LOANABLE FUNDS THEORY OF INTEREST

According to the loanable funds theory, interest rates are determined by the supply of and demand for loanable funds, which can be thought of as monies that can be lent and borrowed. Therefore, in order to explain this theory, we must begin by considering loanable funds supply and demand.

The Supply of Loanable Funds

There are two components of the supply of loanable funds:

(1) Changes in the money supply.
(2) Savings out of current income.

Let us consider these two components in turn.

> *The supply of loanable funds consists of changes in the money supply and current savings.*

Changes in the Money Supply: As we saw in Chapter 3, the money supply consists of coin and currency, plus deposits at financial institutions. We also saw that a nation's money supply can be influenced by its central bank which determines both the availability of reserves and the required reserve ratio. If we assume the size of reserves and the required reserve ratio are not affected by interest rates then the money supply is not affected by interest rates. This simplifying assumption allows us to represent the change in money supply by a vertical line like ΔM^S in Fig. 7.1. This line is vertical because the change in the money supply is assumed to be the same whatever the interest rate is. The more expansive is the central bank's policy, the further to the right is the vertical line, ΔM^S.

If instead of assuming that the money supply is not influenced by interest rates, we assume the central bank determines the rate of growth of the money supply according to interest rates, the line ΔM^S in Fig. 7.1 is no longer vertical. For example, if we assume the central bank reduces the growth of the money supply when interest rates are low, and increases the

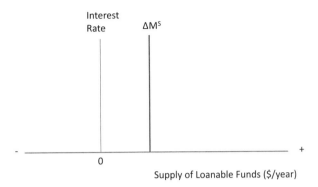

Fig. 7.1. Additions to the money supply are a flow supply of loanable funds. *The greater the increase in the money supply the further to the right is* ΔM^S. *As drawn we assume the money supply does not depend on the interest rate.*

growth in the money supply when interest rates are high — done to stabilize interest rates — the change in the money supply is an upward-sloping line; the higher are interest rates, the larger is ΔM^S. We shall assume ΔM^S is vertical as in Fig. 7.1, although the way we draw ΔM^S can be altered to accommodate different central bank objectives, if necessary.

The change in the money supply is primarily determined by the central bank.

Savings out of Current Income: The part of income which is not spent or paid as taxes is saved and placed in banks or other financial institutions. In turn, the financial institutions make the saved funds available to borrowers. Savings are in this way a component of the supply of loanable funds. Furthermore, the financial institutions provide the service of channeling, or intermediating, the funds between savers and borrowers.

The proportion of national income that is saved depends on interest rates. We must consider in what way interest rates affect savings before we can determine how the total supply of loanable funds varies with interest rates.

When a person decides to spend his or her income rather than save, the opportunity cost is the forgone interest income they would have earned.[1]

---

[1]For the time-being we ignore inflation. Later we shall see that it is the **real** interest rate, described in Eq. (4.11), that determines savings.

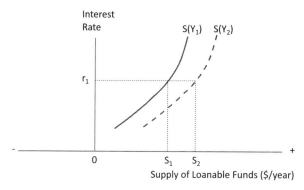

Fig. 7.2. Savings increase with interest rates and national income.
The opportunity cost of spending increases with the interest rate, meaning greater savings. At all interest rates, savings increase with national income.

The higher is the interest rate, the more interest income is lost from a given amount spent today. In other words, the higher is the interest rate, the higher is the opportunity cost of spending rather than saving. For example, if the interest rate is 5%, every dollar spent today means forgoing $1.05 of spending next year, whereas at a 10% interest rate, the cost of spending each dollar today is $1.10 of forgone spending next year. It follows that as interest rates increase, the opportunity cost of spending today increases, and so a larger proportion of the national income is saved. This is shown in Fig. 7.2 by the curve S(Y), which has an upward-slope, showing higher savings at higher interest rates.

The quantity of savings is higher the higher is the interest rate.

The position of the curve S(Y) depends on national income, Y; this is why we put Y in parentheses. The larger is the national income, the more is saved at every interest rate, and therefore, the further to the right is the curve S(Y). For example, if national income increases from Y_1 to Y_2, the savings curve shifts from $S(Y_1)$ to $S(Y_2)$ in Fig. 7.2. This means that at a given interest rate, r_1, savings increase from S_1 to S_2 as income increases from Y_1 to Y_2.

Savings increase with increases in national income.

The total supply of loanable funds consists of savings plus the change in the money supply. Therefore, to obtain the curve representing the total

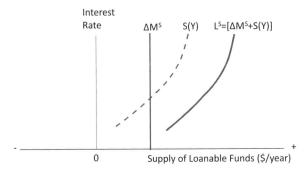

Fig. 7.3. The supply curve of loanable funds.
The supply curve for loanable funds is the horizontal sum of the change in money supply and the savings curve at each interest rate.

supply of loanable funds, we take the horizontal sum of S(Y) and ΔM^S. (The horizontal sum of S(Y) and ΔM^S is the sum of savings and the change in money supply at each interest rate.) This is labeled L^S in Fig. 7.3. Since savings increase as interest rates increase, the supply curve of loanable funds slopes upwards vis-à-vis interest rates. This upward-sloping supply curve of loanable funds must be combined with the demand curve to determine the interest rate at which the supply of and demand for funds are equal.

The Demand for Loanable Funds

There are two components of the demand for loanable funds:[2]

(1) Changes in the demand for money.
(2) The demand for funds to finance capital investments.

Let us consider these two components in turn.

The demand for loanable funds consists of the change in demand for money, and the demand for funds to finance capital investment.

Changes in the Demand for Money: If people want to hold more money than they are already holding the extra amount of money demanded is part

---

[2]A further demand for funds occurs when governments raise funds because of fiscal deficits. We consider this later.

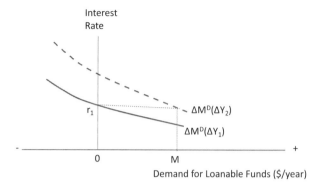

Fig. 7.4. The demand curve of loanable funds.
The demand curve for loanable funds slopes downwards against the interest rate, and shifts right with increases in nominal GDP.

of the demand for loanable funds. The extra amount of money is a *flow* demand, dimensionally matching the change in money supply.

When we discussed the demand for money in Chapter 4, we mentioned that the quantity of money demanded depends on interest rates. Specifically, *ceteris paribus*, the quantity of money demanded is smaller, the higher is the interest rate; the interest rate is the opportunity cost of holding money so that less money is held at higher interest rates.[3] This means that when we plot the change in demand for money curve, ΔM^D, as in Fig. 7.4 it has a downward-slope.

Another factor affecting the demand for money is the GDP, or national income. This is because the more people earn and spend, the larger the money holdings they need to facilitate their transactions. *Ceteris paribus*, the greater is the *change* in the GDP and national income, the larger is the *change* in the demand for money ΔM^D. This is true whether the GDP and national income change as a result of an increase in the price level, or from

---

[3]In fact, the opportunity cost of holding money is the interest rate that could be earned on some other asset such as a bond, minus any interest earned on money. Some forms of bank deposits included in the money supply earn interest, and therefore the opportunity cost is less than the interest rate on bonds and other such non-money assets. For our purposes here we can ignore interest earned on money. We can do this either by assuming we are dealing with a narrow definition of money which excludes interest-earning deposits, or by assuming any interest earned on money changes little relative to interest rates on bonds or other such assets.

a change in real GDP. For example, if the price level doubles people need twice as much money to make their payments, just as if the quantity of goods and services purchased doubles.

The demand for money curve $\Delta M^D(\Delta Y_1)$ in Fig. 7.4 shows that with real GDP changing by ΔY_1 and at the interest rate r_1, there is no demand for additional money. The curve $\Delta M^D(\Delta Y_2)$ shows that if the GDP is increasing by ΔY_2, which is larger than ΔY_1, there is a demand for more money equal to the distance 0M at r_1.

The quantity of money demanded is higher the lower is the interest rate. At any interest rate, the demand for money is higher the more rapidly nominal GDP is increasing.

Capital Investment: The higher is the interest rate the lower is the rate of capital investment. This is because the higher is the interest rate, the lower are the present values of incomes generated by capital investments.[4] This means that if there are many potential investments with different possible pay-offs, the higher is the interest rate, the fewer investments will have present values of incomes that exceeds the cost of the investments. That is, the higher is the interest rate the smaller is the investment.

The effect of interest rates on investment is shown by the curves $I(\Delta Q_1)$ and $I(\Delta Q_2)$ in Fig. 7.5. These curves show the rate of investment, and hence

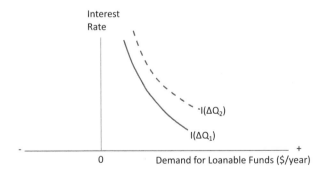

Fig. 7.5.   The demand for loanable funds for capital investment.
The demand curve for loanable funds declines with increases in interest rates and increases with increases in the rate of growth of real GDP. This occurs via capital investment.

[4]This was explained in the backgrounder in Chapter 2.

the demand for loanable funds to finance investment, sloping downwards vis-à-vis the interest rate. The investment curves have (ΔQ) in parentheses because, as in the case of the change in demand for money, changes in GDP affect investment and hence the position of the investment curve. In the case of investment it is changes in *real* GDP that have an effect. Real GDP affects investment because the number of machines and size of plant that firms want to have depend on the outputs of goods and services they are producing, and in aggregate, the output firms produce is the real GDP. The greater is the increase in the real GDP, the larger is the desired increase in number of machines and size of plant, and the greater is investment. That is, the larger is the growth in *real* GDP, the higher is investment at any interest rate, and therefore, the further to the right is the curve I.[5] Therefore, we show the position of the investment curve in Fig. 7.5 depending on ΔQ, the change in *real* GDP. The larger is ΔQ or rate of economic growth, the further to the right is the investment curve. For example, $I(\Delta Q_2)$ is to the right of $I(\Delta Q_1)$ if ΔQ_2 is greater than ΔQ_1. In other words, the more rapid is economic growth the larger is capital investment at any given interest rate.

> *The quantity of funds demanded for investment is higher, the lower is the interest rate. At any interest rate, investment is higher, the larger is the increase in real GDP.*

The total demand for loanable funds is the sum of the change in demand for money and investment at each interest rate. This is shown in Fig. 7.6, where the curve labeled L^D is the horizontal sum of curves $\Delta M^D(\Delta Y)$ and $I(\Delta Q)$. L^D slopes downwards because the curve $\Delta M^D(\Delta Y)$ and the curve $I(\Delta Q)$ both slope downwards. Furthermore, L^D is further to the right the more rapidly the *real* GDP is increasing, via capital investment, and the more *nominal* GDP is increasing, via increases in the demand for money. That is, increases in real GDP increases both the components of loanable funds demand — demand for money and demand for investment — whereas increases in the price level increase loanable funds demand only via the demand for money. (Recall from Chapter 1 that $Y = P \times Q$, so that nominal GDP can be increased by higher prices, P, or higher real GDP, Q).

---

[5]The link between real GDP and investment is explained more precisely in the appendix to this chapter.

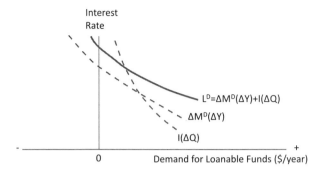

Fig. 7.6. The demand for loanable funds.
The demand curve for loanable funds slopes downwards with respect to the interest rate and increases with increases in the rate of growth of nominal and real GDP.

We should note carefully that whether we are talking about real or nominal GDP, it is the *change* in the GDP that shifts the *demand* curve for loanable funds, L^D, whereas it is the *level* of the GDP that shifts the *supply* curve of loanable funds, L^S. This is why we have Y in parentheses in Fig. 7.3 which shows L^S, and ΔQ and ΔY in parentheses in Fig. 7.6 which shows L^D. The reason L^D shifts with the change in GDP is that funds are demanded if there is a demand for *extra* money holdings and if firms need *extra* capital, and both of these occur when the GDP is *increasing*. On the other hand, the supply of loanable funds is influenced by the level of GDP because the amount saved during any period depends on peoples' incomes and hence on the level of GDP. The importance of distinguishing between the level of GDP and the change in GDP is that *while GDP is increasing* the demand for funds is high, but once GDP ceases to increase and just *stays at the higher level*, the demand for funds declines. However, savings and hence the supply of funds remains unchanged when GDP stays at the higher level.

> *The demand for loanable funds depends on the change in GDP, whereas the supply of loanable funds depends on the level of GDP.*

Market and Equilibrium Interest Rates

According to the loanable funds theory, the interest rate observed in the marketplace, called the **market interest rate**, is the rate equating the supply of and demand for loanable funds. We can find this rate by plotting the

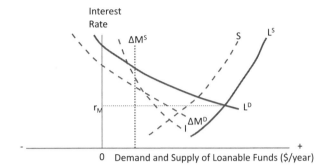

Fig. 7.7. The market interest rate.

The market interest rate balances loanable funds demand with loanable funds supply. This is not the equilibrium rate if at that rate savings, S, are not equal to investment, I.

supply curve of loanable funds, L^S, from Fig. 7.3, and the demand curve for loanable funds, L^D, from Fig. 7.6, in the same figure. This is done in Fig. 7.7. We see that L^S and L^D intersect at the market interest rate, r_M.

The market interest rate equates the supply of and demand for loanable funds.

As well as showing L^S and L^D, Fig. 7.7 also shows the curves behind the supply of and demand for loanable funds. Because L^S is the horizontal sum of ΔM^S and S, and L^D is the horizontal sum of ΔM^D and I, i.e., $L^S = \Delta M^S + S$ and $L^D = \Delta M^D + I$, at the market interest rate:

$$\Delta M^S + S = \Delta M^D + I. \qquad (7.1)$$

We see that there is no requirement at the market interest rate for savings to be equal to investment, because the change in the supply of and demand for money may not be equal. For example, if ΔM^S is larger than ΔM^D, then Eq. (7.1) tells us that at the market interest rate, I exceeds S. Indeed, the extent to which the change in money supply exceeds the change in money demand is equal to the extent investment exceeds savings. This is the situation shown in Fig. 7.7. From examination of the figure, we can see that at the market interest rate the excess of ΔM^S over ΔM^D is equal to the excess of I over S.

With it being possible for S to differ from I at r_M the market interest rate is not an equilibrium rate. This is because if, e.g., I exceeds S at r_M, so that injections into the circular flow of income exceeds withdrawals, then *ceteris paribus*, the GDP will increase to a higher level. The increase in GDP will shift the savings curve to the right until $S = I$.[6] With $S = I$, and also with the market interest rate such that $L^S = L^D$, i.e.,

$$\Delta M^S + S = \Delta M^D + I,$$

it must also be the case that $\Delta M^S = \Delta M^D$. This rate of interest at which $S = I$ *and* $\Delta M^S = \Delta M^D$ is called the **equilibrium interest rate**.

> *The equilibrium interest rate equates savings and investment. Over time, the market interest rate moves towards the equilibrium interest rate via adjustments in GDP.*

The changes in GDP that move the market interest rate to the equilibrium interest rate are likely to occur only gradually, allowing the market rate to differ from the equilibrium rate for some time. During that time the market rate moves up and down with the factors affecting L^S and L^D, i.e., the market interest rate changes with variations in ΔM^S, S, ΔM^D and I in Fig. 7.7.

FACTORS AFFECTING INTEREST RATES

Monetary Policy

Monetary policy is reflected in the *growth rate* of the money supply, rather than the *level* of the money supply. This is because the demand for money grows along with the GDP, and it is normal for central banks to allow the money supply to grow along with money demand. Monetary policy is more **expansionary** — designed to allow the economy to expand — or more **contractionary** — designed to slow the economy down — according to how rapidly the central bank allows the money supply to grow.[7] The higher is the rate of growth of the money supply the more expansionary is monetary policy. The loanable funds theory is well suited to show the effects of changes in the growth rate of the money supply: a faster rate of

---

[6]*While* GDP is increasing, ΔM^D and I are also shifting because ΔM^D and I depend on ΔY. However, the shifts in ΔM^D and I cease after the level of Y, GDP, has increased sufficiently so that S has risen to equal I; after $S = I$, ΔY returns to zero.

[7]Frequently, interest rates are viewed as a measure of monetary policy. However, as we shall show, interest rates are the *result* of monetary policy.

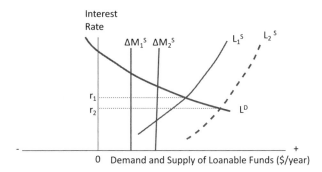

Fig. 7.8. The interest rate and the money supply.
The market interest rate balances loanable funds demand with loanable funds supply. This is not the equilibrium rate if at that rate savings, S, is not equal to investment, I.

growth of the money supply simply means that the vertical line ΔM^S in Fig. 7.7 is further to the right.[8]

Figure 7.8 shows the effect of an increase in the growth rate of the money supply and the consequent rightward shift of ΔM^S from ΔM_1^S to ΔM_2^S. Since ΔM^S is part of the supply of loanable funds, the rightward shift in ΔM^S also causes L^S to shift to the right. (We recall that L^S is the horizontal sum of ΔM^S and S.) We find that an increase in the rate of growth of the money supply reduces the market interest rate from r_1 to r_2, given the positions of all other curves. However, this so-called **liquidity effect** is only temporary if at the market interest rate, savings are not equal to investment so that the GDP changes. These changes in the GDP have further effects on interest rates. Let us therefore consider the effect of changes in the GDP.

An increase in the rate of growth of the money supply reduces the market interest rate via a liquidity effect. However, this effect is only temporary.

Growth in the GDP

The faster is the growth in GDP, i.e., the greater is ΔY, the greater is the demand for loanable funds via both the demand for money and investment.

---

[8]Strictly speaking, in Fig. 7.7 we plot the change in money supply rather than the *rate* of change. To calculate the *rate* of change we need to calculate the change as a percentage of the initial stock of money. However, given the initial stock, the larger is the change, ΔM^S, the larger is the rate of change. Therefore, we can think of variations in ΔM^S as implying variations in the rate of change.

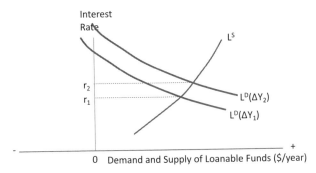

Fig. 7.9. The interest rate and GDP growth.
Faster growth in real GDP increases loanable funds demand via increasing investment, and faster rising prices increase loanable funds demand via the demand for money. Therefore, ceteris paribus, interest rates are higher the faster is the growth of the nominal GDP.

(The demand for money goes up with nominal GDP, and hence with the price level as well as real GDP, while investment goes up with real GDP.) Therefore, the larger is the increase in the GDP, the further to the right is the demand curve for loanable funds, L^D. This is illustrated in Fig. 7.9 where ΔY_2 is larger than ΔY_1. The figure shows that the larger is the growth in GDP, the higher is the market interest rate.

> *More rapid growth in the GDP increases the demand for loanable funds via increasing the demand for money and investment, and thereby increases market interest rates.*

We have explained that whereas the **market** interest rate is where the supply of and demand for loanable funds are equal, the **equilibrium** interest rate is where savings equals investment. We have just shown that faster growth in the GDP shifts the demand curve for loanable funds to the right by shifting both the demand for money curve, ΔM^D, and the investment curve, I. The fact that the investment curve shifts means the equilibrium interest rate increases at the same time as the market interest rate. However, because the shift in demand for loanable funds, L^D, involves shifts in both ΔM^D and I, the increase in the market rate exceeds the increase in the equilibrium rate; the curve I in Fig. 7.7 shifts to the right by less than L^D because L^D is also shifted by ΔM^D. The conclusion that equilibrium interest rates are higher when economic growth is faster means, *ceteris paribus*, that more funds are available to pay the higher interest rates.

Changes in Anticipated Inflation

In Chapter 4, we introduced a link between anticipated inflation and interest rates, namely:

$$\text{Nominal rate} = \text{Real rate} + \text{Anticipated inflation.} \qquad (4.11)$$

We pointed out that if the real interest rate is unaffected by anticipated inflation, increases in anticipated inflation cause equal increases in the nominal interest rate. Let us now consider how Eq. (4.11) relates to the loanable funds theory by showing how anticipated inflation affects the positions of the demand for loanable funds curve, L^D, and the supply of loanable funds curve, L^S. We shall concentrate on the effects of anticipated inflation only on the savings, S, and investment, I, curves behind L^S and L^D. That is, we ignore ΔM^D and ΔM^S. We do this because to deal with ΔM^D and ΔM^S as well as S and I makes the analysis substantially more complex without affecting the qualitative conclusions. In addition, S and I are the components of loanable funds that alone determine the *equilibrium* interest rate.

Anticipated Inflation and Savings, S: The curve labeled $S(\%\Delta P^* = 0\%)$ in Fig. 7.10 shows the amount saved at different nominal interest rates when anticipated inflation is zero. For example, at an interest rate of r_1

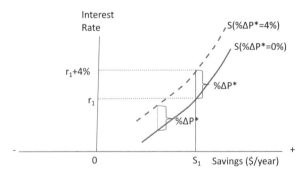

Fig. 7.10. Savings, interest rates, and anticipated inflation.
Savers care about real interest rates, which are nominal market rates minus anticipated inflation. Therefore, the amount saved is unchanged if nominal interest rates change by the size of the change in anticipated inflation.

savings are S_1. Let us suppose there is suddenly an increase in anticipated inflation from 0% to 4%. This means savers anticipate needing 4 cents of interest on each dollar saved for one year to maintain their real buying power. If with zero anticipated inflation savers were prepared to save S_1 per year at an interest rate of r_1, then with 4% anticipated inflation they would require $(r_1 + 4\%)$ to continue saving S_1; with 4% anticipated inflation this preserves the real interest rate. In terms of Fig. 7.10, this means we have a new point on a new savings curve $S(\%\Delta P^* = 4\%)$ which shows savings of S_1 at $(r_1 + 4\%)$. Indeed, for any given quantity of savings the required nominal interest rate is 4% higher with 4% anticipated inflation than with 0% anticipated inflation. This means the entire savings curve is shifted upwards by the anticipated rate of inflation.

The savings curve shifts vertically upwards by the anticipated rate of inflation.

Anticipated Inflation and Investment, I: Capital investment, I, is made when it is profitable to do so. It is profitable when the current or present value of profits generated by the investment exceeds the cost of the investment. When there is anticipated inflation the nominal dollar values of profits anticipated from investments grow along with the anticipated inflation. However, the higher anticipated ***nominal*** profits with inflation do not make investments more profitable. This is because if we compute the present values of anticipated profits that are growing with inflation using an interest rate that is increased by the anticipated rate of inflation, the present values of profits are the same with and without inflation.

The present values of future profits are unchanged by inflation if computed at an interest rate that is increased by the rate of inflation.

The cost of an investment, such as the price of a piece of capital equipment, is not affected by anticipated *future* inflation if this cost is incurred immediately; inflation affects only *future* costs, so that today's price of capital equipment is the same whether or not there is anticipated future inflation. Furthermore, as we have just explained, the present value of expected future profits is also unchanged by anticipated inflation ***if computed at an interest rate that is increased by the anticipated rate of inflation***. This means that if interest rates increase by anticipated inflation, the same rate

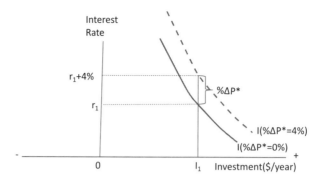

Fig. 7.11.   Investment, interest rates, and anticipated inflation.
Capital investment occurs when the present value of profits generated by the investment exceeds the cost of the investment. If nominal interest rates increase by anticipated inflation the present value and cost of investment are unchanged and therefore so is the amount of investment.

of investment would occur with inflation as would have occurred without inflation at the correspondingly lower interest rate; neither today's cost of investment nor the current or present value of profits are changed. The implication of this for the investment curve, I, is to move the curve vertically upwards by the anticipated rate of inflation as shown in Fig. 7.11. That is, investment is unchanged provided interest rates increase by anticipated inflation.

In Fig. 7.11, $I(\%\Delta P^* = 0\%)$ is the investment curve with zero anticipated inflation, and $I(\%\Delta P^* = 4\%)$ is the investment curve with 4% anticipated inflation. Therefore, as with savings, the investment curve shifts up by the increase in anticipated inflation.

> *The investment curve shifts vertically upwards or downwards by the rate of anticipated inflation.*

Figure 7.12 puts together the upward-shifts in the savings and investment curves from Figs. 7.10 and 7.11. Figure 7.12 shows that the equilibrium nominal interest rate increases with anticipated inflation, and by the amount of anticipated inflation. That is, with 0% inflation and relevant savings and investment curves $S(\%\Delta P^* = 0\%)$ and $I(\%\Delta P^* = 0\%)$, the equilibrium nominal interest rate is r_1, while with 4% inflation and relevant savings and investment curves $S(\%\Delta P^* = 4\%)$ and $I(\%\Delta P^* = 4\%)$, the equilibrium nominal interest rate is $r_1 + 4\%$. That is, the nominal interest

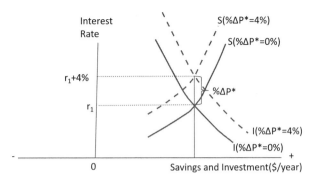

Fig. 7.12. Interest rates, and anticipated inflation.
As a result of savers demanding compensation for inflation and of borrowers being willing to pay, nominal interest rates increase with increases in anticipated inflation.

rate is increased by the anticipated rate of inflation. This provides the rationale for Eq. (4.11).

> *The shifts in savings and investment curves caused by anticipated inflation cause the equilibrium nominal interest rate to increase by anticipated inflation.*

Other Influences on Interest Rates

The loanable funds theory can be extended to explain additional influences on interest rates, such as the effects of fiscal deficits and foreign borrowing. The extensions illustrate the flexibility of the loanable funds theory for describing the wide range of factors that can influence interest rates.

The Effect of Fiscal Deficits: When explaining the loanable funds theory we considered only two sources of demand for loanable funds, from people wanting to hold more money, and from investors buying new plant and equipment. However, when a government spends more than it receives in taxes, i.e., when a government has a fiscal deficit, the government also demands loanable funds. This adds to the other two demands for funds and shifts the total demand for funds curve L^D to the right.[9] The larger is the fiscal deficit the greater is the shift in L^D. This is illustrated in Fig. 7.13.

---

[9]When governments finance their deficits by selling Treasury bills or bonds to the central bank rather than to commercial banks or the public, there is both a demand for and supply of loanable funds; the demand for funds is that of the government, and the supply of funds is that of the central bank. In such a situation the loanable funds demand and supply curves **both** shift to the right.

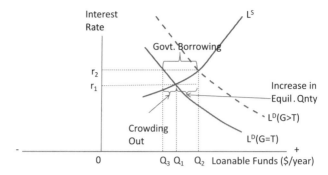

Fig. 7.13.   Interest rates and government borrowing.
Government borrowing increases interest rates, and thereby increases the equilibrium quantity of loanable funds. However, the equilibrium quantity of funds increases less than government borrowing, and so fiscal deficits cause crowding out of private investment.

In Fig. 7.13 we assume the government borrows the amount given by the distance $(Q_2 - Q_3)$, whatever the interest rate is. Therefore, the effect of government borrowing is to shift the total demand curve for funds to the right from $L^D(G = T)$ to $L^D(G > T)$ where we recall G is government spending and T is taxes. This increases the equilibrium interest rate from r_1 to r_2. The equilibrium quantity of loanable funds supplied and demanded increases by $(Q_2 - Q_1)$ as a result of the government borrowing. However, this extra equilibrium quantity of funds, is less than the amount the government borrows, which is distance $(Q_2 - Q_3)$. Therefore, when the government borrows, the quantity of loanable funds that remains available to private investors and money holders is reduced by distance $(Q_1 - Q_3)$; this is the difference between what the government borrows, $(Q_2 - Q_3)$, and the increased equilibrium quantity of loanable funds resulting from the government borrowing, $(Q_2 - Q_1)$. That is, government borrowing to finance fiscal deficits **crowds out** private demanders of funds and increases their borrowing costs.

Fiscal deficits crowd out private demanders of loanable funds and force up equilibrium interest rates.

The extent to which the financing of fiscal deficits causes crowding out depends primarily on the slope of supply of loanable funds curve, L^S. If there is a fixed supply of loanable funds then every dollar of government borrowing is a dollar of crowding out: the government and the private sector have to share the fixed supply. In Fig. 7.13, this would be the case if L^S is vertical. On the other hand, if the supply curve of loanable funds is flat there is no crowding out. In turn, since the supply curve of loanable funds has been constructed from the savings curve, the critical factor is the interest sensitivity of savings: how much do savings increase when interest rates rise due to borrowing by the government.

The Effect of Foreign Lenders: With the increasing globalization of financial markets that has occurred over the years, loanable funds are now generally available from foreign suppliers of funds, as well as being demanded by foreign users of funds. It might be thought that the presence of foreign suppliers of and demanders for loanable funds simply means rightward shifts of the L^S and L^D curves in, e.g., Fig. 7.7, with the effect on interest rates depending on foreign demand for funds versus foreign supply. However, since most individual countries' financial markets are small relative to the global financial market, the effect of foreign suppliers of and demanders for funds can more appropriately be characterized as in Fig. 7.14. The figure shows an individual country's supply of and demand for loanable funds curves, L^S and L^D respectively. We assume the individual country's borrowing represents a small amount relative to the supply of funds from all other countries combined so the country can borrow more from offshore without raising the interest rate. Therefore the supply curve of funds from

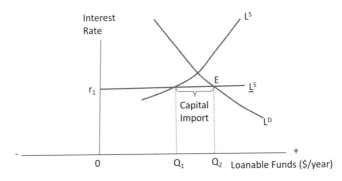

Fig. 7.14.   Interest rates and foreign lenders.
When a country can borrow from foreign lenders at a given interest rate, the supply curve for loanable funds becomes horizontal at that foreign lending rate. Then the quantity of funds demanded can exceed the quantity supplied domestically.

the rest of the world is perfectly elastic at the international interest rate, r_1. That is, the supply curve of funds facing the individual country is L^S below the horizontal line $\underline{L}^S$ and then it is line $\underline{L}^S$.

At the international interest rate, r_1, the quantity of funds demanded by the individual country is Q_2, given off the L_D curve, and the quantity of funds supplied by the country itself is Q_1, given off the L^S curve. (Recall that L^S is the country's own supply of loanable funds). The excess of the quantity of funds demanded over the quantity supplied by the country itself is $(Q_2 - Q_1)$. This amount is borrowed from the other countries, and constitutes a **capital import**. That is, the equilibrium is point E in Fig. 7.14, with the country facing an interest rate of r_1 and loanable funds demand of Q_2. Of this equilibrium quantity demanded, Q_1 is supplied by the country itself — from its savers and via increased money supply — and the remainder, $(Q_2 - Q_1)$, is supplied from other countries.

Consideration of Fig. 7.14 shows that shifts in the country's own loanable funds demand and supply curves do not affect the country's interest rate. Rather, shifts in L^S and L^D in Fig. 7.14 affect only the quantity of capital imports. For example, if the L^D curve shifted to the right capital imports would increase, but the interest rate would not change. However, there would be implications of the capital import for further flows of funds out of the country as interest is paid on foreign debt. Issues such as these are discussed in the next chapter, which considers the balance of payments and exchange rates.

If the supply of funds to a country is perfectly elastic at the international interest rate, shifts in the local demand for and supply of loanable funds do not change the equilibrium interest rate. Rather, they cause variations in the size of capital imports.

SUMMARY

(1) Interest rates can have significant effects on spending by consumers and businesses, and thereby a significant impact on an economy.

(2) The loanable funds theory explains how interest rates are determined by the supply of and demand for loanable funds.

(3) The supply of loanable funds consists of additions to the money supply and savings out of current income.

(4) The money supply is controlled by the central bank, and may or may not depend on interest rates. Savings are determined by the public and increase with increasing interest rates and higher levels of national income.

(5) The demand for loanable funds consists of additions to the demand for money and the demand for financing capital investments.

(6) The increase in the quantity of money demanded is larger the larger is the increase in nominal GDP. Also, because interest earnings are forgone when holding money rather than bonds, the higher is the interest rate the smaller is the quantity of money demanded.

(7) Fewer investments are profitable the higher is the interest rate, and therefore, investment is lower the higher is the interest rate. Also, investment is higher the faster is the growth rate of real GDP because larger output requires more plant and equipment.

(8) The market interest rate is the interest rate at which the supply of and demand for loanable funds are equal. In general, savings do not equal investment at the market interest rate.

(9) The equilibrium interest rate is the rate at which savings equals investment. Over time the market interest rate moves towards the equilibrium rate.

(10) An increase in the rate of change of the money supply causes a rightward shift in the supply of loanable funds curve, lowering market interest rates. However, because savings and investment are not affected, the equilibrium interest rate is not affected.

(11) Increases in economic activity as measured by the change in GDP increase the demand for money and investment. Therefore, increases in the change in GDP cause increases in market and equilibrium interest rates.

(12) The savings curve shifts upwards by the increase in anticipated inflation because only at a nominal interest rate that reflects anticipated inflation is the real interest rate earned by savers unchanged. The investment curve also shifts upwards by anticipated inflation because only at a nominal interest rate that reflects anticipated inflation is the profitability of investment unchanged. As a result of the shifts in the savings and investment curves, nominal interest rates increase by the change in anticipated inflation.

(13) Financing a fiscal deficit represents a demand for loanable funds, and causes an increase in market and equilibrium interest rates.

(14) When loanable funds are available from other countries, variations in a country's supply of and demand for loanable funds cause variations in capital imports, but do not change the interest rate.

QUESTIONS

(1) Why would a central bank policy of maintaining a given, targeted interest rate make the curve showing the change in money supply a horizontal line? How would such a horizontal money supply curve affect, e.g., the consequences of larger fiscal deficits?

(2) Do you think a central bank could maintain an artificially low nominal interest rate for an indefinite period of time?

(3) What could make ΔM^S slope upwards? Would an upward-slope to ΔM^S make much difference to the supply curve for loanable funds?

(4) Can you redraw Fig. 7.7 so that the market interest rate is also the equilibrium interest rate?

(5) Why is it changes in *real* GDP that affect investment, while it is changes in *nominal* GDP that affect the demand for money?

(6) What determines the amount of crowding out from fiscal deficits? Think in terms of slopes of curves in Fig. 7.13, and the underlying savings and investment curves?

(7) Why might the supply curve of funds from abroad to a large economy such as the United States have an upward-slope? How would this influence the conclusion concerning the effect of government borrowing on interest rates, savings, and capital imports?

(8) Is the increase in interest rates in Fig. 7.13 an increase in the market rate, the equilibrium rate, or both?

(9) Redraw Fig. 7.14 to describe the situation of a country that exports capital?

(10) The demand for money depends on the nominal, not the real interest rate. Therefore, the ΔM^D curve does not shift with anticipated inflation. Similarly, ΔM^S does not shift with anticipated inflation. Therefore, L^S and L^D do not shift upwards by the full extent of anticipated inflation; only the S and I components of L^S and L^D shift by

anticipated inflation. Show what this implies for market versus equilibrium interest rates with anticipated inflation?

APPENDIX: INVESTMENT AND REAL GDP

To determine the link between investment and real GDP, assume the number of machines and size of plant firms want is proportional to their output. Because the national output is the real GDP, this allows us to write:

$$K^D = \alpha \cdot Q. \qquad (7A.1)$$

In Eq. (7A.1), K^D is the aggregate desired real capital stock, Q is the real GDP, and α is a constant showing by how much K^D changes with Q. The equation tells us that the desired *stock* of capital moves up and down with real GDP. However, the equation does not yet tell us how *investment* varies with real GDP.

Investment is by definition the *change* in the capital stock. What this means is that if firms achieve their desired stock of capital by the end of each period of time, we can write investment as:[1]

$$I_t = K_t^D - K_{t-1}^D. \qquad (7A.2)$$

In Eq. (7A.2), I_t refers to investment during time period t, e.g., during year t, and K_t^D refers to the desired stock of capital for the end of period t. Equation (7A.2) says that if firms always have the stock of capital they want, then investment during period t is the difference between the stock of capital they want to have by the end of t, K_t^D, and the stock they began with at the beginning of t, or end of period t − 1, K_{t-1}^D.

If we put time subscripts on the K^D and Q in Eq. (7A.1) in order to show the desired stock of capital for the end of each period to be proportional to the real GDP during that period, we have:

$$K_t^D = \alpha \cdot Q_t. \qquad (7A.3)$$

---

[1]In fact, it is *net* investment that is equal to the change in the capital stock. However, the demand for loanable funds comes from all investment, which is *gross* investment. By definition, gross investment is the sum of net investment and depreciation. Therefore, Eq. (7A.2) gives only part of investment, but is sufficiently accurate for our purposes.

Similarly, since we assume the link between K^D and Q also occurs in other time periods such as in period $t - 1$, we can also write

$$K^D_{t-1} = \alpha \cdot Q_{t-1}. \tag{7A.4}$$

Substituting Eqs. (7A.3) and (7A.4) into Eq. (7A.2) gives

$$I_t = K^D_t - K^D_{t-1} = \alpha \cdot Q_t - \alpha \cdot Q_{t-1} = \alpha(Q_t - Q_{t-1}).$$

This can be abbreviated to

$$I_t = \alpha \cdot \Delta Q_t. \tag{7A.5}$$

This tells us there is a relationship between investment and the **change** in the real GNP. The faster real GNP is growing, the higher is investment and hence the larger is the demand for loanable funds.

CONNECTIONS

A LONG HISTORY OF INTEREST

While the term "usury" originally referred merely to the charging of interest, today it usually connotes *exorbitant* interest, as in the expression, "usurious interest". This change in the meaning of usury reflects a general shift in attitude towards an acceptance of the charging of interest, with only excessive, or gouging rates of interest being viewed as unethical.

The potential oppression of interest payments and of debt permeates language. For example, an instrument of debt is the "bond", with its meaning of "binding" and consequent denial of the borrower's freedom. A bond is to give "security" to the lender, where the securing of, e.g., something lose, means tying it down so that it cannot move. The "collateral" on loans comes from the word meaning "subordinately connected", the subordination of the borrower to the lender being in the same vein as being bound and secured. Lending against real property on a "chattel" mortgage, again connotes being tied or enslaved.

Repayment of a bond involves "redemption", a freeing from the oppression of being in debt. A feature of a bond, is a "covenant", a term reflecting a solemn and binding agreement as, e.g., was made with the Jewish People. The obvious parallel between religious values and matters related to interest rates extends even to the factors which are behind the determination of interest rates as described in this chapter. For example, the piety associated with the act of "saving" is evident in the common root of this word and that of "salvation". And on the other side of interest rate determination is the act of "investment", a word which according to *Webster's* means to "clothe; array; adorn ... to furnish with power, privilege, or authority," as when a priest is employed in office.

Investment, specifically investment in inventory stocks, is a feature of the Biblical account of the ascent of Joseph, son of the Patriarch, Jacob, to the Court of Pharaoh. After earning a reputation for interpreting dreams, the Israelite Joseph is brought to the mighty Pharaoh to be told of his troubling dream of seven fat cows and seven thin cows, and of seven fat ears of corn, and of seven withered, thin ears; Genesis 41:17–24. Joseph explains that this foretells of seven years of bountiful harvests to be followed by seven years of famine. He advises that one fifth of the product of the good years be stored as inventory for feeding people in the bad years. The stockpile is indeed sold in the ensuing famine — Genesis 41:25–57 — providing great relief for Egypt and for its neighbors, and an early example of the socially productive role of successful inventory management.

Investments provide a "yield," as does the planting of crops. Indeed, the sowing of seed, which could itself provide sustenance if eaten right away, occurs because when "invested" in the ground the seed yields increased future amounts of food, the essence of successful investment. As with investments in stocks and bonds, higher crop yields may come only at the price of higher risk. For example, the planting of strains of wheat developed during the "Green Revolution" has sacrificed diversity for the sake of higher expected yields. This has increased the risk of total crop failure; today's vast, contiguous fields planted with a common strain of wheat allow insects and diseases to spread more easily than in the past, when between fields with a particular crop or strain of wheat were other crops or strains. We see that in agriculture as in finance, there is a trade-off between maximizing expected yield and the risk this incurs.

The Biblical admonition on the charging of interest is based on three Old Testament commands. The first, in Exodus 22:25–26, states: "If you lend to one of my people among you who is needy, do not be like a money lender; charge him no interest. If you take your neighbor's cloak as a pledge, return it to him by sunset, because his cloak is the only covering he has . . ." This command makes it clear that the prohibition is on charging interest to those with whom a lender resides, such as a family or clan member, or a resident alien. The reference to the pledge, which is what occurs today with mortgages where buildings are pledged, has implications for both borrowers and lenders. For the borrower, the loss of a cloak was an annoying reminder that it is necessary to repay all debts. For the lender, the inconvenience of having to go to the debtor's house every evening to return the cloak, and every morning to collect it again, served to discourage the taking of pledges.

The second Biblical admonition on charging of interest in Leviticus 25:35–37, extends the restriction from money to food, for which the need to return more food than was borrowed constituted the charging of interest: "If one of your countrymen becomes poor and is unable to support himself among you, help him as you would an alien or a temporary resident . . . Do not take interest of any kind from him . . . You must not lend him money at interest or sell him food at a profit." This makes explicit the restrictions on collecting interest from a resident alien, who was likely to be a sojourner, without land and probably poor. As in the case of the first mention of interest, the guiding principle is to provide help to the needy, and not to profit from their misfortune; in a largely agricultural society of the time and place, drought, locusts and other natural events could rapidly turn a person's fate.

The third Biblical reference to interest in Deuteronomy 23:19–20, while reinforcing the restrictions on charging interest on food and loans to countrymen, removes the ban on interest when lending to "foreigners", who from the context, are probably travelling merchants: "Do not charge your brother interest, whether on money or food or anything else that may earn interest. You may charge a foreigner interest, but not a brother Israelite . . . ." It is likely that the permission to charge interest to a foreigner was designed to make a distinction between commercial lending which constitutes an investment, as when lending to a (foreign) merchant, and personal lending which went towards consumption, as when lending to a poor countryman. Further consideration of this final Old Testament reference to interest led to the acceptance of what is, in effect, the practice of financial intermediation when rabbinical interpretation suggested that a third party, the intermediary, could charge interest to the borrower and compensate the provider of credit. Whatever the detailed interpretation, it is clear that in certain circumstances the charging of interest is acceptable.

Christian and Islamic scriptures echo the concern over usurious interest. For example: "And if you lend to those from whom you expect repayment, what credit is that to you? . . . But love your enemies, do good to them, and lend to them without expecting to get anything back": Luke 6:34–35. Again, lenders are commanded to be charitable, even to the point of forgiving repayment. Nevertheless, the commercial needs for credit stretched the interpretation of legitimate circumstances for the charging of interest, although the term "interest" has sometimes been replaced with "dividend," "service charge," "credit fee" and other such euphemisms for interest payments.

The Hebrew world for interest, *neshech*, has the same root as the word for "bite". This common meaning has not been lost by those who know how interest can grow to the point of total ruin. For example, the great Biblical interpreter Rabbi Shemuel ben Meir, 1085–1174, also known as Rashbam, when commenting on the common meaning of *neshech* as "interest" and "bite", points out that as with the bite of a snake, there is no pain at the time it is incurred, but it spreads to affect the entire body, just as interest can become a crushing sum. This power of interest, with its deceptively innocent beginnings, is behind the Old Testament institution of the sabbatical, whereby debts were to be cancelled after seven years, although all ties and bonds, including debts and relationships between slaves and their masters, could be renewed by mutual consent. However, in the Jubilee Year, which occurred in the fiftieth year after seven sabbaticals, forgiveness of all debts and other contracts was unequivocally required, even if there was mutual consent to continue. Indeed, the word "finance" has its roots in the Latin, *finis*, "to end."

CHAPTER 8

EXCHANGE RATES

"As for foreign exchange, it is almost as romantic as young love, and quite as resistant to formulae."

H.L. Mencken

Key Concepts: Importance of exchange rates; balance of payments account; the balance of trade; factors influencing exchange rates; terms of trade and exchange rates; exchange rates and living standards; gold standard; Bretton Woods system; currency "wars"; Mercantilist Fallacy; China and the emerging economies.

THE IMPORTANCE OF EXCHANGE RATES

From day to day, few of us have anything to do with foreign exchange, and it might therefore seem that exchange rates have limited relevance for most people. Such a conclusion is totally unwarranted. For example, exchange rates have important effects on a country's competitiveness. Not only exports are affected, but competition at home between domestic goods and imports depends on exchange rates. For example, the ability of U.S. auto-makers to sell automobiles abroad *and* in the United States is affected by the foreign exchange value of the dollar; competition in the domestic U.S. auto market from Japan, Germany and elsewhere is more severe when the U.S. dollar is high versus the Japanese yen and the **euro**, the currency shared by the countries in the Euro-zone. Exchange rates also influence the direction and extent of **outsourcing**, directly influencing wages and jobs. Another important effect of exchange rates is on international borrowing and investment. *Ceteris paribus*, countries with "weak" currencies have trouble attracting foreign capital to finance business investment and fiscal deficits. These and other effects of exchange rates eventually translate into effects on the standard of living.

Living standards are affected by exchange rates because they affect how much has to be paid for goods and services that trade in international markets, including a country's own products that are priced and sold internationally. For example, *ceteris paribus*, U.S. dollar prices of U.S. supplied oil as well as foreign oil increase when the foreign exchange value of the U.S. dollar declines. More generally, if you think of the combined Gross Domestic Products (GDPs) of all the world's countries like a gigantic pizza, the share of that pizza enjoyed by the citizens of any one country depends on that country's currency. The more a country's currency is worth, the less of it is required when making purchases and the more the country's citizens can buy. Furthermore, the larger is the slice of pizza enjoyed by some countries the less there is for others. With so much of global GDP being tradable, the effects on living standards can be profound. This chapter deals with such consequences of exchange rates, and at the same time explains the factors which can cause exchange rates to change.

THE NATURE OF EXCHANGE RATES

The rate at which domestic currency exchanges for foreign currency is the **exchange rate**. The exchange rate can also be thought of as the price of one country's currency in terms of another country's currency, e.g., the number of Swiss francs required to purchase a U.S. dollar.

> *The exchange rate is the amount of one country's currency it takes to purchase one unit of another country's currency.*

For each currency, the exchange rate can be quoted in two ways, in terms of the amount of foreign currency to buy one U.S. dollar and in terms of the number of U.S. dollars needed to buy one unit of the foreign currency. The amount of foreign currency needed to buy one U.S. dollar is simply the inverse, or reciprocal, of the number of U.S. dollars needed to buy the foreign currency. For example, if it takes 1.25 U.S. dollars to buy one euro, it therefore takes, 0.80 (or $1 \div 1.25$) euros to buy one U.S. dollar. Similarly, if it takes 100 Japanese yen to buy a U.S. dollar, it takes 0.010 (or $1 \div 100$) U.S. dollars to buy a Japanese yen.

It is possible to determine the exchange rate between any two currencies from their exchange rates vis-à-vis the U.S. dollar. For example, it is possible to find the exchange rate between the Japanese yen, written as ¥, and the British pound, written as £, from the exchange rates of the yen versus the dollar, and the pound versus the dollar. For example, with (¥/$) = 100.0, and ($/£) = 1.50, the number of yen per British pound is (¥/£) = (¥/$) × ($/£) = 100 × 1.50 = 150. More generally, we can find the amount of currency i needed to buy one unit of currency j from

$$(i/j) = (i/\$) \cdot (\$/j). \qquad (8.1)$$

The exchange rate between any pair of currencies can be obtained from the exchange rate of each of the currencies against the U.S. dollar.

While the dollar has become the conventional **reference currency** for quoting exchange rates, in theory any currency would do. Indeed, a commodity such as gold can also be used. In fact, as explained later in this chapter and in the Connections section, gold was used until the early part of the 20th century. The U.S. dollar offers advantages over gold and other currencies because there are numerous international commercial transactions involving dollars, and therefore very frequent exchange rate quotations vis-à-vis the U.S. dollar.

When exchange rates are freely determined according to market forces and there is an increase in the amount of foreign currency per U.S. dollar, the U.S. dollar is said to have **appreciated**, and the foreign currency is said to have **depreciated**. For example, when the number of yen per U.S. dollar goes from 100.0 to 105.0 the U.S. dollar has appreciated — it has become worth more — and the yen has depreciated — it had become worth less.

When the number of units of foreign currency per U.S. dollar increases, the U.S. dollar has appreciated and the foreign currency has depreciated.

The terminology "appreciation" and "depreciation" is used with **flexible** (or **floating**) **exchange rates**, which is where exchange rates are determined by market forces. With **fixed exchange rates**, which is where exchange rates are set by central banks, instead of appreciating, a currency is said to have been **revalued**, and instead of depreciating it is said to have been **devalued**.

THE BALANCE OF PAYMENTS ACCOUNT

The numerous different factors that can cause an appreciation or depreciation of a country's currency are summarized in the **balance of payments
account**. The balance of payments account provides a tabulation of the
amounts of a country's currency that are demanded and supplied for various purposes during an interval of time. The factors giving rise to a demand
for a country's currency are listed as **credits** and are preceded by a (+) in
the balance of payments account. The factors giving rise to a supply of a
country's currency are listed as **debits** and are preceded by a (−). In this
chapter, we shall show how the various factors behind the supply of and
demand for a currency influence the exchange rate when the exchange rate
is flexible.

> *The balance of payments account lists the reasons why a currency is demanded
> and why it is supplied, and shows the amounts demanded and supplied for various
> purposes during an interval of time.*

Table 8.1 is a stylized summary of the U.S. balance of payments
account.[1] We see that the largest credit item giving rise to a demand for U.S.
dollars is exports, consisting of merchandise and of services. (U.S. exports
are, of course, U.S. goods and services sold abroad.) The largest debit item
giving rise to a supply of U.S. dollars is imports, which also consist of merchandise and of services. (U.S. imports are, of course, foreign goods and services purchased by U.S. residents.) U.S. exports represent a demand for U.S.
dollars because foreigners must buy dollars to pay Americans for the goods
and services that the Americans sell. U.S. imports represent a supply of U.S.
dollars because Americans supply dollars to the foreign exchange market in
exchange for the currencies they need to pay for foreign goods and services.

> *Exports cause a demand for the exporter's currency. Imports cause a supply of
> the importer's currency.*

Because exports and imports constitute such important components of
the total supply of and demand for a currency, they have major effects on
exchange rates. In turn, exchange rates have major effects on the quantity
and value of exports and imports. We shall describe both the effects of
exports and imports on exchange rates, and the effects of exchange rates on

---

[1]Values used are for illustrative purposes only and do not correspond to actual data.

Table 8.1.   Simplified and stylized U.S. balance of payments account.

Line	(credits +; debits −)		Billions of dollars
1	Exports		+362
2	Merchandise	+220	
3	Services	+142	
4	Imports		−453
5	Merchandise	−328	
6	Services	−125	
7	Unilateral transfers (net)		−11
8	U.S. private holdings of foreign assets (net change)		−13
9	Direct investment abroad	−6	
10	Foreign securities	−7	
11	Foreign private holdings of assets in the U.S. (net change)		+90
12	Direct investment in U.S.	+21	
13	U.S. securities	+69	
14	U.S. Government holdings of foreign assets (net change)		−5
15	Foreign official holdings of U.S. assets (net change)		+3
16	Change in U.S. official reserves		−3
17	Statistical discrepancy		+30
			0
Memoranda:			
1.	Balance on merchandise trade (lines 2 and 5)		−108
2.	Balance on goods and services (lines 1 and 4)		−91
3.	Balance on current account (lines 1, 4 and 7)		−102
4.	Increase (+) in foreign official reserves (line 15)		+3
5.	Increase (−) in U.S. official reserves (line 16)		−3

exports and imports. Let us begin by focusing on how exports and imports represent a demand for and supply of a nation's currency.

EXCHANGE RATES AND CURRENCY SUPPLY AND DEMAND[2]

Exchange Rates and Currency Supply

The supply curve of a currency shows the amount of that currency being supplied on the horizontal axis, and the price of the currency, the exchange

---

[2]This section of this chapter is adapted from Maurice Levi, *International Finance:* Fifth Edition: Routledge, London, 2009.

rate, on the vertical axis. When we draw the supply curve of a currency, we do not plot *quantities* on the horizontal axis as we do with normal supply curves — so many barrels of oil or wheat produced per month or year. Rather, we plot monetary *values* on the horizontal axis — the number of dollars, British pounds or euros being spent on imports. Values involve multiplication of prices and quantities, and respond differently than do physical quantities.

The supply curve of a currency derives, at least in part, from the value of imports. This is because when paying for imports somebody must sell the importer's currency for the needed foreign exchange. Let us see how to plot the value of currency supplied against the exchange rate by considering British imports of wheat. Let us suppose that the world price of wheat is $3/bushel, and that Britain buys such a small proportion of global wheat output that the world price of wheat is not influenced by the amount that Britain imports.

At an exchange rate of $1.5/£ the pound price of wheat is $3 ÷ ($1.5/£) = £2 per bushel. Figure 8.1(a) reveals that at £2 per bushel the quantity of wheat imports is zero, point *A*. That is, at £2 per bushel Britain's production of wheat equals Britain's consumption of wheat so that Britain is precisely self-sufficient at this price. With zero imports the number of pounds supplied is therefore zero at the exchange rate $1.5/£. This is shown by point *A'* on the supply curve of pounds, S£, in Fig. 8.1(b). If the exchange rate is $1.7/£, the pound price of wheat is $3 ÷ ($1.7/£) = £1.76 per bushel. Point *B* on the import demand curve in Fig. 8.1(a) shows that at this

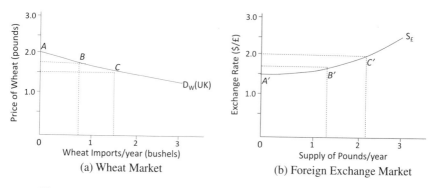

Fig. 8.1.   (a) The demand curve for wheat. (b) The supply curve of pounds.

price, wheat imports are approximately 0.75 billion bushels. The number of pounds supplied per year at exchange rate \$1.7/£ is therefore £1.76 × 0.75 billion = £1.32 billion per year. This quantity of pounds supplied is plotted against the exchange rate \$1.7/£, point B' on $S_£$ in Fig. 8.1(b). Similarly, at the exchange rate \$2/£ the pound price of wheat is \$3 ÷ (\$2/£) = £1.5 per bushel. Figure 8.1(a) shows import demand of 1.5 billion bushels at this price, point C, which involves an annual expenditure of £1.5 × 1.5 billion = £2.25 billion. This gives pointC'on $S_£$ in Fig. 8.1(b). By continuing in this way we can construct the supply curve of pounds, which in this case happens to slope upward. (Depending on the elasticity of demand for imports, it is possible for the currency supply curve to be downward sloping and, depending on the currency demand curve, for the exchange rate to be unstable. We do not consider these possibilities here.[3])

Exchange Rates and Currency Demand

The demand curve for a currency shows the value of the currency that is demanded at each exchange rate. A currency's demand curve can be derived from the country's export supply curve. This curve shows the quantity of exports sold at each price of exports. The value of exports at each exchange rate is then obtained by multiplying the price of exports and the quantity of exports.

Figure 8.2(a) shows the supply curve of British exports. For simplicity of reference, we assume that Britain exports only oil. The quantity of pounds demanded to pay for Britain's oil exports is equal to the value of these exports. Therefore, in order to construct the demand curve for pounds we must calculate the value of oil exports at each exchange rate. Let us suppose that the world price of oil is \$100 per barrel and that Britain has no effect on this price when it changes its oil exports.

If we begin with an exchange rate of \$2/£, the pound price of oil is \$100 ÷ \$2/£ = £50 per barrel. Figure 8.2(a) shows that at £50 per barrel oil exports are zero, point D: at £50/barrel the country is exactly self-sufficient. With zero oil exports, the quantity of pounds demanded to pay

---

[3]For the conditions underlying an unstable exchange rate, see Maurice Levi, *International Finance*: Fifth Edition, Routledge, London, 2009.

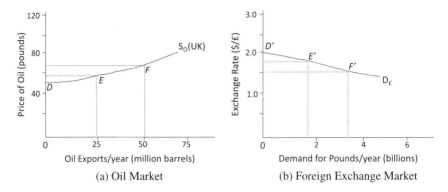

(a) Oil Market   (b) Foreign Exchange Market

Fig. 8.2.   (a) The supply curve for oil. (b) The demand curve for pounds.

for Britain's oil is therefore also zero at $2/£. This is shown by point D' on the demand curve of pounds, $D_£$, in Fig. 8.2(b).

If the exchange rate is $1.8/£, the pound price of oil is $100 ÷ $1.8/£ = £55.55 and oil exports are approximately 25 million barrels per year; point E in Fig. 8.2(a). The value of oil exports and quantity of pounds demanded per year at $1.8/£ is therefore £55.55 × 25 million = £1.389 billion. This is shown by point E' on $D_£$ in Fig. 8.2(b). Finally, at $1.50/£ the price of oil is $100 ÷ $1.5/£ = £66.67 per barrel, and exports are approximately 50 million barrels — point F in Fig. 8.2(a). Therefore, the value of oil exports and hence number of pounds demanded at $1.5/£ is £66.67 × 50 million = £3.33 billion per year — point F' in Fig. 8.2(b). Joining the points gives the demand curve for pounds.

FACTORS AFFECTING EXCHANGE RATES

Terms of Trade

If we plot the supply and demand curves for pounds together, as in Fig. 8.3, we can find the exchange rate that equates the value of exports and value of imports, and hence that equates the supply of and demand for the country's currency resulting from these activities. We see that equality of British pound supply and demand occurs at an exchange rate of approximately $1.75/£. Let us consider what happens to the exchange rate that balances the value of exports with the value of imports when the international prices of exports and imports change. Let us begin by assuming that the price of

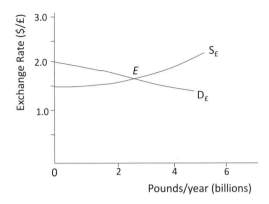

Fig. 8.3. Exchange rate that balances trade.

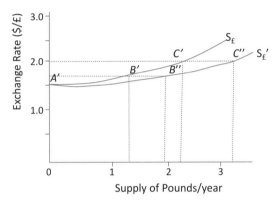

Fig. 8.4. Import prices and the supply curve of pounds.
The supply curve for pounds moves to the right at each exchange rate by the percent increase in import prices.

wheat, Britain's import, increases by 50% from $3/bushel to $4.5/bushel, while the price of oil, Britain's export, remains unchanged at $100/barrel.

With the price of oil unchanged nothing happens to the demand curve for pounds, $D_£$: it remains as in Fig. 8.2(b) and in Fig. 8.3. On the other hand, the higher price of wheat will shift the supply curve of pounds, $S_£$, to the right. This is because when wheat prices are 50% higher, each quantity of wheat imported now costs 50% more pounds than before.

Consider first point A in Fig. 8.1(a) where the quantity of wheat imported is zero. In this case, the supply of pounds remains zero: 50% more pounds when imports are zero is still zero. This means that point A' on the supply curve for pounds in Fig. 8.4 is the same as in Fig. 8.1(b).

However, this is not the case for the other points on the supply curve for pounds.

Consider point *B* in Fig. 8.1(a) and its corresponding point *B'* in Fig. 8.1(b), also shown in Fig. 8.4. At point *B* wheat imports are 0.75 billion bushels. At the beginning world price of $3/bushel the British pound cost is £1.76 per bushel, which means a British pound supply of [0.75 billion bushels × £1.76/bushel], i.e. £1.32 billion. This is shown as point *B'* in Fig. 8.1(b), and is also shown in Fig. 8.4. With world U.S. dollar wheat prices moving 50% higher than before, at each exchange rate the British pound price and hence the British pound supply is also 50% higher. That is, the quantity of pounds supplied corresponding to point *B* is no longer £1.32 billion, but 1.50 × £1.32 billion, i.e., £1.98 billion. That is, point *B'* on the initial pound supply curve is now point *B''* on the new pound supply curve in Fig. 8.4. Similarly, after the assumed 50% increase in the world price of wheat the new point corresponding to point *C'* in Fig. 8.1(b) is at 1.50 × £2.25 billion, i.e., £3.375 billion. That is, in Fig. 8.4 the higher price of wheat has moved point *C'* to *C''*. More generally, a 50% increase in the world price of Britain's import shifts the supply curve of pounds to the right by the same percentage. This effect is shown in Figs. 8.4 and 8.5 by a rightward shift in the supply curve for pounds from $S_£$ to $S_£'$ and a consequent decline in the foreign exchange value of the pound: compare

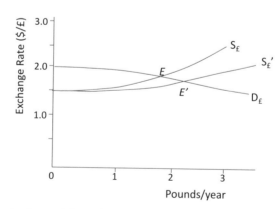

Fig. 8.5. Import prices and the exchange rate.
The supply curve for pounds moves to the right at each exchange rate by the percent increase in import prices. Hence, higher import prices cause currency depreciation.

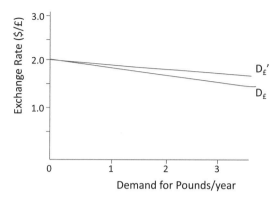

Fig. 8.6. Export prices and the demand curve for pounds.
The demand curve for pounds moves to the right at each exchange rate by the percent increase in export prices.

the equilibriums E and E'. Our conclusion: *ceteris paribus*, higher import prices lower the value of a currency.[4]

> *Higher import prices, ceteris paribus, reduce the foreign exchange value of a country's currency.*

Let us next consider what happens to the foreign exchange value of the pound when the world price of Britain's export, oil, increases. *Ceteris paribus*, an exogenous increase in the value of exports at each exchange rate shifts the demand curve for pounds, $D_£$, to the right as in Fig. 8.6. The demand curve for pounds shifts to the right by the same percentage as the increase in the world price of oil. With an upward sloping pound supply curve this results in an increase in the value of the pound: see Fig. 8.7.

> *Higher export prices, ceteris paribus, increase the foreign exchange value of a country's currency.*

The price of a country's exports relative to the price of its imports is referred to as the country's **terms of trade**. A country's terms of trade are said to improve when the price of its exports increase relative to the price of its imports. A country's terms of trade are said to worsen when import prices increase relative to export prices. In the event that export and import

---

[4]There is also an increase in the quantity of pounds bought and sold: compare the equilibriums in Fig. 8.5 being *E* before the increased price of wheat and *E'* afterwards.

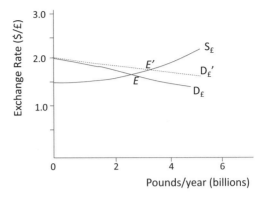

Fig. 8.7.   Export prices and exchange rates.
Higher export prices shift the currency demand curve to the right and hence result in currency appreciation.

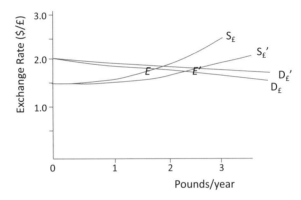

Fig. 8.8.   Inflation and exchange rates.
The supply and demand curves for pounds both move to the right at each exchange rate by the percent increase in prices. If inflation in import and export prices are the same exchange rates are unchanged.

prices increase by the same percentage, the exchange rate will not change. However, there will be an increase in the quantity of currency bought and sold. This is what will happen from inflation when export and import prices are rising in tandem. Such a situation is shown in Fig. 8.8.

Quantities of Imports and Exports: the Absorption Principle

Changes in the *values* of imports and exports can occur via changes in the *quantities* of imports and exports as well as from changes in the *prices* of imports and exports: values are quantities multiplied by prices. In turn, changes in quantities of imports and exports can occur either because of changes in a country's production or because of changes in the extent to which the country's production is taken up satisfying domestic needs. The extent to which production is used up domestically is called **absorption**. We can explain the nature of absorption and the importance of absorption versus production by considering the national income accounting identity that was discussed in Chapter 1 and written as Eq. (1.9):

$$Y \equiv C + I + G + (Ex - Im). \tag{1.9}$$

The national income accounting identity shows that what is produced in a country is either for consumption, C, for investment including additions to inventory stocks, I, for government, G, or for export, Ex. However, C, I, G and Ex all include imported goods and services as well as domestically produced goods and services. For example, C includes consumption of domestic oil as well as imported oil, domestic autos as well as imported autos, and so on. As a result, in order to obtain a country's GDP it is necessary to subtract imports, Im.

A rearrangement of the national income accounting identity allows us to express the trade balance as:

$$(Ex - Im) \equiv Y - (C + I + G),$$

or alternatively

$$(Ex - Im) \equiv Y - A,$$

where $A \equiv (C + I + G)$ stands for absorption. We see that the value of exports, which is a demand for a country's currency, can increase relative to the value of imports, which is a supply of a country's currency, if the country's production increases relative to its absorption. It follows that, *ceteris paribus*, a country's currency will appreciate if production in the country, perhaps from increased productivity, expands more than the demands on the production by the country's residents.

OTHER FACTORS AFFECTING EXCHANGE RATES

Prices and quantities of imports and exports of merchandise such as wheat and oil, while being potentially important influences on exchange rates, are by no means the only influences. Other factors affecting demand and supply for a country's currency include:

Service Exports and Imports (lines 3 and 6 in the Balance of Payments, Table 8.1): Exports and imports of most services, such as travel, shipping, banking, consulting, and so on respond to exchange rates and other economic factors in the same way as merchandise exports and imports. However, while most services behave the same way as merchandise, one service does not. This is **debt service**, which consists of interest and dividend payments made to foreigners and received from foreigners. Interest and dividends are considered debt "service" because they can be thought of as maintenance payments for funds provided by or to foreigners in the past. The amount of interest residents pay to foreigners is a service import, while interest received from foreigners is a service export. Interest payments are an import and a debit item because they give rise to a supply of the payer's currency, and interest receipts are an export and a credit item because they give rise to a demand for the recipient's currency.

Interest payments and receipts depend on the amount borrowed from or loaned to foreigners in the past, and on the interest rate. Similarly, dividend payments made to foreigners or received from foreigners depend on previous equity or direct investment by foreigners in the country or previous investment by residents abroad, as well as on the profitability of these investments. *Ceteris paribus*, the larger is the amount invested in a country in the past by foreigners, the greater is the current supply of the country's currency via interest or dividend payments to foreigners. This is because the country's currency is sold either in order to make interest and dividend payments to foreigners, or by the foreign recipients of these payments. Similarly, the larger the amount residents of a country have invested abroad in the past the greater is the current demand for that country's currency from the payment by foreigners of interest and dividends on those investments. In addition, the higher are a country's interest rates or dividends, the greater is the supply of that country's currency arising from income on past investments in that country by foreigners, and the greater is the demand for the currencies of those who made the past investments.

Debt service consists of interest and dividends paid to foreigners or received from foreigners. The size of debt service depends on past foreign investments and returns on investments.

Countries whose residents have invested more abroad than has been invested in their own country are **net creditors**. The demand for the currencies of net creditor nations from interest and dividends received exceeds the supply of these currencies from interest and dividend payments made. Switzerland, Japan, Saudi Arabia and Bahrain are net creditors, as was the U.S. until it became a **net debtor** in approximately 1985. Net debtor nations include Brazil, Greece, Mexico, Italy, Spain and Venezuela. *Ceteris paribus*, the greater is a country's net indebtedness, and the higher are interest rates and dividend yields, the greater is the supply of the country's currency, and therefore the lower is the foreign exchange value of its currency.

The extent to which there is a difference between the supply of and demand for a currency as a result of merchandise and services combined is called the **balance on goods and services**. This is shown as the second memorandum item in the U.S. balance of payments account in Table 8.1.

The balance on goods and services is the difference between the supply of and demand for a country's currency from merchandise and service payments and receipts.

Unilateral Transfers (line 7 of Table 8.1): Unilateral transfers involve the receipt or payment of foreign aid and gifts. The size of foreign aid is determined more in the political than the economic arena, and the size of private gifts is more the result of perceived needs and the benevolence of providers than of a country's terms of trade and the other economic factors affecting exports and imports.

Richer countries such as the U.S. and Japan make far more unilateral transfers abroad than they receive from abroad. Therefore, there is a greater supply of a currency like the U.S. dollar or the Japanese yen on account of unilateral transfers than there is a demand for such a currency. Poorer countries such as Bangladesh, Egypt, Ethiopia, India, and Pakistan, with receipts of remittances from citizens working overseas as well as foreign aid, face the opposite situation for their currencies. Unilateral transfers represent a net demand for their currencies. However, since a large part of aid is frequently tied to the recipients buying goods and services from the donor country, there is often an offsetting item in merchandise or service imports that cancels much of the effect of increased aid on a country's exchange rate.

When we add unilateral transfers to the balance on goods and services we obtain the **balance of payments on current account**. This is shown as the third memorandum item in the balance of payments account in Table 8.1.

The current account of the balance of payments is the balance on goods and services plus unilateral transfers.

Private Holdings of Foreign Assets (lines 8 and 11 in Table 8.1): Net investments made by residents in foreign assets are preceded by a minus sign in the balance of payments capital account because they give rise to a supply of the investors' home currency. If and when foreign assets are sold so that there is a net **divestment** of foreign assets, there is a demand for the investors' home currency, and a plus sign in front of the "change in residents' holdings of foreign assets" in the balance of payments capital account. Similarly, an increase in the amount foreigners invest in a country gives rise to a demand for that country's currency, and therefore is preceded by a plus sign in the balance of payments. A divestment by foreigners gives rise to a supply of the country's currency and is therefore preceded by a minus. In terms of the stylized U.S. balance of payments in Table 8.1, there is a large demand for U.S. dollars as a result of foreign private investment in the United States amounting to almost as much as the deficit in the U.S. current account.

The balance of payments account divides changes in residents' holdings of foreign assets and changes in foreigners' holdings of domestic assets into two components, the part which is in securities like stocks and bonds, and the part which is in **direct investment**. A direct investment is one where the foreign investor controls the operation of the business, as when a multinational corporation builds a new factory overseas.

"Control" is difficult to define. It certainly occurs when the investor owns more than 50% of the voting shares in a company. However, since there are often numerous shareholders each with only a small proportion of the outstanding shares, a much smaller fraction of the shares than 50% can often give effective control. The division in the balance of payments account is made at 10%. When 10% or more of voting shares is held by the investor the investment is classified as a direct investment.

Direct investments are those where the foreign investor holds 10% or more of voting shares.

Different factors affects direct investment than investment in securities. Therefore, it is worth discussing these investments separately.

Direct Investment (lines 9 and 12 of Table 8.1): The most obvious factor determining how much direct investment takes place in a country is the expected rate of return in that country versus the expected rate of return elsewhere. In turn, expected rates of return depend on the strengths of the markets served by the businesses in which direct investment takes place. Rates of return also depend on wage rates, tax rates charged by host governments, and depending on the type of industry, the availability of raw materials and energy, costs of satisfying environmental and safety regulations in the host country, and so on. For example, whether a U.S. sporting goods manufacturer builds a plant in Korea depends on how much it can sell in Korea and in other countries from its Korean plant, the wage rate in Korea, and the tax rate on profits in Korea. Furthermore, since the rate of return in Korea is compared to what it is in other countries, the ultimate determination of whether a plant is built in Korea depends on Korean wages *relative* to wages in other countries, *relative* tax rates, and so on. These days, with so much production being in the hands of giant multinational corporations which can examine the numerous possible locations for a plant with relative ease, direct investment in a country is sensitive to even small changes in relative wage rates, tax rates, and so on.

The relative expected rates of return from direct investments in different countries are compared with the associated risks. The relevant risks include not only the ordinary business risk that is present wherever an investment takes place, but also the political risk which takes prime importance for direct foreign investment. Political risks include the possibility of **expropriation** — which is a takeover of foreign-owned investment by a government *with* compensation to owners — and **confiscation** — where the takeover is *without* compensation. Evaluation of political risk involves an examination of the strengths of different political parties and their attitudes to a company and to the company's home government. The latter attitude is relevant because action may be aimed not at a company itself but at its government, and yet the company may lose its assets.

> *Expropriation occurs when foreign-owned investments are taken over by a government with compensation. Confiscation occurs when there is a takeover without compensation.*

The calculation of political risk is complicated by the fact that it can be influenced by how direct investments are financed. Specifically, participation by local investors can reduce the chance of expropriation or confiscation. Local participation can take the form of a **joint venture** with a local company, or borrowing from local banks. Political risk can also be reduced by producing different components of a product in different countries so that the facilities in any one country cannot profitably function alone. However, despite the various ways political risk can be reduced, it is clear that any event which affects the perceived political stability of a country can have a damaging effect on direct investment. For example, the election of a socialist government in place of a pro-business government may damage direct investment, and hence reduce demand for a country's currency and its exchange rate. Even an increased possibility an unfriendly government might eventually be elected can reduce direct investment and, *ceteris paribus*, cause a depreciation. Alternatively, favorable political events cause an increase in direct investment and hence in the demand for the currency, and a consequent appreciation.

> *Direct investment in a country depends on the expected rate of return from businesses in that country relative to elsewhere, and on relative economic and political risks. An increase in perceived risk reduces investment, and ceteris paribus, causes depreciation.*

Private Holdings of Domestic and Foreign Securities (lines 10 and 13 of Table 8.1): Increases in holdings of a country's securities such as bonds and stocks result from increases in the country's interest or expected dividend rates relative to interest or expected dividend rates in other countries. This is because investors move funds internationally according to expected rates of return in different countries. However, exchange rates are also relevant. *Ceteris paribus*, the more a country's currency is expected to increase in value, the greater is foreign investment in that country's securities. This is because part of the return earned by investing in foreign securities comes from changes in the value of the foreign currencies.[5]

---

[5]Indirectly, by affecting interest rates the borrowing requirements of government and business can affect foreign holdings of a country's securities; see Example 8.1.

Example 8.1. Fiscal Deficits versus Trade Deficits

It is no mere coincidence that America's twin deficits have grown in tandem, with the fiscal and trade shortfalls both exploding into unchartered territory since the early 1980s. The two deficits are linked via the foreign exchange value of the dollar, and we can follow this connection most easily from the balance of payments account.

The U.S. fiscal deficit has to be financed. The Treasury bills and bonds that raise the funds for the Federal deficiency of taxes versus spending could all be sold to Americans. That is, they could all be sold to Americans if Americans saved enough to buy them all. But with all the other demands on Americans' savings, such as the bills, stocks, bonds, and mortgages that finance business and household needs for capital, there are not enough savings left to finance the fiscal deficit. And so the U.S. government has to raise part of its borrowing requirement overseas, selling its Treasury bills and bonds to European and Asian investors.

Just as with other exports, when foreign buyers pay for U.S. government securities they must first purchase U.S. dollars. The more securities foreign investors buy, the larger the demand for dollars, and the higher goes the foreign exchange value of the dollar. That is, the greater is the extent that the fiscal deficit is financed by borrowing offshore, the higher is the foreign exchange value of the dollar. This means expensive U.S. exports and cheap imports. In turn this hurts exports, increases imports, and puts the trade balance deeper in deficit. That is the consequence of a bigger fiscal deficit — a bigger trade deficit. And it works via the exchange rate.

The balance of payments account explains the linkage well. The sum of all the credits and debits in the account is zero. If there is an inflow of funds from foreigners increasing their holdings of domestic securities — a positive entry in the account — there must be an offset via negative components somewhere else in the account. This comes in the form of the trade deficit. Indeed, the trade deficit arises from the higher-valued dollar caused by the inflow of funds that finances the fiscal deficit.

What does the double deficit linkage tell us? Since there are limits on the size of trade deficits that a country can sustain, it is not

possible to indefinitely finance fiscal deficits offshore. Either the
government borrowing must be reduced, or more of the fiscal deficit
must be financed at home. Domestic financing requires domestic saving.
Only when Americans' savings increase or when the fiscal deficit
declines will the U.S. trade deficit disappear.

The same factors increasing foreigners' holdings of a country's securities also result in residents holding relatively more of their own country's
securities. For example, an increase in U.S. interest rates relative to rates
elsewhere will cause U.S. investors to hold more U.S. assets relative to
foreign assets, at the same time as foreigners hold relatively more U.S.
assets.

*Increasing interest rates and expected dividend rates in a country relative to other
countries increases investment in the country's securities.*

The impact of changes in foreigners' and residents' holdings of a country's assets on the foreign exchange value of its currency can be substantial.
For example, a relatively small increase in interest rates in the U.S. can
cause a large increase in demand for dollars — via Americans and foreigners moving into U.S. assets — and a large decrease in supply of dollars —
via fewer Americans and foreigners moving funds abroad. In this way, a
small increase in U.S. interest rates can cause a substantial increase in the
value of the dollar. The size of the effect of interest rates on exchange rates
is large because the *stock* of assets is so large that minor shifts in the proportion of investment portfolios allocated to a particular country's assets
constitute substantial changes in currency *flows*.[6]
Variations in investment flows have more effect on exchange rates in
the short-run than do variations in exports and imports or any of the other
factors considered earlier. That is, when considering what it is that causes
short-run variation in exchange rates, the principal factor at work is flows
of investment into domestic and foreign securities. Particularly volatile are
flows of funds in and out of short-term securities such as Treasury bills,

---

[6]The stock of assets is the amount held at a point in time. The stock of assets is the result
of many years of investment, and is large relative to the amount invested during a period of
time, where the latter is a flow.

bank deposits, and money market "paper," which consists of securities representing borrowing by businesses, finance companies, investment dealers and so on. While these securities may have maturities of several months, some have maturities of only a few days. Indeed, money moving into and out of bank deposits may be only "overnight." The funds invested for these short maturities are shuffled from country to country in search of the tiniest interest rate advantage, moving so quickly such funds are called **hot money**; like a hot potato, nobody holds these funds very long.

Day-to-day fluctuations in exchange rates are largely due to short-term investment flows which respond quickly to small changes in interest rates in one country versus another.

Changes in Official Assets and Reserves (lines 15 and 16 in Table 8.1): Changes in official assets and reserves occur when there is intervention by governments in the foreign exchange markets. Intervention involves central bank buying and selling of its own currency to affect the exchange rate. In the case of U.S. official intervention, this is seen in Table 8.1 by the entry in line 16. This is also given as memorandum item number 5, "Increase (−) in U.S. official reserves." The −$3 billion in line 16 and memorandum item 5 means U.S. official reserves increased by $3 billion; as always, a minus means a supply of U.S. dollars, with these dollars being sold by the Fed in exchange for the foreign reserves. (The minus means U.S. dollars were supplied, and hence foreign currency was demanded.) Similarly, the +$3 billion entry in line 15 and memorandum item number 4, "Increase (+) in foreign official reserves" means dollar reserves held by foreign central banks in the U.S. increased by $3 billion; as always a plus sign means a demand for U.S. dollars.

U.S. official reserves increase when the Fed buys foreign currencies. Because foreign currencies are paid for with U.S. dollars, the Fed supplies dollars when it buys foreign currencies. Similarly, foreign official reserves in the U.S. decrease when foreign central banks sell, i.e., supply, U.S. dollars. *Ceteris paribus*, a supply of U.S. dollars by the Fed or by foreign central banks reduces the foreign exchange value of the U.S. dollar. Official intervention occurs when central banks are trying to reduce or prevent changes in exchange rates. For example, if the Fed wants to prevent an increase in the value of the U.S. dollar, it sells dollars in exchange for foreign currency. This helps to keep down the value of the dollar because it represents a supply of dollars. This shows up in the balance of payments account as an increase in U.S. official reserves.

Statistical Discrepancy: The **statistical discrepancy**, which can be large, is the supply of or demand for a currency that has not been recorded in the other items listed in the balance of payments account. If all sources of supply of and demand for a currency are recorded in the account the sum of all the pluses must equal the sum of minuses. If these sums are not equal, some items must have been missed or incorrectly recorded. This is not surprising given the number of illegal transactions in drugs, the inaccuracy of knowledge of what is spent on travel, problems in matching payments with exports and imports when there is trade credit, and so on. The statistical discrepancy does not suggest any specific factors to add to our list of factors that can change exchange rates.

Exchange Rate Changes in the Short-Run and Long-Run

We have already indicated that in the short-run — from minute-to-minute, day-to-day, or even month-to-month — changes in exchange rates are primarily due to changes in residents' holdings of foreign short-term securities and foreigners' holdings of domestic short-term securities. These changes in short-term security holdings are in turn largely due to changes in interest rates.

Changes in exchange rates in the long-run — over years or decades — are determined primarily by inflation and not by interest rates. Countries with relatively rapid inflation experience depreciations of their currencies versus currencies of slower inflating countries. It might be felt that by maintaining high interest rates a country could keep funds flowing in from abroad and thereby maintain a high exchange rate, even if the country were suffering from rapid inflation. However, high interest rates can only postpone eventual depreciation. This is because if a country's currency does not depreciate over the long-run by as much as its inflation exceeds inflation elsewhere it will suffer recurring current account deficits. This is the result of its products being uncompetitive in the international marketplace. If the country finances its current account deficits via increases in foreign debt, its interest payments to foreigners grow, and as we have seen, interest payments represent a supply of the country's currency. Therefore, the deficit in the current account, which is where interest payments appear, becomes larger. This necessitates further borrowing from abroad, which causes even larger deficits in subsequent years due to additional interest payments, eventually causing the currency to depreciate.

EFFECT OF DEPRECIATIONS AND APPRECIATIONS

An increase in the value of a country's currency caused by, e.g., higher interest rates, makes the country's exports more expensive, and thereby reduces quantities sold and employment. These effects are felt in export-oriented industries and also in industries selling products domestically that compete with imports: imports become relatively cheaper vis-à-vis domestic products. Therefore, we might wonder why a country might ever force up interest rates to support or increase the foreign exchange value of its currency.

The benefit of a high value of a currency is that it makes imports and internationally tradable goods and services cheaper. In this way, it can contribute towards lower inflation and a higher standard of living. The improvement in the standard of living occurs because the country's currency will purchase more on world markets. To see this, imagine the global GDP like a gigantic pizza. The size of the slice any individual country is able to enjoy increases with the value of the country's money. Of course, this means that other countries have a smaller slice of the pizza. That is, when countries experience depreciation their citizens, *ceteris paribus*, have a lower standard of living. We can think of this in at least two ways.

Firstly, as we explained above by reference to the slice of the global pizza, a depreciated currency does not buy as much in the international marketplace. For example, it takes more of the depreciated currency to buy wheat, oil, foreign cars, foreign travel, and other internationally traded items.[7] Secondly, when a country's currency depreciates, residents' average

---

[7]Even a country's own products which are traded internationally will cost its residents more of their own currency after a depreciation. This is because traded products have prices set in the international marketplace so that, e.g., a barrel of oil costs more of the depreciated currency, even if the oil is domestically produced.

incomes, when translated into foreign currency for the purpose of comparing average incomes in different countries, translate into smaller amounts. That is, countries with depreciating currencies move down the "league table" of living standards. Of course, this drop in relative living standards is a manifestation of the fact incomes in the country no longer buy as much internationally, making the second view of the effect of a depreciating currency just an alternative perspective to the first view.

Just as depreciation means a decline in living standards, appreciation means an improvement. Again, this can be seen either in the additional buying power of the currency in the international marketplace, or in the movement up the table of standards of living that appreciation brings about.

> *Depreciation means a reduction in a country's standard of living, and an appreciation means an increase in a country's standard of living.*

Despite the detrimental effects of depreciation on the living standards of a country's citizens, there have been times when a low currency policy has been adopted in order to create jobs and spur economic growth. The purpose of the policy is to expand exports and reduce imports. Because the jobs and economic growth come at the expense of other countries' jobs and growth, a cheap currency policy is referred to as **"beggar thy neighbor policy"**. Devaluation by one country can result in retaliation by others and the outbreak of **currency wars**. Such wars are more likely to occur with fixed than with flexible exchange rates, and since all currencies cannot simultaneously be devalued against each other, currency wars ultimately result in devaluation of money. This tendency for currency wars to lead to devaluation of money is evident if we consider the evolution of the international financial system.

EXCHANGE RATES AND THE INTERNATIONAL FINANCIAL SYSTEM

Until the beginning of the 20th century the international financial system was based on gold, a system known as the **gold standard**. The essential feature of the gold standard was that governments fixed the prices of their paper currencies to gold, and thereby fixed exchange rates between their paper currencies. In order to see why fixing currencies to gold fixes exchange rates between currencies, let us assume the Federal Reserve sets the price of gold at $40 per ounce, and the Bank of England sets the price of gold at £20 per ounce. This fixes the exchange rate between dollars and pounds at two dollars per pound because if the exchange rate were anything else there would be profitable **arbitrage**. For example, suppose the exchange rate was $2.1/£, and that the cost of shipping gold between the U.S. and Britain was so low it could be ignored. Then somebody could take $40, buy an ounce of gold from the U.S. Federal Reserve, send the gold to Britain, and sell it to the Bank of England for £20. With the exchange rate of 2.1 dollars per British pound, they could sell the £20 for $42 (or $2.1/£ × £20). Since the person started with $40, they would make a $2 profit. With many people trying to make this arbitrage profit, there would be so many people going through this process, which at the end involves selling British pounds for U.S. dollars, that this would drive down the price of the pound. This pressure on the value of the pound would continue until the exchange rate was only $2 to the pound.

Similarly, if the exchange rate were the other side of $2/£, e.g., $1.9/£, arbitragers could take £20, buy an ounce of gold in Britain, send it to the U.S., sell the gold for $40, and then sell the dollars for pounds. With $1.9/£, the number of pounds per dollar is $1 \div 1.9 = 0.526$, and so they would receive £21 (or £0.526/$ × $40). Since they began with £20 they would make an arbitrage profit. With many people seeking this profit there would be many people going through the arbitrage process, which at the end involves buying pounds with U.S. dollars. This would push up the price of the pound, i.e., the number of dollars to buy a pound, until it was $2/£. We see that the exchange rate between dollars and pounds if gold is $40 per ounce in the U.S. and £20 per ounce in Britain would be $2/£.

The exchange rate between currencies can be set by governments fixing the price of gold.

The gold standard was in effect until the beginning of World War I, and was again briefly tried in the inter-war period. With World War II following closely on the heels of the Depression, exchange rates became highly regulated, with many nations suspending the conversion of their currencies into gold or foreign exchange. As World War II drew to an end, the Western allies realized the need to have a new exchange rate system that would force countries to again make their currencies convertible. They also wanted to prevent countries from trying to create employment by keeping their exchange rates artificially low, i.e., they wanted to avoid currency wars.

Bretton Woods and the International Monetary Fund

The system which achieved currency convertibility and avoided currency wars was worked out in 1944 at a meeting of experts and officials from the U.S. and the allied powers. They met in the attractive surroundings of Bretton Woods, New Hampshire, and so the agreement they reached became known as the **Bretton Woods Agreement**. The same meeting at Bretton Woods resulted in the establishment of the **International Monetary Fund (IMF)**, to help countries with temporary balance of payments problems, and to monitor compliance with the terms of the agreement.

Under the Bretton Woods Agreement, each central bank maintained a fixed exchange rate, intervening in the foreign exchange markets to keep its exchange rate moving in a very narrow range. Each central bank would buy its own currency in the foreign exchange market when it fell to the lower end of its permitted range, thereby preventing it from falling further. Similarly, it would sell its currency when it approached the top end of its permitted range, thereby preventing it from increasing further. By standing ready to sell unlimited amounts of its currency at the top end of the permitted range a central bank could ensure that the value of its currency never went above its **ceiling value**. Similarly, by standing ready to buy unlimited amounts of its currency at the lower end of its permitted range a central bank could keep its currency above its **floor value**.

The Bretton Woods Agreement fixed exchange rates within a permitted range.

The exchange rate each central bank set out to maintain was that of its own country's currency vis-à-vis the U.S. dollar. Therefore, each central bank bought its own currency with U.S. dollars when the value of its currency was falling against the dollar, and sold its own currency for dollars when the value of its currency was increasing against the dollar. The Bretton Woods system started to break down during the early 1970's, and had been abandoned by 1973. Since the breakdown of the Bretton Woods system, the major international currencies have had flexible exchange rates, whereby exchange rates adjust until the private demands for currencies equal the private supplies. With truly flexible exchange rates there are no changes in official foreign exchange reserves, and market forces are the only influence on exchange rates. These are the forces we have explained in our account of the balance of payments earlier in this chapter.

Mercantilist Fallacy: China and the Emerging Economies

Perhaps the most passionately debated issue concerning exchange rates in the 21st century has been the widening trade surpluses of China, and the lingering trade deficits of the United States. Indeed, the debate has widened to include the impact of newly emerging economies on the trade imbalances of the developed world. At the core of the debate has been the issue as to whether China in particular has purposely undervalued its currency to gain markets from the United States. Those who believe there has been currency manipulation to gain markets point to the trade imbalances themselves. They also point to **Purchasing Power Parity (PPP)**, exchange rates based on a market basket of goods and services. (A currency is said to be underpriced if its actual value is lower than would be indicated by the cost of the market basket. For example, if the basket costs one thousand dollars in the United States and four thousand Chinese yuan in China, the PPP exchange rate is four yuan to the dollar. If the actual rate is five yuan to the dollar, the yuan is underpriced vis-à-vis the PPP value.)

Clearly, establishing whether there has been or has not been currency manipulation would require an investigation that is well beyond the scope of this introductory textbook. However, we can ask whether there is motive for such undervaluation over an extended period of time, say a matter of decades or more. Specifically, would it make sense for China to artificially keep its currency low so as to run an indefinite trade surplus?

According to the absorption principle, running a trade surplus means producing more than you absorb: recall that the absorption principle involves viewing the trade balance as $(Ex - Im) \equiv Y - A$, where $A \equiv (C + I + G)$. Therefore a surplus means producing goods and services for other countries' citizens to enjoy more than enjoying other countries' goods and services. It means living below the country's means.

The false notion that a country should run an indefinite trade surplus is known as the **Mercantilist Fallacy**. The mercantilists thought that the goal of international trade was to run a trade surplus. At the time of the gold standard a surplus meant accumulating gold, and that seemed like a good idea: the bigger the pile the better. But what is the purpose of accumulating piles of gold bars — or dollar balances in a ledger — just to hold on to them. The purpose of international trade is to benefit from producing what you produce relatively cheaply, and selling this in exchange for what other countries produce relatively cheaply. This is the **principle of comparative advantage**. There is no motive for China or any other country to run a trade surplus for ever and ever.

SUMMARY

(1) The exchange rate is the amount of one currency it takes to buy one unit of another currency. Exchange rates are typically quoted in terms of the U.S. dollar.

(2) The exchange rate between any two currencies can be determined from the exchange rates of each currency against the U.S. dollar.

(3) An increase in the amount of foreign currency per dollar means an appreciation of the dollar and a depreciation of the foreign currency.

(4) The balance of payments account is a tabulation of the amounts of a country's currency supplied and demanded for various purposes during a given time period. Items resulting in the supply of a country's currency are debit entries identified by minus signs, and items resulting in the demand for the country's currency are credit items identified by plus signs.

(5) A major reason for a country's currency being supplied is its imports, and a major reason for a country's currency being demanded is its exports.

(6) A depreciation of a country's currency reduces the price of its exports to foreigners. This increases the quantity of the country's currency that is demanded, and means a downward-sloping demand curve for the currency.

(7) A depreciation of a country's currency increases the price of imports, and thereby reduces the quantity of imports.

(8) The balance of merchandise trade is the value of exports of merchandise minus the value of merchandise imports. The balance is in surplus

if the value of exports exceeds the value of imports, and is in deficit if imports exceed exports.

(9) Adding exports and imports of services to the balance of merchandise trade gives the balance on goods and services.

(10) Unilateral transfers involve foreign aid and private gifts, including workers' remittances. When these are added to the balance on goods and services the result is the balance of payments on current account.

(11) Increases in residents' assets held abroad result in a supply of the investor's currency, while increases in foreigners' holdings of domestic assets result in a demand for the borrower country's currency.

(12) Direct investment occurs when a foreign investor owns more than 10% of voting shares. Direct investment depends on the expected rate of return in a country versus expected rates of return in other countries, and on economic and political risks.

(13) Investment in foreign securities depends on interest rates and expected divided yields in foreign countries versus interest rates and expected dividend yields at home, and on expected changes in exchange rates.

(14) The supply of or demand for a country's currency can be affected by the country's central bank if it attempts to fix the exchange rate. Central bank buying or selling of a country's currency cause changes in official reserves.

(15) The gold standard involved central banks fixing the price of gold vis-à-vis their paper currencies. The Bretton Woods Agreement of 1944–1973 required each non-U.S. central bank to buy and sell its currency for U.S. dollars when the exchange rate reached either end of a narrow band.

(16) The Mercantilist Fallacy is the false notion that the purpose of international trade is to run an indefinite trade surplus. There is no reason for a country to continually undervalue its currency: it would be living below its means.

QUESTIONS

(1) Why is a sustained deficit in the balance of merchandise trade undesirable?

(2) Why is a sustained surplus in the balance of merchandise trade unde-sirable?

(3) How do you think changes in real GDP at home versus real GDP abroad are likely to affect currency supply and demand, and hence exchange rates?

(4) In what various ways can interest rates affect exchange rates?

(5) Via what mechanism might an *expected* appreciation of a currency cause the currency to actually appreciate?

(6) Why can we calculate the exact size of the statistical discrepancy in the balance of payments account if we know the change in official foreign exchange reserves?

(7) In what sense does a country with a repeated balance of trade surplus, such as Japan, live below its means, and how might exchange rates correct the situation?

(8) If a currency supply curve slopes downwards, could the exchange rate at which the quantity of currency supplied and demanded are equal be unstable? (An unstable equilibrium is one where small deviations from equilibrium price set up forces which push the price even further away from equilibrium.)

CONNECTIONS

PRECIOUS PARALLEL[1]

When L. Frank Baum penned his much-loved enchanted tale, *The Wonderful Wizard of Oz*, he was not only creating a treasure for generations of delighted children, but was making a sophisticated and penetrating commentary on one of the central economic issues of the day. That issue was whether the United States should remain on the gold standard, or whether it should instead add to the size of the money supply by the free, unrestricted mintage of silver coins at a fixed price vis-à-vis gold.

The *Wonderful Wizard of Oz* was published in 1900, and so if we are to understand the contemporary influences that shaped Baum's characters and plot, we must describe the principal features shaping the economic landscape in the years leading up to its publication. Near the top of the list of high profile issues stood the great monetary debate, sparked by secular deflation that had gripped the United States for several decades. Specifically, from 1869 to the late 1890s the price level in the United States had fallen more than 30%, and food prices had fallen even further, dropping over 50% during the same period.[2] Not surprisingly, with prices of what they had to sell declining so much faster than what they purchased, American farmers were greatly displeased. In the run-up to the Presidential Election of 1896, which was the low point of prices, the farmers' displeasure was channeled directly to President Cleveland in Washington, the "Wicked Witch of the East" who had been instrumental in the repeal of the Sherman Silver Purchase Act that had kept the U.S. on a gold standard rather than the bimetallic standard — one based on gold and silver — favored by western farmers.[3]

---

[1]This commentary has been greatly influenced by Hugh Rockoff's insightful article, "The 'Wizard of Oz' as a Monetary Allegory," *Journal of Political Economy*, August, 1990, pp. 739–760.

[2]See Rockoff, *ibid.*, p. 742.

[3]If not personalized in Cleveland, Baum's reference to the Wicked Witch of the East may have referred to Eastern business and financial interests which largely supported keeping the U.S. on a gold-only standard.

The fight over the choice between a gold standard and a bimetallic standard reached its climax in the presidential nominations and campaign of 1896. Deflation, especially in food prices, was at its most rapid rate as the presidential nomination process gathered steam. The background to this deflation was monetary growth, limited by the U.S. stock of gold that was sufficient to keep up with the growth in U.S. national output and the demand to hold U.S. dollars. (For example, the money supply grew at approximately 2.6% per annum from 1869–1879 while real output grew at approximately 5%. In addition, the demand for money holdings grew rapidly, reducing the ratio of income to money, or in other words, reducing the velocity of circulation of money.[4])

Stirred on by the pro-silver forces at the 1896 Democratic National Convention in Chicago, presidential-leadership candidate William Jennings Bryan gave his celebrated, rousing "Cross of Gold" speech in which he brought the delegates to their feet by commanding the Republicans: "Thou shalt not crucify mankind upon a cross of gold". The enthusiastic outpouring from his inspirational oratory carried the nomination, and so Bryan began his campaign against Republican William McKinley. Bryan entered the election campaign carrying the silver banner, advocating adding it to the U.S. money supply to end the deflation that Bryan and his supporters had attributed firmly to the gold standard.

When writing *The Wonderful Wizard of Oz*, Baum would have witnessed all of this and also the fiercely fought presidential battle that Bryan and the silver forces lost. He would also have seen the buildup to the repeat battle of 1900 in which the incumbent, William McKinley, was again to take on Bryan whose commitment to bimetallism had begun to be doubted by the silver-backers.

As the fanciful story goes, honest, compassionate and principled Dorothy who lived with her hardworking and poor Aunt Em on an impoverished farm in Kansas, in the American West where the silver movement began, is swept up by a cyclone, a metaphor for the gathering storm of discontent. Alone with her dog Toto, Dorothy lands square on top of the

---

[4]The income velocity of circulation is the national income divided by the money supply. *Ceteris paribus*, as with monetary growth less than output growth, a declining velocity means lower inflation.

Wicked Witch of the East in the land of Oz — the standard abbreviation for ounce, as in, e.g., $1,500/oz. for gold — a barely disguised reference to the land of the gold standard and its Eastern base of support.[5] To the delight of the residents of Oz, the Munchkins, who had been subjected to the Wicked Witch of the East, Dorothy's landing disposes of the Witch, leaving only her silver slippers.[6]

The Munchkins are unable to direct Dorothy to Kansas, and so she is sent, along with the silver slippers, to see the Wizard of Oz who lives in the Emerald City (Washington, D.C.) at the end of the Yellow Brick Road where Dorothy, like others, will find that the answer is *not* to be found. The Yellow Brick Road is, of course, the path taken by the gold advocates who, according to those promoting bimetallism, had caused the problems Dorothy and her hard-working relatives had suffered in Kansas.

On her way Dorothy first encounters the scarecrow, a manifestation of the Western farmer. She is told sadly that the scarecrow has no brains as his head is stuffed with straw, but she soon discovers the clear, latent ability the scarecrow possesses. Baum is telling the reader that even on complex issues like those involving the choice between gold and bimetallism, the farmer is most capable of reason. Dorothy then encounters the Tin Woodsman, the personification of America's industrial working-man. The Tin Woodsman has lost his heart and has been subdued by the Wicked Witch of the East, a characterization of the detachment and alienation of American industrial workers.

The fourth leg in the odd coalition is the Cowardly Lion. This is presidential hopeful, Bryan himself. The bimetallic standard advocates had become troubled that Bryan was losing his dedication to their movement as he embraced other issues, and as gold discoveries, good U.S. crops, and an inflow of gold from European purchases of U.S. wheat led to a sudden end to the deflationary period. Indeed, the Cowardly Lion falls asleep in a

---

[5] The bimetallic standard had received backing from the Prohibition Party. Therefore, Toto is a reference to the friendly teetotalers, as the Prohibitionists were popularly called.

[6] In the movie the Witch's slippers are ruby. This is Hollywood's adaptation of the silver slippers, a license also taken with numerous other shining metallic objects that Baum refers to at several other points in the book.

field of poppies, and it is the mice, representative of ordinary, little people, who pull him back to the cause.

When finally they arrive at the Emerald City, the Wizard has a pot of courage waiting for the Cowardly Lion (Bryan), capped by a golden plate to prevent it from overflowing, another reference to the containment of prosperity that the gold standard represented to its opponents. Before entering the city all must wear green-tinted glasses or be locked up forever with a gold buckle; those financiers who direct policy in the city force everybody to see the world through money-colored glasses. Dorothy and her friends then pass through seven passages and up three flights of stairs, a reference to the so-called "Crime of 73," the 1873 legislation that had ended the minting of silver dollars.

The Wicked Witch of the West, William McKinley, uses one of the wishes granted by the Gold Cap — again pointing to the powerful, oppressive, gold standard — to enslave the Yellow Winkies, a thinly veiled reference to McKinley's decision not to grant independence to the Philippines. The Witch deviously seeks to seize Dorothy's silver slippers which the Witch knows to be so powerful, and is delighted to seize one, knowing that divided, the pro-silver forces would lose their power. Dorothy pours water over the witch and the witch simply disappears, demonstrating that all it would take for the farmers' plight to end was good rains on the Western prairie which had suffered years of damaging drought.

With the Wicked Witch dissolved, Dorothy frees her friends. The Tin Woodsman is given a new axe with a gold handle, and a blade that glistened like silver — a clear reference to bimetallism — but Dorothy is still unable to return to Kansas, getting only a ride in a hot air balloon; all the promises she receives are like hot air. So Dorothy tries to find Glinda, Good Witch of the South; the South was generally in favor of adding silver to the monetary system. With the help of the South in the person of Glinda, the problem is solved as Dorothy clicks her silver slippers three times and returns to Kansas.

When she wakes her slippers are gone, just as by 1900 the silver issue had disappeared. The United States Congress passed the Gold Standard Act in that year, ending years of indecision and setting the U.S. firmly on the gold standard, an exchange rate system that was to last until World War I.

INDEX